Process Theology

OTHER BOOKS BY RONALD H. NASH

Poverty and Wealth: The Christian Debate Over Capitalism

Liberation Theology (editor)

Christianity and the Hellenistic World

Christian Faith and Historical Understanding

The Concept of God

Social Justice and the Christian Church

The Word of God and the Mind of Man

Freedom, Justice and the State

Ideas of History (editor)

The Light of the Mind: St. Augustine's Theory of Knowledge

The Case for Biblical Christianity (editor)

The Philosophy of Gordon H. Clark (editor)

The New Evangelicalism

Dooyeweerd and the Amsterdam Philosophy

Process Theology

Edited by **Ronald Nash**

A Mott Media Book

BAKER BOOK HOUSE
Grand Rapids, Michigan 49506

Copyright 1987 by
Baker Book House Company

ISBN: 0-8010-6782-0

Paperback edition, June 1989

Printed in the United States of America

Contents

Introduction

What is process theology? To its proponents, process theology is the most important development in Christian thought since the first century. It is significant, they think, because the movement gives sophisticated moderns an intellectually and emotionally satisfying reinterpretation of Christianity that is compatible with late-twentieth century ways of thinking. Moreover, they add, process thought finally removes from Christianity the dominating influence of Greek and Hellenistic notions that have, in their view, distorted the essence of Christianity for almost two millenia.

To its critics, process theology is the most dangerous heresy presently threatening the Christian faith. Process theology does not eliminate pagan ideas from the faith, its critics argue. Rather, process thought is a total capitulation to paganism. Take any essential Christian belief, these critics state, and one will find that process theologians supplant it with an alien belief. Is God the sovereign, personal omnipotent and all-knowing creator of the universe? Is Jesus Christ the eternal and divine Son of God whose incarnation, death and resurrection were necessary to effect the redemption of human beings? Is faith in Christ the only ground for human forgiveness? To these and other questions that touch the very heart of Christianity, the official process answer is No.

The roots of process thinking can be traced as far back as the ancient Greek philosopher, Heraclitus (500 B. C.). In one form or another, process theology was around during the heydays of liberalism, neo-orthodoxy and the radical death-of-God theologies earlier in this century. However it received relatively little attention prior to the 1960's. But with the decline of other non-orthodox versions of Christianity in the past decade or two, process theology has assumed a position of dominance as the chief competitor to versions of Protestant and Catholic theology that still seek to be faithful to traditional Christian concerns. Process thinkers have in these past two decades produced an immense amount of literature supporting their reinterpretation of Christianity and attacking traditional Christian theism. Traditional theists have been relatively slow to respond to this challenge. A comprehensive critical assessment of process theology therefore is long overdue. This book is an attempt to redress this situation.

The chapters of this book divide naturally into four main groups. The first two chapters (by Nash and Bloesch) introduce process theology by contrasting it to classical theism (chapter one) and to Reformed theology (chapter two). These introductory discussions make up Part One of the book.

Process thought may be approached from either a philosophical or theological direction. Part Two contains four chapters that focus on theological considerations. Bruce Demarest takes note of how process theology rejects both the deity of Christ and the doctrine of the Trinity, two essential and necessarily related Christian beliefs. Demarest draws attention to the frequency with which process thinkers declare that Jesus sinned and made mistakes. Clearly, the Jesus of process theology is neither omnipotent nor omniscient. Demarest offers his criticisms of these defective views of Jesus and the Trinity. William Craig explains how the omniscience of God has traditionally been taken to mean that God has full and complete knowledge about the future as well as the past and present. He takes issue with process thinkers who limit divine foreknowledge in a misguided effort to preserve an element of human freedom. While process thinkers argue that their position offers more plausible answers to the problem of evil, Michael Peterson disagrees. Peterson argues that the process theodicy contains serious difficulties that point to even deeper problems within the process system. The presuppositions of process thinkers lead them to distort the content of major Christian beliefs while, at the same time, trapping them in a number of philosophical difficulties. In the final chapter of Part Two, William Craig defends the Christian belief that the world had a beginning in time from process attacks on creation.

Part Three contains five chapters that are more philosophical in content. The chapters by Arthur Holmes and David Basinger deal with somewhat related topics. While Holmes investigates critically the process claim that God cannot act, Basinger examines the process view that God cannot cause humans to act; God can only lure us.

As Holmes explains, the God of historic Christianity is a God who acts. He acts in creation, in revelation and in redemption. The process denial of this view results in a sub-Christian view of the Incarnation; it also accounts for the process bias against supernaturalism. Basinger argues that process thinkers have failed to make their case that a God who can only attempt to persuade humans is superior to the God of theism who can bring His will to pass. Thus traditional theists are within their rights in continuing to believe that God can control human beings. Roman Catholic scholar W. Norris Clarke explores two areas of tension between process thought and traditional theism. The first is process theology's conflict with the traditional Christian doctrine of creation while the second is the infinity of God. Traditional theism need not surrender, Clarke argues, God's real relatedness to the world. James Mannoia wonders if process thought is logically coherent. He points out several ways in which it is not and concludes that even if a case could be made for its theological adequacy as a framework for Christian doctrine, its logical incoherence is a major stumbling block that no process thinker has succeeded in removing.

Part Four concludes the book by offering three contrasting attitudes toward process theology by writers who are proponents of Christian theism. Clark Pinnock's chapter is the most sympathetic. While he ultimately rejects the process system, Pinnock nonetheless believes that some process criticisms of theistic claims may be justified and he urges traditional Christian theists to consider what they can learn from process theology. Royce Gruenler pulls no punches about the dangers he sees in process thought. Gruenler was himself an advocate of process theology until its theological and philosophical difficulties led him to return to historic Christian theism. Carl Henry's assessment falls somewhere between Gruenler and Pinnock in tone, even though Henry concludes that process thought as a system must be rejected by anyone who accepts the historic Christian faith.

A few words of advice and warning may be helpful. First of all, some subjects are discussed in more than one chapter. I regard this as one of the book's virtues. Every teacher knows how important it is to repeat difficult or complex points in different ways. Secondly, the contributors do not always agree on their approach to or their assessment of process theology. This book is not the product of thirteen like-minded individuals who decided to gang up on process thought. Many of the contributors will disagree sharply with some of the views expressed by their colleagues. I regard this as another virtue of the book. Process theology is not a monolithic movement. Its variant strains call for different responses from orthodox critics. Whatever moments of truth may appear in its writings should be acknowledged. Finally, two gentlemen whose names do not appear elsewhere in this book deserve special mention for their own distinctive contributions to the book. Ed Vandermas read the manuscript and offered many helpful suggestions. The idea for the book originated with Leonard Goss; his editorial skills helped make this a better book.

Ronald H. Nash

PART ONE

Introduction

Process Theology and Classical Theism*

Ronald H. Nash

Ronald H. Nash

Ronald H. Nash is professor of philosophy at Western Kentucky University. He received his M.A. from Brown University and his Ph.D. from Syracuse University. Nash is the author or editor of fifteen books including *Poverty and Wealth: The Christian Debate Over Capitalism*, *Liberation Theology*, *Christianity and the Hellenistic World*, *Social Justice and the Christian Church*, *Christian Faith and Historical Understanding*, *The Concept of God*, *The Word of God and the Mind of Man*, and *Freedom, Justice and the State*. His articles have appeared in such journals as *The New Scholasticism*, *The Intercollegiate Review*, *Augustinian Studies*, *The Reformed Journal*, *Christianity Today*, and *Christian Scholars' Review*.

Ｔhis chapter will introduce process theology by contrasting it with what is often called classical theism. In the next chapter, Donald Bloesch carries the introduction of process theology one step further by contrasting it with Reformed theology.

It is extremely important to recognize that the relationship between classical theism and Christian theism is a matter of some dispute. A number of orthodox Christian thinkers regard the classical theism described later in this chapter as equivalent to Christian theism. I disagree. I regard classical theism as one way in which important concerns of Christian theism can be formulated. But classical theism is not, I contend, the exclusive formulation of Christian theism. The content of classical theism results from the application of several *philosophical* presuppositions to some major theological convictions. Since process theologians believe they can easily criticize major tenets of classical theism, they are delighted whenever they hear someone equate classical theism with Christian theism. That only makes their task of arguing for the superiority of process theology easier, they think. We have yet to see any detailed process response to those traditional Protestant and Catholic writers who refuse to equate classical theism with Christian theism.[1]

Classical Theism

Classical theism or (as it is sometimes called) Thomistic theism has been around for a long time. David Ray Griffin's book *God, Power and Evil: A Process Theodicy* contains a helpful analysis of classical theism from his perspective as an advocate of process theology.[2] Though advocates of classical theism may be unhappy with certain features of Griffin's presentation of their position, it offers some significant advantages for our study. For one thing, it presents in stark contrast the major differences between classical theism (as it is understood by process thinkers) and process theism.

7

Even if Griffin's presentation should prove to be flawed or inaccurate in some respects, he succeeds in demonstrating the simple elegance of classical theism.

Griffin identifies a number of logically connected attributes which he calls "the essential core of theism." He believes this concept of God is a systematic explication of certain views found in Augustine and other classical theists who antedate Thomas Aquinas (1225-1274). To what extent the concept of God Griffin discusses deserves to be identified with the essential elements of biblical Christian theism is an open question; but the package of divine attributes he identifies is sufficiently dependent on the writings of Thomas Aquinas to justify calling it the Thomistic concept of God. Griffin identifies eight attributes that make up the core of Thomistic theism:

> pure actuality
> immutability
> impassibility
> timelessness
> simplicity
> necessity
> omniscience
> omnipotence

Some readers will question the completeness of this list. What has happened, for example, to the attribute of divine love? Process theologians—Griffin and others—believe that properties like love, compassion, and sympathy are logically incompatible with the eight core attributes. In their view, one of the major tasks for classical theism is showing how the God described in the Thomistic package of attributes can be the caring, loving God of the Bible.

Pure Actuality

The medieval doctrine of *actus purus* was the scholastic equivalent of Aristotle's teaching that God is pure actuality. Basic to the philosophy of Aristotle and his followers was the belief that everything that exists is a combination of form and matter. Everything possesses both actuality and potentiality.[3] The form (essence) of a thing determines its actuality; its matter is the ground for the thing's several potentialities. While every existing thing can possess only one actuality at any given time, every existent possesses a number of different potentialities. Because of its essential properties, a given piece of wood, for example, may be in actuality a desk. But that same wood possesses the potentiality to be a number of different things, such as a chair or a table.

Aristotle regarded potentiality as a kind of imperfection. This conviction led him and Aquinas after him to believe that any potentiality in God's being would detract from His perfection.[4] Thus, it became easy for Christian thinkers who accepted this tradition to conclude that God must possess no potentiality; God must be pure actuality. While God can act, He cannot be acted upon. God therefore must be an exception to the doctrine that everything is composed of form and matter. Because potentiality cannot belong to God, God can possess no matter; He must be pure form.

Some of the implications that follow from Aristotle's doctrine of pure form are obviously difficult to reconcile with the Christian doctrine of God. For one thing, Aristotle taught that God cannot think about anything in the changing and imperfect world. The only perfect thing worthy of God's attention is God Himself. For Aristotle's God to think about anything else would detract from His perfection. Aristotle's Unmoved Mover whose only activity is contemplation of his own nature is a far cry from the loving God described in the Bible.

Immutability and Impassibility

Two of the other attributes in Griffin's itemization of Thomistic theism, immutability and impassibility, are related but not equivalent properties. Immutability suggests that God does not change, while impassibility refers to the impossibility of God's being acted upon. Impassibility also suggests that God cannot be "moved" in an emotional sense: God cannot be hurt, grieved, saddened, and so on. While Scripture sometimes speaks of God as subject to such emotions, many interpreters take these passages as metaphorical. As Griffin sees it, the attributes of immutability and impassibility conflict with passages in the Bible that speak of God changing His mind or being affected by the prayers of His people.

Timelessness

Griffin is convinced that Thomistic theism is required to interpret God's eternal existence as timelessness. The doctrine of timelessness entails more than that God's existence is without beginning or end. It implies that God exists totally outside of time. God has neither temporal duration nor temporal location; God's existence does not occur during any period of time and He does not exist at any particular moment of time. God is "outside" of time. For a timeless God, all of time exists in one eternal present. It is true that most classical Christian theologians like Augustine and Aquinas understood God's eternity in the sense of timelessness. But, I argue, the interpretation of Augustine and Aquinas need not be normative for subsequent generations of theists; nor does Griffin argue that it should be.[5]

A number of Christian thinkers who are otherwise committed to biblical theism have had second thoughts about interpreting God's eternal existence as timelessness. They have preferred to say that God is everlasting. By this, they mean to say that while God has always existed and always will exist, it is a mistake to think of God as entirely divorced from the process of time. Classical theists believe that interpreting God's eternal existence as everlastingness rather than timelessness demeans God by making Him subject to a feature of His creation. As David Diehl summarizes this line of thinking: "time is one of the qualities or principles of finite existence to which God has subjected his creation, and unless God is viewed as timeless or 'above time' he is brought within the limitations or laws of creaturely existence."[6] Diehl offers an interesting reply to this kind of claim:

> But the idea that time is strictly a law of creaturely existence is the very point in question. There are other laws to which God is "subject" without being reduced to a creature, e.g. the law of self-consistency, the "law" of honesty, the "law" of love or of mercy, etc. But these "laws" are not laws to which God is subject as though they were *above* him. They are the very characteristics of his own nature or essence, and since God lives out of his own essence he therefore lives with self-consistency, always telling the truth, always showing mercy to repentant sinners, and so forth. So the question becomes, "Is time a characteristic of the very being of God?" If so, then a temporal God is not reduced to creaturely limitations by existing in time any more than he is by telling the truth (as creatures sometimes also do).[7]

Even if a theist wishes to maintain that God's "time" is not our time, it is still true that God has His own time-strand along which events occupy temporal relationships. The Exodus came before the Crucifixion and the Ascension came after the Resurrection. Advocates of the timelessness doctrine *may* be confusing the fact of *God's being Lord over what happens within time* with *God's being outside of time*. The timelessness doctrine seems to assume that if God is "in time", He cannot be Lord of what occurs in time. In my view, the timelessness of God and the sovereignty of God are clearly independent notions. The gods of Plato and Aristotle were timeless beings but they were not the Lord of creation. The important question for theists here is whether God's sovereignty is compromised in any way by the Bible's assertion that God acts in time and is thus an everlasting being.

Necessity

The attribute of divine necessity is a double-barreled property. First it implies that God's existence is necessary in the sense that it is impossible for God not to exist. Everything besides God exists contingently; that is, its nonexistence is possible. But if God exists, He exists necessarily; it is impossible that He might not have existed and it is impossible that He might cease to exist.[8] The other dimension of the attribute of necessity deals with the relationship among the various attributes that make up the concept of God. The divine essence itself—the particular package of attributes God possesses—is necessary. In other words, it is not an accident that God possesses the attributes He does. It is in fact inescapable that God be the kind of being specified by the Thomistic package.[9] There is nothing accidental or nonessential about the being of God.

Simplicity

Griffin thinks the attribute of simplicity may be the key to the Thomistic package since so much seems to follow from attributing it to God. If a being is simple, then it has no parts. If a being has no parts, then it cannot change (since there is nothing to lose or gain). If a thing cannot change (is immutable), then it must be pure actuality in the sense that it cannot possess any potentiality. "Before" and "after" are words that would be inapplicable to such a being, a point which entails that any simple being must also be timeless. It would appear that the Thomistic concept of God cannot do without the property of simplicity.[10]

Omnipotence and Omniscience

The attributes of omnipotence and omniscience refer to God's power and knowledge respectively. Knowledgeable proponents of classical theism have never maintained that divine omnipotence entails God's ability to do absolutely anything. William Rowe may have come as close to a satisfactory definition of omnipotence as possible when he wrote that "God can do anything that is an absolute possibility (i.e., is logically possible) *and not inconsistent with any of his basic attributes.*"[11] As a preliminary definition, divine omniscience means that God knows all truths and holds no false beliefs. While legitimate doubts may be raised about the indispensability of some elements of the classical list of divine attributes for Christian theism, omnipotence and omniscience *are* essential properties of the Christian God. While Christian theists may debate the meaning of the two attributes and the extent of their application to such things as God's having the power to change the past or God's having the power to know human free choices in the future, acceptance of these attributes is one of the watersheds that divides Christian theism not only from process theology but from paganism.[12]

Summary

This then is one account of the influential classical or Thomistic concept of God that has played such an important role in the history of Christian thought. Thomists have usually believed that acceptance of any one attribute logically commits one to accepting the entire package. But if this has been one strength of the Thomistic concept of God, it may also prove in the present debate to be its Achilles' heel. A growing number of philosophers and theologians are persuaded that the Thomistic concept of God is fraught with serious problems. Moreover, those who criticize the Thomistic package of attributes from the perspective of process theology insist, because of the logical relationships among the attributes, that no tinkering with the Thomistic concept of God is possible. Therefore, they argue, if the Thomistic concept of God really is inadequate, it must be abandoned in favor of the kind of competing notion of God offered by process theologians. The next section of this chapter will examine the process concept of God. But I want to make it clear that, in my view, the choice between Thomistic theism and the finite god of process theology is not a forced option; the disjunction between their respective theories of God is not exclusive. It is possible to develop mediating concepts of God that can avoid the major difficulties of the allegedly static God of Thomistic theism and the finite god of process theology. Suggestions about these alternative concepts of the God of Christian theism will be found throughout this book.

Process Theology

We have seen how process theology characterizes classical theism. Even if its characterization is acceptable to classical theists, I argue, it is still possible for one to adhere faithfully to the convictions of Christian theism and alter elements of the classical concept of God. The purpose of this section is to summarize the most important ways in which process theology differs from Christian theism in general and from Thomistic theism in particular.

Three Basic Convictions

Process theology takes its cue from three basic convictions. First, advocates of process theology believe that the Thomistic concept of God is subject to a number of fatal objections. Second, they maintain that Christians should have been suspicious of the Thomistic package of divine attributes because of its heavy reliance upon ideas borrowed from pagan Greek philosophy and because of its alleged incompatibility with several major emphases of the Bible. Third, they believe that a much more satisfactory approach to the concept of God is to be found in the philosophy of the twentieth century philosopher, Alfred North Whitehead.

Major Proponents of Process Thought

Whitehead (1861-1947) is the dominant influence on process theology. The son of an Anglican vicar, Whitehead taught at Cambridge University and was for years best known for his work in the philosophy of science and the philosophy of mathematics. Between

1910 and 1913, he and Bertrand Russell co-authored the highly influential book *Principia Mathematica*. Whitehead eventually made his way to America and Harvard University where new interests began to develop at a fairly late stage in his career. His writings began to evidence a greater interest in speculative philosophy and traditional metaphysics. In books like his famous *Process and Reality*, he developed a metaphysical system in which the notion of process was paramount.

Whitehead's most influential interpreter, Charles Hartshorne, has himself written much that has stimulated the development of process theology.[13] Other major proponents of the process system include Schubert Ogden,[14] John B. Cobb, Jr.,[15] Norman Pittenger, Daniel Day Williams, Bernard Loomer, H.N. Wieman, David Ray Griffin, Peter Hamilton, and Ewert Cousins, among many others.[16]

Major Views of Process Theology

Process theology views both pantheism and Thomistic theism as unacceptable extremes. In order to distinguish their position from pantheism, process theologians often call their theory panentheism. Whereas pantheism identifies God and the world in some way, panentheism denies that God and the world are identical. But while God and the world are not identical, they are interdependent, a claim that distinguishes panentheism from theism. Panentheists suggest that God be thought of as in the world much the way a mind is in a body. In fact, they often state, the world can be thought of as the body of God. Process theologians reject every one of the eight elements of the Thomistic package of divine attributes. They deny that God is pure actuality and they reject both the immutability and the impassibility of God. The God of process theology is not outside of time; His existence is inextricably involved in the process of time. The process God is not simple. To the extent that the necessity of God is understood in the sense of aseity (God's independence from the world), this doctrine is rejected as well.[17] Process theologians make it clear that their God is neither omnipotent nor omniscient in any sense that would satisfy a traditional Christian theist. The process concept of God can be summarized in eleven theses which it offers in direct contrast to the tenets of Thomistic theism.[18]

1. In process theology, Thomistic theism's emphasis upon *being*

is replaced with its own stress upon *becoming*. According to process theologians, Thomistic theists view God as static and impassive substance. In process thought, substance is exchanged for process. Panentheists think of God and reality by means of models that stress interrelationship. One useful model for them is that of a society in which each component contributes something to the others. In a process universe, everything affects everything else—including God; the process God is no exception to this universal interdependence.

2. While the God of Christian theism is an independent Creator, the God of process theology is an interdependent cooperator. Whether or not Christian theists accept the Thomist model in every respect, they believe that God is Creator. The doctrine of creation means that while the world is dependent upon God, God is not dependent on the world. Process theology denies God's independence of the world. For panentheism, God and the world are mutually dependent on each other. As Ewert Cousins explains:

> Aristotle views relation as involving change and dependence and hence imperfection. As a result, the Aristotelian-Thomistic school holds that the world can be related to God because it is dependent on him, but God cannot be really related to the world. If he were, then he would be dependent on creation and would not be the unmoved mover required by the Greek idea of perfection.[19]

Process thought, Cousins points out, opposes all such thinking.

The classical Christian doctrine of creation *ex nihilo* was one way early Christian thinkers marked off the ontological distance between God and the world. They used this doctrine as a conscious repudiation of Plato's explanation of the origin of the world. Plato had taught that the world began when a finite god, much like an artist fashioned the world out of pre-existing material. Christianity found Plato's view objectionable because it clearly limited the power and sovereignty of God. The process view of creation resembles Plato's to the extent that the creation comes out of a pre-existent pole of God's own being. Whereas the classical Christian doctrine of creation implied God's control over the world, the God of process thought is not so much the controller of the world as he is its director. The process God works in the world;[20] he cooperates with the world. But he does not control the world; he is an interdependent partner with the world. For process theologians, neither God nor the world would be complete without the other. God's being has always been counterbalanced or complemented by things which exist independent of His will. The God of process theology is not the sovereign Lord of the universe.

It follows then that process theologians also reject the traditional doctrine of divine transcendence. In classical Christian theology, God's transcendence was understood to mean His distinctness from the world. But the panentheist belief that the world is God's body rules out the notion of transcendence.

3. The classical Christian doctrine of divine immutability is replaced by the notion of a changing God. Process thinkers attempt to support their rejection of divine immutability by appealing to the biblical picture of God. How, they ask, could a totally unchanging God respond to the prayers of his people? For this reason, Cousins believes that the God of process thought

> is closer to the Christian experience and to the Biblical witness than is the timeless Absolute of Greek philosophy. For the Christian God is concerned with the world; he is involved in its suffering and its tragedy. The world, man, and human events make a difference to him. The deepest reality of God is seen not in his detachment or in his power, but in his love. In contrast with the static Absolute and the all-powerful monarch, the process God is the God of persuasive love revealed in Jesus Christ.[21]

Process theologians stress the apparent incompatibility between the biblical picture of God as truly personal and the classical emphasis on immutability and impassiveness. The impassive God of scholastic philosophy, they say, is inconsistent with the biblical God who is personal, loving, and caring.

4. In the writings of some process thinkers, the personal God of theism appears to be replaced by an impersonal God. This is a point of major disagreement among process thinkers. It is unlikely that Whitehead's God can be regarded as personal since his God was not really distinct from other beings. The personal character of Pittenger's God is also debatable. According to Pittenger, while God is the ground of the personal, he nevertheless transcends personal categories. Other process thinkers, however, like John Cobb, Jr., attempt to allow for a view of God as a living person.[22]

5. Process theologians unanimously reject the timelessness doctrine of Thomistic theism. They believe "it is self-contradictory to think of God as both alive and changeless. If God is alive, then he must experience some change. And this means that God literally experiences and exemplifies process. That is, he enjoys the experience of before and after. He is everlasting and omnitemporal, but not timeless."[23] Instead of being timeless, God is "temporal, relative, dependent, and constantly changing."[24] It is important to note, however, that the dispute over divine timelessness is not unique to process thinkers. An increasing number of Christian theists find a reinterpretation of God's relationship to time compatible with other elements of their concept of God.

6. While both theists and panentheists describe God as perfect, representatives of the two movements understand perfection in significantly different ways. For Christian theists, God's perfection means (among other things) that nothing more can be added to God's being: He is complete or fulfilled perfection. For the panentheist, however, God's perfection is being attained successively; God is continually growing or developing in perfection. As the amount of value within the universe (God's body) increases, God's own perfection evolves and grows. As Ewert Cousins states:

> Classical theism applied to God the Greek notion of perfection, claiming that God is absolutely perfect in all respects and in no way surpassable. In Hartshorne's view, God is perfect in love, in goodness, in the omnipresence and the omnicompetence of his sensitivity to the world. But his perfection must be defined in such a way that it includes the possibility of his self-surpassing experience of new value. This involves some limitations on classical doctrines of perfection, especially on omnipotence.[25]

7. Theists and panentheists disagree as to whether God should be understood as absolute or relative. "Absolute" in this context means that God cannot be involved in any *real* relationship with the world. "Relative" carries with it the notion of being related to something, in this case, being related to the world. Traditional theism affirms that while God gives meaning to the world, it is impossible for the world to give any meaning to God. Process thinkers disagree. God needs the world, they maintain, in order to "enrich his everlasting existence and to give it stimulus and meaning, as well as 'embodiment'. "[26]

To state that God needs some world is not to say that he needs this particular world or the particular creatures in this world. He might be able to get along just as well with a different world. But God does need some world to complement his existence. Process thinkers insist that God actually receives something from the world; the world adds something to God, something which he would otherwise lack. According to Lewis Ford, if God's experience were not actually enriched by the world, "the existence of the world would be wholly gratuitous, devoid of any ultimate significance."[27] Since God includes all experiences within his own being, the finite creatures who exist within God "are not simply the passive effects of God but are also *causes* having an impact on one another and consequently on or in God."[28]

Process thinkers, however, give little attention to the apparent equivocation their position contains on this subject. Even if God is related to everything that exists, how does it follow that God is therefore relative? Recognizing this, Schubert Ogden has admitted that God's "being related to all others is itself relative to nothing, but the absolute ground of any and all real relationships."[29]

8. Another disagreement between theism and panentheism concerns the question whether God's omniscience is unqualified or restricted. Theists have traditionally viewed God as omniscient in the strong sense; God knows all things including future contingent actions. Since God's knowledge is complete, there is no sense in which it can be said to grow. Process thinkers like Hartshorne explain God's knowledge as a process of God becoming aware of the experiences and knowledge of the creatures who exist within his own being. Because God knows all of the past and present experiences of such creatures, because his own being encompasses all such entities and their experiences, Hartshorne's God is omniscient with respect to all past and present events. But for Hartshorne, it is impossible for even God to have knowledge about the future. The future is open and indeterminate and not even God can know it.

9. Christian theism emphasizes God's role as efficient cause of the world; process thought stresses God's role as final cause. In other words, God, who is the goal or lure of the entire cosmic process, draws it to its final fulfillment. God is the final cause or *telos* of the world. But process theologians are wrong if they think it would

be inconsistent for a theist to maintain that God is both the efficient *and* the final cause of the world.

10. In a sense, the foundation for most of the distinctive doctrines of process theology is its insistence that the monopolar notion of God found in Christian theism should be replaced by a dipolar view of God. The monopolar view of God conceives of God as absolutely perfect; His absoluteness is unqualified. But according to Hartshorne, God should be thought of as comprising two contrasting poles. The dipolar view originated with Whitehead who regarded the world as the *actual pole* of God. But, Whitehead insisted, if the world were all there is to God, the result would be pantheism. And so, he held, there is also a *potential pole* to God's being which is beyond the world. With respect to his potentiality, Whitehead's God is absolute, eternal, and infinite. With respect to his actual pole (the world), God is relative, temporal, and finite. God's *primordial nature* (the potential pole) is what God is eternally; God's *consequent nature* (or his actual nature) is what God is at any given moment. As Hartshorne interprets the doctrine, the two natures or poles of God are as follows:

God's Primordial Nature	God's Consequent Nature
transcendent	**contingent**
abstract	concrete
necessary	contingent
transcendent	immanent
eternal	temporal
potential	actual
one	many
infinite	finite
cause	effect
absolute	relative
immutable	mutable

Whitehead expressed this dipolar characteristic of God by writing:

It is as true to say that God is permanent and the World fluent, as that the World is permanent and God is fluent.

It is as true to say that God is one and the World many, as that the World is one and God many—

19

> It is as true to say that the World is immanent in God, as that God is immanent in the World.
>
> It is as true to say that God transcends the World, as that the World transcends God.
>
> It is as true to say that God creates the World, as that the World creates God.[30]

The primordial pole of God can be thought of as the mind of God; it is akin to Plato's realm of eternal objects. The consequent or actual pole is the sum total of everything that exits at any given moment. The two poles can be thought of as representing God's mind and his body. The eternal objects of God's primordial nature lack an independent existence; they are potentialities which may or may not come to be actualized in the universe. Until they are actualized, the eternal objects exist only as concepts in the minds of such actual entities as God. Therefore, God's primordial nature can be viewed as an envisagement of all the possibilities which could someday become actual.

The dipolar God is involved in an endless process of change. Everything that exists is in a continual state of process; it is constantly becoming something else through its interaction with other entities. God contributes permanence to temporal beings while temporal beings dispense flux to God. God's source of diversity is the world and the world's source of unity is God. "Creativity" is the process thinker's name for the all-encompassing process. The concrete pole of God's being, the world, describes, for some particular moment of the process, what God is. Therefore, the world is the physical realization or actualization of God's conceptual vision. No contradiction is supposed to exist between the two poles of God's being since they describe different aspects of God.

11. The final difference between theism and panentheism to be noted here is their attitude to the question of God's ultimate triumph over evil. Traditional theism affirms the ultimate victory of God over all forms of evil; panentheism, sometimes with regret, disagrees. According to panentheism, no ultimate triumph over evil is possible for God. Evil can never be completely conquered or destroyed. Barnhart admits: "No claim is made that God can guarantee that Christians or any other group will enjoy everlasting personal victory over all suffering and death."[31]

The eleven points I have noted draw attention to the major ways in which the God of process theology differs from the God of Christian theism.

Some Problems With Process Theology

A Forced Choice?

Because process thinkers equate Christian theism with Thomistic or classical theism, they maintain that responsible Christians have only two choices; they are confronted by an either/or situation. A Christian must either adopt the entire Thomistic package of attributes or else reject the Thomistic concept of God and accept the process view of God. Supposedly, there is no third alternative. Once people accept the view that only two choices are available, and begin to see the serious problems that attend the Thomistic theory of God, the appeal of the process concept of God increases immensely. There is, however, one major catch to all this. The disjunction, either Thomistic theism or panentheism, is not exclusive. There are other alternatives. It may be best to think of Thomistic theism and process theology as opposite poles of a continuum along which a variety of other alternatives can be found. Rejection of the Thomistic package as described earlier in the chapter does not necessarily require one to accept the process concept of God. Even if Thomistic theism is found unacceptable, panentheism is not the only alternative.

Many process thinkers seem to be drawn into this forced choice by their uncritical identification of the God of theism with Aristotle's Unmoved Mover, who was unrelated to the world, impassive, and unconcerned. But as Bruce Demarest argues:

> The Christian faith emerged out of the matrix of Judaism with its conception of God as a living, active being relentlessly operative in the ordinary events of nature and the supernatural display of miracles. The God of the Jewish-Christian tradition is changeless in being, attributes and purposes, but in His dealings with the creation God does enter into changing relations. Thus, the divine immutability in no wise implies that God is unconcerned, inactive, or unrelated—It is wholly irresponsible to replace the God of theism with a finite, evolving Deity in order to affirm relatedness to the world. Biblical faith unhesitatingly affirms that the perfection of God includes creative interaction consistent with His changeless character and purposes.[32]

Traditional theists like Demarest maintain then that God's perfection does not preclude but rather includes relations with His creation. The recognition of this fact does not conflict with the belief that God's character and purposes are unchanging.

Greek Philosophy

Especially ironic is the oft-recurring panentheist claim that Thomistic theism is dominated to an inordinate degree by the influence of pagan Greek philosophy. Perhaps this is true. But it is just as true that process theology is equally indebted to ancient Greek thought; it simply elevates a different Greek tradition to prominence. The conflict between Thomistic theism and process theology is basically a revival of the struggle between competing schools of Greek philosophy, one emphasizing *being*, the other stressing the dominance of *becoming*. A process theologian chiding a Thomist for his dependence on Greek thought is like the pot calling the kettle black.

The Bible

Equally ironic is the effort process theologians expend trying to make it appear that their position is more consistent with the teaching of Holy Scripture than the position of the Thomistic theist. Since the process theologian himself introduces faithfulness to Scripture as a criterion of theological adequacy, it is legitimate to inquire about the extent to which process theology itself satisfies this test. Most process theologians appear to have a highly selective biblical hermeneutic. Scripture is welcomed as authoritative when it agrees with panentheist opinions. But when Scripture conflicts with panentheist beliefs, it is conveniently ignored or casually discarded.

For example, serious questions can be asked about the Christology of process theologians. Their rejection of the deity of Christ comes across clearly.[33] Hartshorne readily acknowledges, "I have no Christology to offer, beyond the simple suggestion that Jesus appears to be the supreme symbol furnished to us by history of the notion of God genuinely and literally 'sympathetic'—receiving into his own experience the sufferings as well as the joys of the world."[34] Some process thinkers disassociate themselves from Hartshorne's position on the grounds that Hartshorne himself recognizes how his theological convictions differ from traditional Christian teachings.

But even the Christian theologians within the process movement make it clear that their Christology is a radical reinterpretation of traditional dogma. Cobb and Griffin admit that "Process theology is not interested in formulating distinctions within God for the sake of conforming with traditional Trinitarian notions."[35]

Nor does process theology line up any better with a host of other basic Christian beliefs: the Incarnation, the bodily Resurrection, the Atonement. Traditional Catholics and Protestants deplore the extent to which process thinkers cut the ties to the historic Christian faith and in effect offer the world a distinctly new religion. If process theologians disqualify Thomistic theism on scriptural grounds, they cannot ignore Scripture as a possible ground for disqualifying process theology. To the extent that process theologians present their position as an expression of *Christian* thought, the fidelity of their views to the normative documents of the Christian faith is a valid consideration. It is certainly a point at which they have major problems.

Is the Process Concept of God Coherent?

But process theology has philosophical problems as well. Many critics have sensed that a major difficulty lies somewhere within panentheism's dipolar view of God. One writer who struggled to make this problem explicit was E. L. Mascall. He noted that Whitehead, to cite just one example, "has concentrated his thought so thoroughly upon the *way in which things behave* as never to inquire *why they are*. He has never properly understood what finite being *is* and so has never apprehended its radical contingency."[36] Mascall seems to be saying that the dipolar God of process thought deprives the process theologian of any answer to the question, *why* does the actual world exist? Since the potential nature of God is eternal, it is easy enough to grant that the realm of potentialities requires no sufficient reason for its existence. But the things that exist within the actual world (the consequent nature of God) are contingent.[37] Why do these contingent things, these particulars that happen to be, exist? Why were some potentialities actualized and not others?

Mascall says:

> We still want to know why [existing finite things] are there at all. To
> say that they are units of Creativity explains nothing, unless we are
> also told why they are the particular units that they are, manifesting
> the particular kinds of Creativity that they do. The one thing that
> they are clearly not is self-explanatory, but this is the one fact that
> Whitehead never allows himself to think about. He postulates God
> as the ground of rationality, but never as the ground of being.[38]

In short, Whitehead and other process thinkers develop a
metaphysical system that leaves unanswered the most fundamental
of all metaphysical questions, *why is there anything at all?* It is a
system of explanation that fails to provide any ultimate explanation.

Philosopher Norman Geisler picks up the same point and takes
it in a slightly different direction. Geisler argues:

> If God has both an actual pole and a potential pole, one is faced with
> disturbing metaphysical questions. How can God actualize his own
> potentialities? Potentialities cannot actualize themselves any more than
> empty cups can fill themselves. Capacities do not fulfill themselves;
> they must be activated by something outside themselves. Anything
> passing from potentiality to actuality, from what is not to what is,
> depends on some actuality to ground it. Nothing does not produce
> something; possibilities to exist do not materialize on their own.[39]

The point is that in process thought, God's eternal and potential
nature is given. But then, in some way, some of God's infinite potentialities are actualized in the things that make up the concrete world
which is also God's consequent nature. Geisler wants some explanation of how those potentialities become actualities. After all, potentialities do not have the power to actualize themselves; if they did,
they would be something other than potentialities.

Much the same concern is felt by W. Norris Clarke who suggests
that Whitehead's dipolar view of God and rejection of the Christian doctrine of creation out of nothing

> brings us back to an older Platonic primal dualism of God over against
> the world . . . where neither of these two primal poles is ultimately
> responsible for the other. What then is the ultimate source or explana-
> tion of the unity of the universe, of why its two correlative poles, God
> and the multiplicity of the world, are attuned to each other so as to

make up a single system, since neither one ultimately derives all of its being from the other? If there is to be any ultimate source of unity in the universe at all—which is dubious, just as it was for Plato—it seems to be pushed back beyond even God to an inscrutable, faceless, amorphous force of creativity which is just *there*, everywhere in the universe, as a primal fact with no further explanation possible—a kind of generalized necessity of nature, with striking similarities to the ancient Greek *ananke*.[40]

In response to the kinds of questions raised by Mascall and Geisler, many process thinkers do exactly what Clarke notices: they appeal to something they call creativity in order to explain what makes it possible for God to actualize his own potentialities. But this move appears to raise even more serious problems for the pantheist. Geisler explains:

It is self-destructive to the [panentheistic] system to posit something like Whitehead's "creativity" with reality status outside the bipolar actual entities of the world. Only actual entities actually exist in the world, and beyond the world only potentialities exist, namely, eternal objects. Creativity cannot be a real ground in a Whiteheadian system: only actual entities are real causes.[41]

Dipolar theism starts out with a system in which everything is either an actual entity that concretely exists in the world or one of the eternal potentialities existing in the primordial nature of God. But this dualism excludes anything that can serve as a sufficient reason for the existence of any actual entity. When a solution to the problem is sought by appealing to something else called creativity, the original dipolar emphasis of panentheism is effectively abandoned and a third thing, whatever creativity turns out to be, is held to exist outside the world. But this appears to elevate creativity above God.

Should a panentheist wish to revise the Whiteheadian system by giving a reality status to something beyond God in which he [God] is grounded, then his "God" turns out not to be God after all. For if there is a real creative ground for the bipolar [i.e., dipolar] "God," then it is this pure actuality beyond the bipolar potentiality-actuality that is really God. In short, panentheism needs a theistic God in order to ground its "God," which turns out after all not to be God but to be a giant creature needing a more ultimate and real cause of itself.[42]

In other words, attempts to explain why actual entities exist which appeal to Whitehead's "creativity" seem to end in an appeal to something that is more ultimate than the dipolar God. Thus, the rationality of the dipolar system seems to depend on a more ultimate monopolar principle.

For Bruce Demarest, the dipolar God of process thought is a hoax or mirage. Echoing some of the points already made, he charges: "The primordial pole of God, which possesses no actuality, in fact possesses no reality. The attempt to impose upon the system a transcendent, timeless anchor in the form of the primordial nature smacks of a desperate attempt to forestall the system's collapse into the radical immanentism and pantheism."[43] Demarest regards dipolar theism not as a brilliant stroke of genius, but as a desperate act of expediency. Without it, panentheism would have nothing to prevent its inevitable collapse into sheer pantheism.

Conclusion

Process theologians would love to have their contemporaries believe two things: (1) that process theology is superior to classical theism; and (2) that the choice between process theology and classical theism is forced in the sense that there is no third alternative. Some contributors to this book offer defenses of various tenets of classical theism; they argue that process theology is not superior to Thomistic theism. Other contributors argue that even if there are issues where process theology appears to get the better of Thomistic theism, those who would equate Thomistic theism with Christian theism are mistaken and thus whatever problems Thomistic theism may have do not require an acceptance of the process system.

Clearly, one need not choose between Thomistic theism and process theology. We are not confronted by an exclusive disjunction that obliges us to select either the entire Thomistic package of divine attributes or the panentheistic concept of God. I happen to be one of the contributors to this volume who believes that certain features of what has been called the classical concept of God require modification. But it is quite another thing to demand that the whole traditional Christian concept of God be scrapped in favor of a God who is neither omnipotent nor omniscient. This is as bad a bargain as exchanging Aladdin's old lamp for a shiny new one.

All of the contributors to this book do agree, however, that another choice before us *is* forced—the choice between theism and panentheism. Here there is no middle ground. At several points, the panentheist challenge to Thomism may be warranted. But that does not require an acceptance of panentheism. Modifications of the classical concept of God can be made so as to ease the objections raised against that notion by process thinkers. Once we realize that the choice before us is not an either/or option, the plausibility of the process alternative fades considerably. In the decision between theism and panentheism, the choice seems clear. A being who is not essentially omnipotent or omniscient, who is not the sovereign and independent Creator, is neither worthy to receive our worship nor to bear the title "God."

NOTES

* This chapter is adapted from material originally published in *The Concept of God* by Ronald Nash. Copyright by the Zondervan Corporation. Used by permission.

1. Besides myself, those contributors to this book who consciously distinguish between classical theism (as described later in this chapter) and Christian theism are Donald Bloesch, Clark Pinnock, Thomas Morris, David Basinger, James Mannoia, Arthur Holmes and, no doubt, one or two others. But this certainly does not mean that the people included in this list agree on every point.

2. David Ray Griffin, *God, Power and Evil: A Process Theodicy* (Philadelphia: Westminster, 1976).

3. Of course, for Aristotle, God is an exception to this. This is the whole point to his claim that God is pure form or actuality.

4. For Aquinas's views on this point, see his *Summa Contra Gentiles* I. 16. 1.

5. Many contemporary theists find the notion of timelessness incompatible with the biblical picture of God. See Nicholas Wolterstorff's essay, "God Everlasting," in *God and the Good*, ed. Clifton Orlebeke and Lewis Smedes (Grand Rapids: Eerdmans, 1975) or chapter 6 of Ronald Nash, *The Concept of God* (Grand Rapids: Eerdmans, 1983). Royce Gruenler's contribution to this book illustrates the importance that some spokesmen for classical theism attach to timelessness in its debate with process thought. As I explain in my book, *The Concept of God*, a lot of people including myself find it difficult to sort out all of the issues. I continue to advise theists that, in my judgment, it is not necessary for them to place all their anti-process eggs in the timelessness basket.

6. David Diehl, "Divine Omniscience in the Thought of Charles Hartshorne and Cornelius Van Til: A Systematic Comparative Study," (Ph.D. Dissertation: Hartford Seminary Foundation, 1978), p. 307.

7. Ibid., pp.307-308.

8. This sense of divine necessity has been challenged often in recent years. I defend the notion in chapter 9 of my book, *The Concept of God*.

9. The claim inherent in this second sense of divine necessity is more problematic. In a sense, the whole of my book, *The Concept of God*, is an exploration of the degree to which this claim is true.

10. The doctrine of simplicity raises many difficult questions that lie beyond the scope of this book. I have already addressed these questions in chapter 7 of *The Concept of God* where I express the view that simplicity may be safely eliminated from the cluster of divine attributes that constitute the theistic concept of God.

11. William Rowe, *Philosophy of Religion* (Encino, Calif.: Dickenson, 1978), p. 9.

12. Clark Pinnock, in his contribution to this book, expresses some reservations about whether divine omniscience includes the power to have knowledge about what philosophers call future contingent events. Most of the other contributors to the book, including myself, would part company with him on this position.

13. Hartshorne has been a prolific writer. One place to begin a study of his thought is his book, *The Divine Relativity* (New Haven: Yale University Press, 1948).

14. Schubert Ogden, *The Reality of God and Other Essays* (New York: Harper and Row, 1966).

15. John B. Cobb, Jr., *A Christian Natural Theology* (Philadelphia: Westminster, 1965).

16. More general studies of the movement include: Delwin Brown, et al., *Process Philosophy and Christian Thought* (Indianapolis: Bobbs-Merrill, 1971); and Ewert Cousins, ed., *Process Theology* (New York: Newman, 1971). Both books contain helpful bibliographies.

17. It should be pointed out, however, that since some like Hartshorne are fervent defenders of the ontological argument, they insist that there is some sense in which God is a necessary being.

18. Even though we shall frequently speak of *the* process concept of God, differences of opinion do exist within process thought. When those differences are important, attention will be drawn to them in the text or notes.

19. Cousins, *Process Theology*, p. 15.

20. Theism, of course, through its doctrine of divine immanence, also affirms that God is active in the world. But it rejects the interdependence between God and the world that is such an important element of process thought.

21. Ibid.

22. See Cobb's *Natural Theology*, pp. 188f.

23. J. E. Barnhart, *Religion and the Challenge of Philosophy* (Totowa, N. J.: Littlefield, Adams and Co., 1975), p. 153.

24. John Cobb, Jr., and David Ray Griffin, *Process Theology: An Introductory Exposition* (Philadelphia: Westminster, 1976), p. 47.

25. Cousins, *Process Theology*, p. 14.

26. Barnhart, *Religion and the Challenge of Philosophy*, p. 153.

27. Lewis S. Ford, "The Viability of Whitehead's God for Christian Theology," *Proceedings of the American Catholic Philosophical Association* 44 (1970): 148.

28. Schubert Ogden, "Love Unbounded: The Doctrine of God," *Perkins School of Theology Journal* 19 (1966): 14.

29. Ibid.

30. Alfred North Whitehead, *Process and Reality* (New York: Harper and Row, 1960 reprint), p. 528. Not all process theologians accept a dipolar view of God. John Cobb, Jr., for one, denies the doctrine; see his *A Christian Natural Theology*, pp. 176ff.

31. Barnhart, *Religion and the Challenge of Philosophy*, p. 151.

32. Bruce Demarest, "Process Trinitarianism," in *Perspectives on Evangelical Theology*, ed. Kenneth S. Kantzer and Stanley N. Gundry (Grand Rapids: Baker, 1979), p. 29.

33. For examples, see Cobb, *Christ in a Pluralistic Age* (Philadelphia: Westminster, 1975), pp. 74ff., or Pittenger, *Christology Reconsidered* (London: SCM, 1970), p. 79.

34. Charles Hartshorne, *Reality as Social Process: Studies in Metaphysics and Religion* (Boston: Beacon, 1953), p. 24.

35. Cobb and Griffin, *Process Theology*, p. 110.

36. E. L. Mascall, *He Who Is* (London: Longmans, Green and Co., 1962), p. 158.

37. An important distinction is necessary at this point. Panentheists allow that the world as such can be eternal in the sense that God may have always had a body. But even if the world itself is eternal, the particular things within the world are not. And as contingent beings, they require a sufficient reason for their existence.

38. Mascall, *He Who Is*, p. 159.

39. Norman Geisler, *Christian Apologetics* (Grand Rapids: Baker, 1976), pp. 208-9. Compare also the following comment by William J. Hill: "How can anything that lacks all actuality function as the explanatory principle of the fact that there *are* finite instances of actuality (that there are beings rather than nothing)?" William J. Hill, "In What Sense is God Infinite? A Thomistic Perspective," *The Thomist* 42 (1978): 20.

40. W. Norris Clarke, S. J., *The Philosophical Approach to God* (Winston-Salem, N. C.: Wake Forest University Publications, 1979), p. 72.

41. Geisler, *Christian Apologetics*, p. 209. For additional discussions of problems related to the notion of creativity, see Robert C. Neville, "Whitehead on the One and the Many," *The Southern Journal of Philosophy* 7 (1969-70) 391ff., and David L. Schindler, "Creativity as Ultimate: Reflections on Actuality in Whitehead, Aristotle, and Aquinas," *International Philosophical Quarterly* 13 (1973): 161-171.

42. Geisler, *Christian Apologetics*, p. 209. Other attacks on dipolar theism and its appeal to creativity can be found in Robert C. Neville, *Creativity and God* (New York: Seabury, 1980) and W. Norris Clarke, *The Philosophical Approach To God*, pp.72ff.

43. Demarest, Bruce, "Process Trinitarianism", p. 29.

Process Theology
and Reformed Theology

Donald G. Bloesch

Donald Bloesch

Donald Bloesch is Professor of Theology at Dubuque Theological Seminary. He received the Ph.D. degree in theology from the University of Chicago in 1956 and did post-doctoral work at Basel University, where he studied under Karl Barth. He is the author or editor of twenty-two books including *Essentials of Evangelical Theology* and *The Future of Evangelical Christianity*.

P rocess theology is without doubt one of the most vital theological movements in America since the First World War. It has attracted eminent scholars from a variety of Christian traditions, including Roman Catholic, Episcopal, Congregationalist, Methodist and Presbyterian. Its possible convergence with the newly arising feminist theology could well make it the key theological movement in the English-speaking world in the last part of this century. As one who had the opportunity of studying under some of its leading exponents (Charles Hartshorne, Daniel Day Williams, Bernard Meland), I can testify to its cultural appeal and philosophical profundity.

Two Types of Theology

My reason for choosing to compare process thought and Reformed theology is that process thinkers generally see that particular strand of evangelical theology as their foremost adversary. It is the Augustinian and Calvinist doctrines of the sovereignty of God, the irresistibility of grace, revelation as divine intervention into history, and the shadow of a final, irreversible divine judgment that seem to create special difficulties for process theologians. Just as Augustine and Calvin are considered the *bêtes noires* of the past, so Karl Barth is regarded as the main threat at present. Thomas Aquinas is treated as an adversary but one who can be respected, since his method is basically philosophical (appealing to criteria in nature and experience) rather than theological (calling for submission to a divine revelation). To be sure, there is an undeniable theological side to Thomas as well, and some evangelical theologians, for example, Geoffrey Bromiley, are willing to acknowledge him as basically a theologian of revelation. Yet what makes him attractive to process thinkers is his natural theology. They regard him as a useful foil who can help them to articulate their own position by way of contrast.

Reformed theology has been in eclipse in America ever since Jonathan Edwards (who saw revival as the surprising work of God) was supplanted by Charles Finney (who regarded revival as the result of humanly contrived techniques). Modern evangelicalism is by and large much closer to Finney than to Edwards, just as modern liberal theology is much closer to Schleiermacher, Ritschl and Bushnell than to the Bible or the Reformation. Neo-orthodoxy, associated with such names as Karl Barth, Emil Brunner and Reinhold Niebuhr, succeeded for a time in recovering certain motifs associated with Reformation theology, but the religious academic world today is almost totally engulfed in experientialism and subjectivism.

Process theology fits into the American temperament and culture more than Reformed theology ever could. From the revival period onward, American religion has been experiential and relativistic, and this is true of American philosophy as well. The key figures in modern American religious thought are Emerson, Thoreau, William James and Walt Whitman (rather than Augustine, Calvin or Luther), and process theologians readily acknowledge their affinity to this transcendentalist tradition.[1] Instead of upholding the saints of the age-old church, Bernard Meland advocates celebrating the cultural heroes of America's past (he includes Jefferson, Emerson, Thoreau, Lincoln and Whitman).[2] Here we see how process theology is admirably adapted to the *Zeitgeist*, the spirit of the times.

Alfred North Whitehead, perhaps the most influential of all process philosophers, had an admiration for Jesus but not for Paul. Like his disciple Charles Hartshorne, he saw much in Buddhism as closer to true religion than the historic Christian faith—including the priority of becoming over being. Two luminaries in Christian tradition for whom he expresses an appreciation are Origen and Erasmus.[3]

When I refer to process theology, I include those renowned representatives of process philosophy—Whitehead, Hartshorne, Teilhard de Chardin, C. Lloyd Morgan, Samuel Alexander, Henri Bergson, Paul Weiss—as well as men and women who consciously seek to relate the process tradition to the heritage of the Christian church—Daniel Day Williams, John Cobb, Norman Pittenger, Marjorie Hewitt Suchocki, Schubert Ogden, David Griffin, Lewis Ford, Paul Sponheim and Donald Goergen. Henry Nelson Wieman, probably the most creative and innovative of all process theologians, is actually closer to being a philosopher of religion than a theologian.

The same can be said for Bernard Meland and Bernard Loomer, and perhaps this is true of all process thinkers. Process theology also includes theologians influenced by the dynamic side of Hegel's thought, including Jürgen Moltmann and Thomas Altizer.

By Reformed theology, I am thinking not of a narrow Calvinism but of that broad theological tradition that seeks continuity with the mainstream Protestant Reformation—Calvin, Luther and Zwingli. Among the notables in this tradition outside of the Reformation are Zacharias Ursinus, Gisbert Voetius, Philip Schaff, Abraham Kuyper, Herman Bavinck, Benjamin Warfield, P. T. Forsyth, James Denney, Emil Brunner and Karl Barth.[4] Since I align myself more or less with this venerable tradition, I shall be speaking out of this general perspective in my critique of process theology.[5]

Authority

The differences between the two types of theology come to light especially in the area of theological methodology and authority. Whereas Reformed theology appeals to an authoritative divine revelation, which is integrally associated with Holy Scripture, process thought bases its case on what is experientially accessible and scientifically verifiable. While Reformed theology envisions truth as an event breaking into history from the beyond, process thinkers see truth in terms of the correspondence between sensory perception and empirical reality. Logical consistency together with empirical adequacy is normative for the knowledge of God in process thinking. In Reformed theology, the truth of God is inaccessible to both conception and perception and therefore must be given in an act of divine revelation.[6] God is Wholly Other than what man can conceive or imagine (cf. Isa. 55: 8, 9; I Cor. 2: 6—11), though this does not mean that human rationality is totally divorced from divine wisdom, since we are created in God's image. An analogical relation is established between the Word of God and human reason in the illumination of faith, but this does not take away from God's utter transcendence, nor does it underplay the reality of mystery and paradox in Christian faith.

Reformed theology affirms that man is separated from God both by ontological fate and by historical guilt. It is primarily because of sin, which clouds the noetic as well as the volitional aspects of our being, that we humans are incapable of rightly perceiving or appreciating the light of God reflected in nature and history. All of us have an inescapable awareness of the living God (through common grace), but only some of us have a saving relationship to this God (through redemptive grace).

In the Reformed understanding, it is not enough to sense the presence of God: we must be awakened by the power of his grace to the reality of what he has done for us in Christ and then take up the cross and follow Christ in faith and obedience. We must subordinate both our reason and our desires to the claims that God makes upon us in Jesus Christ as we find these in Holy Scripture.

Whitehead, by contrast, concludes: "Ultimately nothing rests on authority; the final court of appeal is intrinsic reasonableness."[7] "All knowledge," he insists, "is derived from, and verified by, direct intuitive observation."[8] For Wieman, valid evidence is the only legitimate ground for accepting a belief, and "evidence is valid only when it has been gathered and tested by observation, reason and experiment."[9] Hartshorne is more circumspect concerning the power of historical argument and empirical induction to give us ultimate truth; he opts for an intuition that can be validated and confirmed in experience.

Reformed theology in its history has admittedly been guilty of heteronomy, that is, locating authority in an external standard or formula accessible to human understanding and open to human control. At its best, when it speaks of the Bible as the Word of God, it means that the Bible is the source and sign of God's redemptive revelation in Christ, which we never possess, even rationally, but which we can receive through the illumination and empowering of the Spirit.

When Reformed theologians affirm the Bible as the infallible standard for faith and practice, they mean that this original witness to what God has done for us in sacred history participates in the event of revelation by means of the creative and ongoing action of the Spirit. They also confess that the scriptural witness gives an adequate and trustworthy account of this revelation by virtue of its inspiration by the Spirit.

Process theology occasionally uses Scripture because it affords provocative lures that lead us into the promise of the future. Scripture derives its concurrence from whether it tallies with one's self-evident, preconceptual experience. The Bible is a story of man's progressive evolving consciousness of the divine presence in human history and nature, one that can be confirmed and corrected by the insights provided by the new science and the new philosophy. When comparing the relative dearth of biblical references in process writings to their conspicuous abundance in such seminal Reformed works as Calvin's *Institutes* or Barth's *Church Dogmatics*, one can only conclude that the Bible's authority is not really taken seriously.

Doctrine of God

Perhaps nowhere does process theology diverge more from the traditional Christian understanding, and especially the Reformed understanding, than in the area of the doctrine of God. Process theologians are unanimous in rejecting what they believe to be an unwarranted amalgamation of biblical and Hellenistic insights with the result that the God of Christian tradition has become unrelated to historical actuality. They repudiate the position of classical theism in which they think God is equated with a static or completed good that excludes pain, suffering and anything else indicating deficiency. The doctrine of the impassibility of God is especially the object of their strictures, since it connotes that God being perfect cannot suffer, thus seeming to call into question whether God can be meaningfully related to history and humanity.

In the light of modern evolutionary theory, process thinkers have sought to resymbolize God in order to bring the conception of deity into accord with modern sensibilities. According to Whitehead, God is "the Divine Eros," "the Eros of the universe," "the principle of concretion" and "the Ultimate Irrationality." Hartshorne describes God as "Eminent Freedom," "Eternal-Temporal Consciousness," "Personalized Becoming" and "the All-Surpassing One." For Wieman, God is "the Creative Event," "the Creative Process," "the Principle of Integration," "the Directive of History" and "Growth in Qualitative Meaning." Teilhard sees God as "the Divine Energy," "Omega" and "Creative Transformation." Cobb prefers to speak of "a dynamic maximum of possibilities" and "Creative-Responsive Love." Ogden opts for "Creative Becoming," "the eminently relative One," "Pure Unbounded Love" and

"Absolute Relatedness."[10] Pittenger's God is the "altogether lovely" and "the Cosmic Lover," Meland's is "the Creative Event" and "the Creative Passage." Marjorie Suchocki depicts God as the "unification" and "harmonization of all possibilities."[11]

In some process thinkers, creativity is considered more fundamental than God, who then becomes a privileged agent in the universe (Whitehead, Lewis Ford). In others God is equated with the first principle—creativity (Hartshorne, Cobb, Wieman).

Some process thinkers envision God as a person or society of persons (Whitehead, Hartshorne). Others conceive of God as beyond personality, since creativity is prior to personality (Wieman). Even those who view God in personal terms do not really think of God as an absolute individual who reigns over the universe as Sovereign Lord (as in Reformed theology); instead he is an all-embracing, sympathetic consciousness who tries to influence history by the lure of love rather than rule over history. He is the Cosmic Persuader rather than King and Lord of all creation.

What distinguishes the process view most from the classical Christian view is that God is held to be inseparable from nature. Process thinkers generally take pains to disassociate their position from pantheism in which God is identified with the substance or reality of the world and the empirical world is then reduced to the multiform appearance of a cosmic unity or an overarching idea. Their position is better referred to as panentheism (Hartshorne) in which God encompasses the world and the world is included in God without being identical with him. God is then the soul of the world, and the world is the body of God (Teilhard, Hartshorne). God is the creative force or creative good within the world drawing it toward the eternal ideals of the good, the true and the beautiful.

God is related to the world as fire to wood. The wood is consumed in the fire, but the fire lives off the wood. What is good and true in the world and in human life is taken up into the life of God, and thereby God is enriched by the world. It is assumed that God needs *some* world in order to be living and creative; otherwise God would simply remain an abstraction or principle. Whitehead distinguishes between the primordial nature of God (the idea of God) and his consequent nature (his concrete life as a creative force in the world). He also speaks of eternal objects or ideals by which God as the creative mover in the world guides and directs the world. Not all process thinkers subscribe to this Platonic vision of a separate world of eternal objects, but they nonetheless speak of the world as moving toward transcendent ideals.

In glaring contradiction to the Reformed view that God created the world out of nothing (*ex nihilo*), process thinkers envisage God as forming the world out of a pre-existent matter (*ex hulas*). God is the unifier and organizer of the world process (Teilhard) rather than an almighty Creator and Lord.

In process theology God does not so much act in history as receive the impressions of history and incorporate them into his own life. He is a spiritual presence that resides in nature rather than a Sovereign Lord who intervenes in history. He moves the world by the magnetic power of his beauty and love rather than judges the world by his holiness; he is the final cause of the world rather than its formal cause. He empathizes with the world in its sorrow rather than judges the world in its sin. God is the sympathy that soothes much more than the fire that burns.[12]

While the God of classical Christian faith is infinite and personal, the process God is actually finite and potentially infinite. He is suprapersonal rather than personal in a realistic or naive sense. He is characterized not by all-sufficiency and impassibility but by transcendent excellence (Hartshorne). He is not surpassed by any other process or being, but he can and does surpass himself as he strives toward new heights and goals. Process thinkers like to state the issue this way: Our choice is between the unchanging and passionless absolute of classical tradition and the creative surge or creative emergence of modern evolutionary thought.

Reformed theologians would retort that the God of the Bible is not a passionless absolute but absolute love and holiness. He is God in action, not a God who grows. He agonizes over human sin rather than simply empathizes with human suffering. Moreover, he acts to rescue people from sin instead of simply resolving the discords of existence in his own life. The process God is not a God who is sovereign over the world but a God who can only influence the world by the magnetic attraction of his beauty and love. No wonder that Whitehead describes God as "the poet of the world" rather than its creator.

41

Anglican theologian Eric Mascall has likened the process view of God's relation to the world to a mutual aid society. This is perhaps a little unfair, since for process thinkers, we owe God our very lives, whereas God depends on us only for his enrichment. Moreover, we generally fall short of the ideals to which God beckons us. At the same time, Mascall's metaphor accurately reflects their belief that God and humanity are co-creators and that we contribute to his perfection just as he contributes to our satisfaction.

The Reformed understanding is a supernatural creationism in which God creates the world out of nothing, distinct from himself but entirely dependent on himself. Process theology, by contrast, is a form of naturalism that envisions God as a creative process within the world or as the creativity that activates the world. British philosopher P. F. Strawson has said that what philosophy can regard as worthy of the veneration formerly directed to God is "the universe." Hartshorne endorses this view provided that the universe is taken to mean the all-inclusive reality—the soul as well as the body of the world and not simply the phenomenal world as such.[13]

Finally, Reformed theology faithful to Christian tradition conceives of God as a Trinity—Father, Son and Holy Spirit. Even though process theologians sometimes use Trinitarian language, their conception is modalistic: God acts in three or more different ways or there are different aspects of the creative process. Basically God is envisaged as binitarian—as finite (in his concrete aspect) and infinite (in his abstract aspect), as relative and absolute. Whitehead did speak of three natures in God—the primordial, consequent and superject—but these are not three subjectivities or agencies of consciousness; instead they represent the ever-continuing cosmic process of God going out of himself and returning to himself. Hartshorne in his latest book portrays God as androgynous or bisexual—with the feminine element predominating.[14] God is both creative and receptive, but he is essentially the receptacle of the world's values. Reformed theology is emphatic that God coexists as a fellowship within himself and is not in need of any world for the completion of his perfection. In process thought God needs the world by a metaphysical necessity; otherwise God is reduced to an empty abstraction apart from the world.

Christ and Salvation

Process theologians make a place for Jesus, but basically he is seen not as the Word made flesh but instead as the universal center of psychic convergence, the model of self-realization. Sharply breaking with Christian tradition, they deny that there was just one incomparable incarnation in history—when God became man in Jesus Christ. In its place they argue for a universal cosmic incarnation of which Jesus is a supreme manifestation. While some hail Jesus as the perfect embodiment of the ideals of goodness, truth and beauty, others see him as only one step, albeit a crucial one, in the upward surge of creative evolution. "I do not think of Jesus as the highest product of the creative process," says Wieman; indeed, "the revelation of God in Christ should never be identified with the man Jesus."[15] For Teilhard de Chardin, Jesus is the bearer and goal of the upward movement of the universe toward the divine. The focus of our attention should be not on the historical Jesus but on the universal Christ, the omega point of evolution, the goal of the evolutionary process.

Jesus is important in the salvific process because in him the power of creative transformation was manifest. In this respect he is the pioneer of our salvation. What rose from the dead was not the person of Jesus but the life-giving power at work within him which gave the disciples a new horizon of meaning (Wieman).

Process thinkers are quick to deny those doctrines that are dear to Reformed theology—Jesus as an expiation for sin or as a propitiation of the wrath of God. Such beliefs, they say, belong to a mythological past. Teilhard prefers to speak of "the cross of evolution" instead of the cross of substitution, meaning that Jesus bore the weight of a world in evolution as we also do when we are incorporated into his body.

Salvation is a growth of qualitative meaning rather than the forgiveness of sins or deliverance from bondage to the powers of darkness. To be saved means to muster the courage to realize our potential as bearers of creativity. It is to "enjoy rich harmonies of living, and pour this richness into the one ultimate receptacle of all achievement, the life of God," where it will be forever immortalized in the memory of God.[16]

Whereas Reformed theology envisages a world lost in sin, process theology sees the world as teeming with infinite possibilities. Sin, in this new understanding, is basically a resistance to creativity, a failure to live up to moral ideals. It is stubbornness and resistance to change rather than transgression of a moral law that carries with it the penalty of damnation. Evil is an obstruction rather than a curse that cripples and paralyzes the human race. It is to be traced to a deficiency in understanding and a reluctance to break with the past rather than an inborn lust for power that pits man against the living God (as in Reformed theology). It is to be linked with the inertia of nature (Whitehead) or the intractability of matter (Plato).

In the process view, God can mitigate but not eradicate evil, since every new breakthrough into freedom brings with it new possibilities for temptation and sin. The discords of life are transformed in the life of God into a higher unity rather than nailed to the cross as that which God negates; in this sense what we regard as evil is seen as contributing to a higher good.

In the Reformed view, evil signifies an assault upon the good and must be overcome and defeated rather than altered or transfigured. There is no satisfactory rational explanation for the possibility of evil, but there is a spiritual solution to the presence of evil—the cross and resurrection of Christ whereby God takes upon himself the sin, guilt and shame of the world so that all who believe might not perish but have eternal life. This victory over sin is already secured, but it needs to be enacted and fulfilled in concrete human experience.

Following in the tradition of Neo-Platonic mysticism, process thinkers see as the ultimate evil not human sin but the "perpetual perishing of time" (Whitehead). In contrast to the mystics, they realize that we cannot escape from time, but the values of our life can be immortalized in the memory of God.

Process theologians deny the resurrection of the body and, for the most part, the immortality of the soul as well. What is immortal is not the human ego, which is in a constant state of flux, but the ideals that give meaning to human existence and the actions that manifest these ideals. Our good deeds are remembered by God and thus made to serve the ultimate harmony and beauty toward which the world is moving. According to Hartshorne, "The only immortality we need is opportunity, by our joyous and beneficent earthly living, to enrich the divine life, which alone is imperishable and alone is able to appreciate the values we create in all their worth."[17]

Reformed theology envisages the kingdom of God breaking into history but always standing in judgment over history; process thought, on the other hand, sees a kingdom of freedom at work in history eventuating in the christification of the universe (Teilhard). The idea of progress seems to be an invariable concomitant of the idea of process, though this is not always obvious in all process thinkers. Whitehead interprets the history of the world as "the victory of persuasion over force."[18] Wieman believes that "we are passing over one of the great divides of history; possibly it is the last high pass over the top mountain range before we enter the valley of abundance."[19] Yet the march onward and upward is not without tragic interruption. There may be relapses and diversions, though basically the surge of evolution cannot be turned back. Creative evolution will inevitably go forward, even if it is through much darkness and misery.

Ethics and Spirituality

This optimism concerning the human situation also leaves its imprint in the areas of ethics and spirituality. It is not the corruption of human virtue but the release of human possibilities that engages process thinkers.

Although process theologians speak much about love, they generally have in mind the *eros* of Hellenistic philosophy and religion, not the *agape* of the New Testament. In their view, eros is the love of the good, the true and the beautiful. Whitehead even describes God as "the eros of the universe" and "the eternal urge of desire." As Anders Nygren has ably shown, eros is the love that proceeds from emptiness to fulness, whereas agape is the love that proceeds from strength and fulness to emptiness.[20] Eros is self-enriching while agape is self-denying.

For process thinkers, the primary motivation in both divine and human action is the will to satisfaction. We love others in order to fulfill the deepest yearnings within the self and in the universe. This is the ethics of eudaemonism, defended in its classical form by both Plato and Aristotle.

A place is made for altruism, but altruism is really in the service of egoism. Our love is directed toward possession of the perfect good. We love others by recognizing the presence of the same God in the depth of their being (Teilhard); consequently, our neighbor is a stepping stone to union with God. We love both ourselves and others in order to enrich the life of God and thereby to fulfill ourselves in God (Hartshorne). Our worship of God is a "a means to successful living" or an aid in attaining "the supreme good" (Wieman). God, moreover, is motivated to help humanity by a desire to satisfy his own yearning for fulfillment.

Against this view of love, theology in the Reformation tradition stresses the incompatibility of agape and eros (Luther, Nygren, Barth). God loves us not in order to fulfill himself (he is already fulfilled) but in order to redeem the sinner. We are led to love our neighbor not because we see in him a reflection of the God within us but because we genuinely wish to help our neighbor even in his sin. Self-love must be crucified so that other-love may develop and grow. Our love for God is born not out of the desire to possess the greatest good (as in Neo-Platonic mysticism and process thought) but out of the joy of knowing that our sins are forgiven.

One of the striking features of process theology is the subordination of ethics to aesthetics. For Whitehead, "The real world is good when it is beautiful."[21] Such thinkers are inclined to speak of the holiness of beauty rather than the God of holy love who makes moral demands. This is a God, as Whitehead says, whose love "neither rules, nor is it unmoved; also it is a little oblivious as to morals."[22] How utterly different is the conviction of Calvin and Luther that God sees, knows and judges every sin!

This aesthetic bent is evident in Hartshorne's remarks on child rearing:

> If I were bringing up a child, I should not start by burdening him with a lot of moral rules. I should begin by trying to help the child see that life can be beautiful and can be lived beautifully. Then I should not need to bother so much about how moral ideas would develop.[23]

Whitehead sees an eternal divine ideal for creation—that of harmony and intensity. It is toward this ideal that all of creation is moving—an ultimate harmony of opposites that will be impressive for the sheer impact of its beauty. While Reformed theology locates the key to peace in reconciliation between God and a fallen humanity, Whitehead regards peace as "primarily a trust in the efficacy of beauty."[24]

Because of their tendency to understand sin as a failure to realize the good rather than an unfailing proclivity to corrupt the good, process thinkers are inclined to be naive in the area of power politics. Whitehead applauded Chamberlain's accommodation to Hitler at Munich as a promise of better relations between the two countries. Hartshorne advocates a unilateral reduction in our nuclear arsenal in the hope that the Soviet Union will follow our example of common sense. In contradistinction to Reformed theology, process thinkers rest the hope of the world on the persuasive power of reason rather than on the resurrection of Jesus Christ and the outpouring of the Holy Spirit.

In the area of spirituality, scholars in the process tradition regard worship as an adventure into creativity rather than as submission before a holy God who demands loving obedience from his people. Worship is the celebration of the power of creativity to overcome all obstacles rather than the commemoration of a unique and incomparable event in the past when God in the person of his Son dealt the death blow to the powers of darkness, the reverberations of which continue to resound throughout history (the Reformed view).

Prayer in the process view is not personal petition to a God who has the power to alter world history but instead an attitude that brings us into contact with the power of creative transformation or the hidden possibilities within ourselves and others. Prayer is meditation on the wonder and joy of living rather than the pouring out of the soul before a merciful and almighty God. In Reformed theology it is not the rhapsody of nature or the exuberance of a creative life but the cross of Christ that is the focal point of spirituality.

Process thinkers do not deny the petitionary dimension in prayer, but for them petition is basically a formula for self-realization. "As we pray," Marjorie Suchocki says, "we change . . . ourselves in our deepest orientation."[25] Wieman offers this prayer as a model for the believer: "God, quicken every cell of my body, and all the love of my heart, and every impulse of my flesh, to the creativity of beautiful forms of intellectual and artistic achievement."[26] He urges us to repeat this petition until our whole nature "spontaneously expresses itself in artistry." It is therefore not so much a petition as auto-suggestion; it is what the New Thought movement would call an "affirmation."

The prayer of praise and thanksgiving is likewise altered in this latest brand of modernism. In Reformed theology we are called to praise and thank God primarily for what he has done for us in Jesus Christ, for the gift of reconciliation and redemption. We also thank God for his creation and providential care. In process theology we praise God in order to bring ourselves into contact with his transforming power. We thank God that we can be included in the surge of evolution and celebrate the fact that evolution cannot be defeated or overthrown. In his *Hymn to Matter* Teilhard says: "Blessed be you, mighty matter, irresistible march of evolution, reality ever new-born."[27]

Whereas Reformed theology avers that man's chief concern should be to glorify God and enjoy him forever (Westminster Shorter Catechism), process theology places the accent on human beings sharing the glory of God in the creative advance into novelty. One process thinker puts it this way: "The work of the church . . . is not to glorify God in the traditional sense, but to enable the individual to fulfill himself by acting wisely and effectively, to find himself through fellowship, and to gain release from inner constraints which render ineffective the flow of creativity."[28]

As might be expected, the traditional goal of missions is radically subverted in favor of "mutual understanding" and "creative interchange."[29] Wieman is not opposed to seeking conversions so long as we are willing to subordinate our limited visions of truth to the higher vision that arises from the encounter between faiths. The religion we should strive for is the one that is most inclusive. To hold uncompromisingly to the particularity of the biblical claims is to place an unnecessary impediment to interreligious dialogue.

A Biblical-Modern Synthesis

Process theology is best understood as an attempted synthesis between biblical and modern thought born out of an apologetic concern to make the gospel credible and palatable to its cultured despisers. This pronounced apologetic thrust is evident in the fervent desire of process theologians to reconcile religion and modern science. It can be seen in their concerted effort to bring into the service of religion such ideas as evolution, relativity, organism and creativity, all of which are derived from either the natural or social sciences.

Unabashedly capitulating to the cultural pressures around him, Wieman makes clear why the Christian message must be recast in a new mold: "The apologist for religion should present all our most sacred beliefs and programs of action as tentative and experimental. Until he does that he can never make Christianity acceptable to this age."[30]

That process thought signifies an accommodation of the faith to evolutionary naturalism and romanticism is incontrovertible. But it also contains elements of the very same biblical-classical synthesis that it condemns in orthodox theology. Hartshorne in particular believes that we must continue to find points of contact between the Judeo-Christian tradition and classical philosophy if we are to do justice to the search for wisdom in all ages. It can be shown that process thought has a definite affinity to the philosophy of the pre-Socratic Heraclitus, who affirmed the priority of becoming over being. It also has a pronounced Platonic and Neo-Platonic cast; indeed it was Plato who spoke of the world soul as self-moved and interpreted creation as the attempt by God to bring structure and form to chaotic matter in the light of eternal ideas. Aristotle, who envisaged God as the final cause of the world moving the world by the sheer force of attraction, also resonates with the process view. The philosophies of both Whitehead and Hartshorne might be regarded as idealistic as well as naturalistic because of the role of eternal or divine ideals in the evolutionary process.

While it is indisputable that process and Reformed theologies represent two different types of religion, this does not mean that Reformed theologians cannot learn positively from this new adversary of historic Christian faith. On the basis of the doctrine that all people are created in the image of God and that sin can blur but not eradicate this image as well as the doctrine that God's Spirit is at work in the world outside the church preserving that world from chaos, we can detect glimpses of truth in the process position, truth that has sometimes been suppressed in historical orthodoxy. It can be said that in every heresy there is a remnant of orthodoxy, just as in every orthodoxy there is some intimation of heresy. We as evangelical and Reformed theologians need to be aware of our own susceptibility to heresy as well as the accidental wisdom in systems of thought that are obviously heretical.

First, we should acknowledge that the process insistence on the unavoidability of metaphysics in theology and philosophy is well-made. Too often theologians have skirted metaphysics and focused only on ethics, soteriology or spirituality. Because the gospel is a report of the saving deeds of God rather than a life- and world-view, some Barthians regard the latter as of little concern. But even though not itself a world view, does not the gospel carry with it metaphysical implications that contrast it with the claims of non-Christian religions and philosophies? Whitehead has even declared that both scientific theory and method cannot be divorced from the unconscious metaphysics which they assume.[31]

Again, the insights of the process thinkers on the subject of language and symbolism can be helpful to evangelical theologians. Whitehead rightly recognized that when applied to ultimate reality, "words and phrases must be stretched towards a generality foreign to their ordinary usage."[32] Both Hartshorne and Ogden admit the need for analogical as well as univocal language in the description of God and his activity in the world. My criticism here is that they relegate the biblical depictions of God to the level of poetry and myth, whereas philosophical generalizations are believed to be closer to literal truth.

Whitehead's stress on the interrelatedness in the world is salutary and indeed may reflect certain themes of his Anglican background. His emphasis on the solidarity of the human race can be useful in clarifying the doctrine of original sin and also the doctrine of the church as the body of Christ.

The process insistence on human dignity and freedom may be a welcome antidote to certain strands within Reformed thought that have overemphasized the depravity and helplessness of man. The impression is sometimes given in Reformed circles that to glorify God is to reduce man to nothing. Irenaeus was closer to the biblical vision when he affirmed that "the glory of God is man fully alive." Karl Barth has recaptured the original Calvinist vision that God's glory means the redemption and elevation of humanity. For Barth, even human eros can be redeemed, although it must never be confused with agape, which remains always other-directed.

Finally, we should recognize that there is much truth in the process allegation that orthodox Christian theology has been adversely affected by a synthesis of biblical insights and classical philosophy. The biblical-classical synthesis is discernible not only in the tradition of Christian mysticism but even in the traditions of the Reformation and Protestant orthodoxy. The classical idea of perfection as all-sufficiency and completeness has indubitably penetrated Christian thinking and prevented the church through the ages from giving due justice to the biblical idea of God sharing in the pain and suffering of his people. It was said that God is impassible, impervious to pain and suffering, and this is why not only the church fathers and medieval scholastics but also Calvin and other mainline Reformers insisted that Christ suffered only in his human nature, not in his divine nature. Calvin and Reformed orthodoxy also contended that the biblical descriptions of God "repenting" or "changing his mind" are to be taken metaphorically, not literally. Here again Karl Barth has helped us to reappropriate a neglected side of the biblical tradition.

The principal contrast between Reformed and process theologies is to be found in the area of basic orientation. Reformed theology is unashamedly theocentric. The goal in life is to glorify God and serve the kingdom of God. Process theology, on the other hand, is essentially anthropocentric. Life's goal is to realize human potential in the service of a better world in which we are included as participants and contributors. We contribute to the enrichment of God, but God also contributes to our enrichment and fulfillment. Wieman put it this way: "God is that in the universe which will yield maximum security and increase of human good when lives are properly adjusted to him."[33] Process theologians would have considerable difficulty in affirming with the early Calvinists in New England that we should be willing to be damned for the glory of God.

The divergences between the two theologies are also glaringly apparent in the area of authority (as we have seen). Reformed theology confesses that God in his self-revelation in Jesus Christ as attested in the Bible has final and unconditional authority for faith and life. Process theology affirms that our authority lies in what can be felt and perceived empirically and what can be tested scientifically. Faith in the process view is emptied of cognitive content: it becomes an open-ended search for truth. In Reformed theology, on the contrary, faith is a steady and certain knowledge of God's promises to us and his beneficence to us (Calvin).[34]

The fact that process theology locates authority in cultural experience betrays its ideological character. An ideology is here understood as a complex of ideas that appeal more to emotion than to reason and that serve vested interests in society, thereby preventing one from perceiving the full reality of the human situation. Democratic liberalism is one such ideology, and it cannot be denied that the process vision of an open universe and its stress on the decisive role of individuals in shaping their own destiny are intimately bound up with the virtues emphasized in liberal democracy: freedom, autonomy, relativity and pluralism. Indeed, Wieman calls for a new formulation of faith in tune with democracy in which "the guide and standard will be the fullest self-expression and mutual understanding of particular individuals."[35] Hartshorne regards the Calvinist appeal to an infallible divine revelation as compromising "the essential principle of democracy, that none of us is divinely wise, that we all may make mistakes."[36] He complains that to insist upon "the classical view of revelation" is to impose "a fearful burden on our democracy."[37] Moreover, the process view that being is to be understood in terms of doing fits in well with such values of the modern technological society as productivity, efficiency and utility.

In making this kind of criticism, however, we should keep in mind that all theology has an ideological taint, including Reformed theology. The emphasis on predestination and subordination in classical Reformed thought may be partly derived from feudalistic and monarchial ideologies of the past, though this is not to imply that these doctrines do not have biblical roots as well. Christians should at all times endeavor to transcend ideological bias, and we can be partly successful in this task because we are in contact with a God who transcends human culture even while he is actively at work within it. Yet we should always be circumspect in our claims, especially in the political and social arena, knowing that we are probably more children of our times than prophets to our times.

Process theology represents an excursus religion, calling people out of a past faith orientation into one more in tune with the spirit of the times. Reformed theology on the other hand is a confirmatory religion, seeking to maintain continuity with past traditions but endeavoring at the same time to communicate the insights of the past in a fresh way. It is the same faith but phrased in new language, though this new language is a supplement, not a substitute for the original symbolism of Christian tradition, what Barth calls the language of Canaan and the language of Zion. Process theology heralds a new faith, one that is closer both in spirit and in content to the Renaissance and Enlightenment than to the Reformation. Its symbols and metaphors are derived for the most part from physics, biology and psychology and are to be seen as substitutes for the traditional language of faith.

Nicolas Berdyaev, who is welcomed by process thinkers as an ally in forging a dynamic view of God, contrasts the modern view with the classical one: "The revelation of a suffering and yearning God is higher than the revelation of a God whose sufficiency and satisfaction are in himself."[38] I would have to agree that the modern process conception of a God who shares our suffering is probably closer to the biblical view than the Hellenistic conception of a God who is wholly self-contained, who is removed from temporality and exempt from vulnerability. But are these the only alternatives? Much better is the biblical view of God, rediscovered though not always maintained in Reformed theology, a view in which God is pictured not as the Unmoved Mover (Aristotle) nor as the creative process but as being in act, the One who decisively enters into history irrevocably altering its course. Such a God changes only in his ways with humankind, not in his innermost being nor in his overriding will and purpose. He is therefore a God who can be depended upon. Can a God limited in knowledge and deficient in power be depended upon in times of trial and distress? Is such a God even worthy of worship?

At its best, Reformed theology affirms a God who is in himself impassible and omnipotent but who enters into our suffering not to satisfy his yearning for fulfillment (as in Berdyaev and process thinkers) but out of compassion for a lost human race. This is a God who basically does not need the world because he coexists as a fellowship of love within himself. Yet this God chooses freely to relate to the world in order to share the richness of his love and mercy; in so doing he makes himself vulnerable to affliction and suffering, which can only touch him where he touches the world—in the person of Jesus Christ. This is a God, moreover, who does not simply empathize with us in our sufferings but who rescues us from pain and suffering through the sacrificial life and death of Jesus Christ and his glorious resurrection from the grave.

Reformed theology insists that in Jesus Christ the whole world has been changed, since God in Christ took upon himself the burden of the world's afflictions, the penalty for human sin. It is not God who needs to be changed (as in the process view) but fallen humankind, and this change is enacted not through the will to creativity but through the mystery of supernatural regeneration. The hope of humanity rests not on our cooperation with the power of creative transformation but instead on a divine intervention into human history that happened in the past and will happen once more when Jesus Christ comes again to bring in the kingdom that shall have no end.

NOTES

1. Reinhold Niebuhr might also be included in this list except that his impact was restricted primarily to intellectual circles and then only for a brief period—the 1940s and 50s. Niebuhr's political thought continues to have an influence on the moderate right wing of the political spectrum. His emphasis on tragedy, irony, ambiguity and the inaccessibility of God represents a foreign intrusion into the American religious scene. It stands in direct opposition to the optimistic, romantic and Pelagian character of American philosophy and religion, which is reflected in process philosophy and theology, the New Thought movement and the electronic church movement. Niebuhr is closer to what I have called Reformed theology than to process theology, although he seeks a synthesis of Renaissance and Reformation insights.

Paul Tillich, who is also worthy of mention, stands closer to the American dream, despite his preoccupation with fate and tragedy. His this-worldly mysticism and ecstatic naturalism reveal an affinity to both process and feminist theologies.

2. Bernard E. Meland, *America's Spiritual Culture* (NY: Harper and Bros., 1948) pp. 93, 135.

3. Alfred North Whitehead, *Religion in the Making* (NY: Macmillan Co., 1957), p. 148.

4. I am closer to the theological methodology of Calvin, Kuyper, Forsyth and Barth than to that of Charles Hodge and Benjamin Warfield. But they all had a common devotion to the glory of God above all else and a zealous adherence to the sovereignty of divine grace.

Process Theology and Reformed Theology

5. Because this chapter is basically a critique of process thought from the perspective of Reformed theology, I shall concentrate on delineating the position of process theologians on various questions and then present what I believe is the proper Reformed alternative. In order to save space, I have refrained from giving substantial corroboration for my understanding of Reformed theology, but the reader should know that Calvin and Barth are my chief mentors.

6. Heinrich Heppe summarizes the position of Reformed orthodoxy thus: The truth of revelation "is not imparted to man by flesh and blood, but solely by the Spirit of grace, who opens a man's eyes and directs his heart, that he may achieve a certain knowledge of revealed fact." Heinrich Heppe, *Reformed Dogmatics*. Trans. G. T. Thomson (Grand Rapids: Baker, 1950), p. 7.

7. Alfred North Whitehead, *Process and Reality* (NY: Macmillan Co., 1929), p. 63.

8. Alfred North Whitehead, *Adventures of Ideas* (NY: Macmillan Co., 1933), p. 228.

9. Henry Nelson Wieman and Regina Westcott-Wieman, *Normative Psychology of Religion* (Westport, Conn.: Greenwood Press, 1971), pp. 114-115.

10. See Schubert Ogden, *The Reality of God and Other Essays* (NY: Harper & Row, 1966), pp. 56-70.

11. Marjorie Hewitt Suchocki, *God-Christ-Church: A Practical Guide to Process Theology* (NY: Crossroad, 1982), p. 85.

12. Alan Gragg acknowledges that Hartshorne tries to make a place for this last notion but that he does not develop it sufficiently. See Alan Gragg, *Charles Hartshorne* (Waco: Word Books, 1975 3rd Printing), p. 112.

13. Charles Hartshorne, *Omnipotence and Other Theological Mistakes* (Albany, NY: State University of New York Press, 1984), p. 123.

14. Ibid., pp. 56-60.

15. Robert W. Bretall, ed., *The Empirical Theology of Henry Nelson Wieman* (NY: Macmillan, 1963), p. 191.

16. Charles Hartshorne, *The Divine Relativity: A Social Conception of God* (New Haven: Yale University Press, 1948), pp. 127-128.

17. Charles Hartshorne, *Insights and Oversights of Great Thinkers* (Albany: State University of New York Press, 1983), p. 186.

18. Whitehead, *Adventures of Ideas*, p. 31.

19. Henry Nelson Wieman, *The Source of Human Good* (Chicago: University of Chicago Press, 1946), p. 52.

20. See Anders Nygren, *Agape and Eros*. Trans. Philip S. Watson (Chicago: University of Chicago Press, 1982).

21. Whitehead, *Adventures of Ideas*, p. 345.

22. Whitehead, *Process and Reality*, pp. 520-521.

23. Cited in Norman Pittenger, *The Lure of Divine Love* (NY: Pilgrim Press, 1979), p. 25.

24. Whitehead, *Adventures of Ideas*, p. 367.

25. Suchocki, *God-Christ-Church*, p. 206.

26. Henry Nelson Wieman, *The Wrestle of Religion with Truth* (NY: Macmillan, 1927), p. 79.

27. Cited in Hans Küng, *Does God Exist?* Trans. Edward Quinn (Garden City, NY: Doubleday & Co., 1980), p. 175.

28. Wayne Shuttee, "The Work of the Church" in *The Empirical Theology of Henry Nelson Wieman*, ed. Robert W. Bretall (NY: Macmillan Co., 1963), [pp. 211-221], p. 220.

29. Wieman, *The Wrestle of Religion with Truth*, p. 169.

30. Henry Nelson Wieman, "Wrong Ways to Justify Religion," *The Christian Century*, vol. 46, no. 51 (Dec. 18, 1929) [pp. 1571-1573], p. 1573.

31. Whitehead, *Adventures of Ideas*, p. 198.

32. Whitehead, *Process and Reality*, p. 6.

33. Wieman, *The Wrestle of Religion with Truth*, p. 59.

34. Cf.: "Now, we shall have a complete definition of faith, if we say, that it is a steady and certain knowledge of the Divine benevolence towards us, which, being founded on the truth of the gratuitous promise in Christ, is both revealed to our minds, and confirmed to our hearts, by the Holy Spirit." John Calvin, *Institutes of the Christian Religion*. Trans. & ed. John Allen (Phil.: Presbyterian Board of Christian Education, 1936), III, II, 7, p. 604.

35. Henry Nelson Wieman, *Now We Must Choose* (NY: Macmillan, 1941), p. 174.

36. Hartshorne, *Omnipotence and Other Theological Mistakes*, p. 6.

37. Ibid., pp. 43, 44.

38. Nicolas Berdyaev, *Truth and Revelation*. Trans. R. M. French (NY: Collier Books, 1962), p. 56.

PART TWO

Theological Considerations

The Process Reduction
of Jesus and the Trinity

Bruce Demarest

Bruce Demarest

Bruce Demarest, Professor of Systematic Theology at Denver Conservative Baptist Seminary, is a graduate of Wheaton College (B.S.), Adelphi University (M.S.), Trinity Evangelical Divinity School (M.A.) and the University of Manchester (England) where he received his Ph.D. Dr. Demarest is the author or editor of four books including *A History of Interpretation of Hebrews 7:1-10 From the Reformation to the Present, General Revelation: Historical Views and Contemporary Issues*, and *Challenges to Inerrancy: A Theological Response.* He has contributed to the *New International Dictionary of the Christian Church*, the *New International Dictionary of New Testament Theology*, and the *Evangelical Dictionary of Theology.*

Two crucial features of the Christian faith—without which it would cease to be intrinsically Christian—are the Incarnation of the Son of God, whereby God took upon Himself our humanity, and the Trinity, that loving sociality of three persons within the being of the Godhead. Thus in this article we are dealing with theological concerns that are most thoroughly essential to the Christian way. The person and work of Jesus Christ represents the fundamental datum, the main pillar of the Christian faith. In the words of Emil Brunner, "the center and the foundation of the whole Christian faith is 'Christology,' that is, faith in Jesus Christ."[1] No matter for abstract speculation, Jesus' identity and accomplishment on the Cross is inextricably linked with the hope of salvation and with one's view of God. For if Christ is the eternal Word spoken by the Father and if the unity of God is taken seriously, a plurality of persons within the Godhead immediately follows. Hence the deity of Jesus Christ and the Trinity are necessarily interconnected tenets of the Christian faith.

Another factor that highlights the importance of this topic is that process theology has mounted one of the most potent challenges to orthodox Christian truth in the second half of the twentieth century. The process school of Whitehead, Hartshorne, Cobb and company has promoted its gospel of naturalistic theism with unflagging zeal, such that in many academic quarters it has supplanted classical theism, neo-orthodoxy, or theistic existentialism as *the* viable theological system. If liberation theology is becoming the theology of the masses, process theology is gaining ground as the theology of the non-evangelical scholar. Indeed, the future may witness some form of marriage between process theory and liberation praxis. Thus evangelical faith today confronts process theology as a potent contemporary challenge. The attraction of the Whiteheadian system is seen in the fact that some younger evangelicals, particularly within the Arminian tradition, have bought into aspects of process theology.

Assumptions of Process Theology

Several underlying premises of process thought contribute a priori to its assessment of the person and work of Jesus and the Trinity. The first is its postulate of the universe as panentheistic; namely, that the reality of God includes the world within itself while at the same time transcending the world. Reality, according to process thought, is a single spatio-temporal process consisting of a series of becomings and perishings, with new becomings emerging from that which has perished. The biblical world view of natural and supernatural realms assumes a prescientific vision of the universe which process thought rejects in the name of scientific modernity. Although the Jesus of process thought accepted the world view of his day, process theology rejects the dualism between matter and spirit in favor of a one-order vision of the universe. Thus, according to Pittenger, "the notion of the natural and the supernatural, the belief in angelic and demonic spirits, the methods by which God was supposed to work in his world, etc., are not and cannot be ours."[2] This first assumption excludes any miraculous interruptions in the natural order, any 'intrusions' by God into the natural sphere in which he is ever operative. As Griffin affirms, "since the scientific revolution in the seventeenth century the conviction has grown that all events have natural causes, and that the natural sequence of cause and effect is never interrupted."[3] Of course if God does not supernaturally intrude from without the natural order, divine revelation by definition is excluded. So Griffin acknowledges that "the requirement of rationality seems to imply that theology cannot be based on revelation."[4] With the elimination of divine revelation, process theology takes its stand as a natural theology shaped from human materials alone.

Another important tenet of process theology is its repudiation of a substantial ontology. The movement insists that neither persons nor God can be objectified as an existent or a substantial self. An actual entity or a person, it is said, is constituted by relatedness to other entities or persons, in keeping with the Whiteheadian principle that becoming is more fundamental than being. In consequence of this philosophical assumption, "confidence has gone in the type of supernaturalistic ontology to which Christian theology in its classical presentations has been attached."[5] In particular, this means that process theologians no longer find the creedal formulations of Nicea and Chalcedon intelligible or relevant. The classical Christological and Trinitarian formulations, it is argued, were worked out within a world view that is alien to the modern scientific mindset.

The process school, moreover, comes to the theological task with a low view of Scripture. Theologians in the tradition assert that modern critical study of the New Testament precludes accepting all that is written therein as literally true. The primitive material concerning Jesus' life and teaching, it is argued, was altered by the practical needs of the early Christian community. Thus supernaturalist teachings and miracle stories are dismissed as spurious accretions. Cobb, for example, claims that "the stories of Jesus' temptation in the wilderness, his struggle in Gethsemane, and his forsakenness on the cross are not historically reliable."[6]

A final assumption that follows directly from the above is that process theologians feel free to dismiss or rewrite the orthodox body of Christian doctrine. That a doctrine appears on the pages of the Bible or that it was faithfully upheld by the historic Christian church provides no basis for its acceptance by modern empirically minded people. Hence process theology "will obviously require a rather fundamental reconstruction of the traditional views of Christian theology, for it is precisely the traditional methods and doctrines which have led to the problems."[7] By these words process theology has announced that it intends a significant reformulation of church doctrine, particularly in the areas of Christology and the Trinity.

The Person and Accomplishments of Jesus

Pre-existence of Christ

The purpose of this second section is to explicate several crucial aspects of Jesus' person and work from a process perspective so as to assess the Whiteheadian understanding of Christianity's central figure. With regard to the classical doctrine of pre-existence, process theology refuses to identify Jesus' selfhood with a pre-existent divine person. The orthodox claim that the personal center of Jesus' existence antedated his birth is viewed as a purely mythological notion

and thus meaningless for the modern mind. As redefined by J. A.
T. Robinson, pre-existence means "that a life, power or activity
(whether divine or spiritual) which is not as such a person comes
to embodiment and expression (whether partial or total) in an individual human being."[8] The widely debated concept of Christ's eternal
generation likewise has been reinterpreted in a nonmetaphysical
manner. Again Robinson states, "the Christ has been in the
process—yes, in process—from the start, and in this sense we may
speak of the 'eternal generation of the Son'."[9]

The Incarnation

Consideration of the Incarnation brings us to the heart of process
theology's conception of Jesus as the Christ. Whiteheadians reject
as crassly mythological the idea of the literal enfleshment of the
second person of the triune God. Modern minds must abandon "as
incredible and impossible the Greek idea of a god who comes down
to earth and walks about as a human being."[10] Process thinkers
repudiate the idea that the Incarnation involves an intrusion from
without; rather they insist that Jesus must have participated in the
total evolution of the human race and in the full history of the Jewish
people. In the language of process philosophy, "A self is a specific
routing or series of occasions in which there is a continuity which
includes the memory of the past, the relationships of the present,
and the projective aim toward the future."[11] Thus it is claimed that
Jesus was no outlandish anomaly unrelated to the world, but in the
fullest sense he was a Palestinian Jew who labored at a carpenter's
bench. Process thinkers likewise disavow the doctrine of Jesus' virgin
birth as mythological and nonhistorical. The carpenter was the
humanly conceived son of Joseph and Mary. "The stories told in
the first two chapters of Mathew and Luke are apologetic, or
Christological, in intent, and they cannot be taken as historical narratives. Insistence on a biological virgin birth has been a mistake."[12]
The process understanding of the Incarnation is rooted in its conception of the Logos identified as God in his primordial nature,
namely as that impersonal yet timeless principle of order and purpose
in the universe or the organ of novelty and the lure for feeling.
Process theologians insist that the early church fathers erred in
personifying the Logos as the eternally subsistent second person of

the Godhead. The Word, as the ground of meaning and the source of purpose, is said to be immanent in the world, luring all entities toward optimal creative transformation. The immanence of the Logos in the cosmos process theologians declare to be the Christ. As expressed by Cobb, " 'Christ' refers to the Logos as incarnate, hence as the process of creative transformation in and of the world."[13] It should be underscored that in the process vision, Christ, or the incarnate Logos, is present in all human beings and, indeed, in all creation. The degree, however, to which the Logos is present and operative in the world varies. Here process theology claims that the Logos achieved maximal actualization in the man Jesus of Nazareth. His significance resides in the fact that he represents the fullest incarnation of the Logos or the power of creative transformation. As articulated by Pittenger, to affirm that the Word was "enfleshed" means that Jesus "is the point where the Word is most signally, most intensively, most vitally and dynamically operative."[14] Only in the sense that Jesus is the paradigm instance of the indwelling of the Logos can it be said that the carpenter was the Christ.

The Two-Natures Doctrine

A fundamental tenet of process theology is that the classical two-natures doctrine of Christ presupposes concepts that are out-dated, absurd, and irrelevant to modern minds. It is argued that the substantialist model of the relation between God and Jesus must go, for the reason that two entities (such as God and man) cannot occupy the same space at the same time. This being so, process theologians insist that Deity, viewed as a substance, cannot possibly unite with humanity, likewise viewed as a substance, without creating a displacement of one substance by the other. Thus Cobb concludes that "Jesus is not 'consubstantial' with the Father, for the notion of any two entities being of the 'same substance' is rejected."[15] Whiteheadians are fond of referring to the so-called "havoc" wreaked in traditional theology by the orthodox formulation that involves an alleged displacement of two substances. Rather they insist that the old relation of essences must give way to the new model of an experiential relation in which societies of actual occasions or momentary experiences merge in creative synthesis. Expressed otherwise, one must view Jesus of Nazareth not in terms of two natures, but in terms of the structure of actual occasions that constituted his self.

67

Process theology begins with the claim that the Jesus who lies at the heart of the Christian faith was really and fully a man. The classical assertion that in Jesus Deity united with humanity would mean that some aspect of Jesus' humanity was displaced by God. Nothing, Whiteheadians insist, must stand in the way of affirming his complete manhood. The Nazarene should be regarded as the man whom God sent, in whom God worked, and through whom the reality of God was seen. "He was a fully human person who was related to God in a very special way."[16] Pittenger argues for the movement that neither Jesus nor his earthly companions ever entertained the idea that the son of Joseph and Mary was ontologically divine. Whiteheadians claim that Jesus was no more divine than any other person.

In lieu of a union between two substances (which is held to be logically impossible), process theology posits the immanence of God in the man Jesus. The distinctive Christian claim, it is argued, is that God indwelt the personal humanity of Jesus, providing Jesus with his initial aim and the lure to fulfillment. What process theology envisages is the mutual interaction of God the divine Lover and Jesus the human responsive lover in a moral union that is rich and complete.

> The most complete, the fullest, the most organic and integrated union of Godhead and manhood which is conceivable is precisely one in which by the gracious indwelling of God in man and by manhood's free response in surrender and love, there is established a relationship which is neither accidental nor incidental, on the one hand, nor mechanical and physical, on the other; but a full, free, gracious unity of the two in Jesus Christ.[17]

John 10:30 ("I and the Father are one") and John 14:11 are understood in the sense of the interpenetration of divine and human activities. The human self of Jesus was open to and responsively acting in concert with the working of the divine self. Thus process theology understands the old doctrine of the hypostatic union as "the coincidence of the divine and human acts, the act of God and the act of man."[18] Jesus, according to Pittenger, should be viewed not as the God-man but in terms of the rubric "God-in-man."[19]

Process theology is willing to talk about the Deity of Jesus only if it is defined in the sense of God's special presence and working in the man from Nazareth. Jesus is divine not because he is absolutely different from other men, but because he is the personalized instrument of God's self-expressive activity. That is, Jesus "is the primordial exemplification of God's immanence in the world, and our ultimate immanence in God."[20] The title, "Son of God," to the early Christians meant "privileged creature of God" by virtue of the activity of Divinity within him.[21] Process theologians insist that because Jesus is intrinsically a man (albeit a man who specially reveals God), he must not be the object of worship. God alone is worthy of the Christian's worship.

Process theologians make no attempt to camouflage their position regarding the person of Jesus Christ. When measured against the traditional orthodox view, process theology concedes its explication of Christianity's founder is, in fact, Ebionite.[22]

Jesus and Human Sin

Process theology's overriding concern to ensure the humanity of Jesus has led to the conclusion that the Nazarene shared the human experience of sin. The school argues that if Jesus were somehow exempted from human deficiency and sin he could not have been a real person. Thus, in the first place, Whiteheadians conclude that Jesus was neither omniscient, omnipotent, nor omnipresent. In addition, they claim that Jesus erroneously believed that physical and mental illness was caused by demons and that the world was headed toward some grand eschatological climax. Says Pittenger, "We need not hesitate to say that in these matters he was mistaken."[23] Believing that sin connotes a distortion of God's divine intention or aim for a person, process thinkers state not only that Jesus was tempted like we are, but that, in fact, he yielded to the force of temptation. In short, Jesus sinned in truly human fashion. Pittenger carries this line of thought further by suggesting that Jesus, like many of his contemporaries, engaged in homosexual activities. Pittenger, however, cautions against our adopting a negative view of homosexuality. To do so "is to denigrate God's creation, to succumb to a Manichean view of nature, and to deny the goodness of the sexuality with which God has endowed his human creatures."[24] Pittenger would have us be more understanding of Jesus, for manifestly "he [*was*] not of the marrying kind."[25]

Jesus' Speciality

Modern theologians have debated extensively the question of whether Jesus differed from other men in degree or in kind. Process theologians respond as one that Jesus could not have differed in kind from other persons, otherwise he would have been removed from the realm of the human and the historical.

> If some absolute difference in kind from other instances of God's revelatory and salvatory work in the world is predicated of Jesus, . . . , then it becomes apparent that our Lord is in fact removed from the concrete human situation and to what God is 'up to' in it; he seems irrelevant to us and to whatever else seems to speak of and from God to men.[26]

Assuming that Jesus differed from his contemporaries in degree rather than in kind, process theologians have debated the nature of the distinctive quality with which Jesus was endowed. Whiteheadians articulate a variety of responses to this issue.

Pittenger and Hamilton claim that the difference between Jesus and other persons was chiefly due to Jesus' total obedience to the will of the Father. The Logos is at work at all times, in all places, and in all persons and traditions. In this respect Jesus cannot be considered unique. However, the element of speciality or eminence in Jesus lies in the fact that he brought forth a greater fullness of response to the divine working than did other persons. That is, Jesus' total obedience to God's general aim or purpose provides the clue to the specialness of the Christ-event. The above line of argument suggests that Jesus cannot be considered final, for the reason that the God who is ceaselessly operative in the world has not stopped expressing himself. As affirmed by Pittenger, "to speak of Jesus, that particular individual man who lived in Palestine at a given time and place, as final is a mistake."[27]

Ford and Griffin, however, claim that whereas complete obedience to the divine purpose may be a necessary condition for Jesus' decisiveness or speciality, the fact is that God provided Jesus with a specifically Christological aim. In other words, what set Jesus apart from his brethren is the special aim God provided him and then his conformity to this specific aim. Because Jesus actualized God's Christological aim to an optimum degree, Christians regard Jesus as especially revelatory of God's character and ways. "The Christian believes that Jesus was God's supreme act of self-expression, and is therefore appropriately apprehended as God's decisive revelation."[28]

John B. Cobb, Jr., who has explored this issue more extensively than any other process thinker, insists that God's presence in Jesus is "unique." He claims that "Christians can think of Jesus' relation to God as decisively unique without involving themselves in absurdity, or irrational acceptance of dogma."[29] Although God is present in all occasions, Cobb maintains that God's presence in Jesus was unique in several respects: 1) With Ford and Griffin, the content of the initial aim presented to Jesus was unique; 2) With Pittenger, Jesus' actualization of God's initial aim for him was remarkably complete; and 3) most significantly, Jesus' structure of existence— his 'I'—was co-constituted by the incarnate Logos. With regard to the third and most crucial point, "Jesus' structure of existence . . . was one in which the tension of the self and the Logos was overcome in coalescence."[30] While maintaining that Jesus represents the full Incarnation of the Logos, Cobb strives to retain an open-ended religious pluralism by affirming the effective, albeit unconscious, working of the Logos in all persons and religions. The Logos is incarnate in the entire world, particularly in the spiritually sensitive religions of the East. He insists:

> The universalist claims of Christianity are that the divine Logos is present in all things and that it is fully incarnate and redemptively effective in Jesus. This leaves open the possibility that the Gautama might also have incarnated the Logos in a redemptive manner.[31]

Cobb not only claims that Buddhism may be a salvific faith, but that as Christianity opens itself to Buddhism and the religious traditions of Asia it may find itself positively transformed by the Logos in their midst. In sum, for Cobb, "Christ is the way that excludes no ways."[32]

Process theologians, then, uphold the uniformity of God's activity in the world, while claiming some specialty for Jesus as the focal point for God's working in the world. The orthodox assertion that Jesus Christ is the only way to God is regarded as a crude imperialist assertion. In an evolutionary cosmos, thinkers in the school want to allow room for the possible further development of truth after the historical person of Jesus of Nazareth.

Jesus' 'Saving' Work

Process theologians devote relatively little attention to the Cross, believing that the focus of Jesus' accomplishment resides in his life rather than in his death. Process thinkers acknowledge that whereas orthodoxy concentrates on the benefits of Jesus' death, White-headians largely concentrate on his life. Before launching into a consideration of Jesus' work, however, a brief mention of the process understanding of sin is in order. Process thinkers caution against holding an exaggerated picture of human sinfulness. Indeed, they maintain that there is no being that is inherently evil. Sin is viewed not as a radical evil that is rooted in human nature as such, but as a deviation of aim, a failure of achievement, in short, as an absence of love. Process anthropology is thus markedly Pelagian.

The traditional Christian teaching that the Cross of Christ propitiated God's anger against sin and effected reconciliation between the creature and the Creator is viewed by process theology as mythology that cannot be taken seriously in the modern world. Pittenger observes that the traditional notions of ransom, redemption, satisfaction, etc., are merely *symbols* devised to articulate the experience of Christians in a first century Near-Eastern culture. He adds, "The old legend of the garden of Eden portrays the way we seek to fulfill our own desires and in so doing deny our true nature."[33] Salvation, in the process understanding, does not mean deliverance from the penalty and power of sin. Rather it means right integration, the realization of one's significance, health, wholeness, healing of the split within the person, and exchange of egocentricity for concern for others. Salvation is viewed as that *process* of conformation to God's aim by exposure to the divine field of force. In brief, "it is a unity of life, on the way to full integration, where men and women are so related to . . . the cosmic thrust or drive."[34]

When it comes to interpreting the work of Jesus in the spiritual realm, process theologians insist that what was accomplished on the Cross cannot be fully explained. "There is a mystery here which we must accept . . . but which we can never hope to explicate with utter clarity."[35] Whiteheadians observe that God failed Jesus on the Cross by his inability to provide those lures that would have afforded Jesus the tranquility he needed in that hour of crisis. Still Whiteheadians venture that what Jesus accomplished on the Cross involves at least three elements. The first is the *example* he provided. Here the process view is not unlike that of the Socinians and Unitarians in the Reformation and post-Reformation eras. Jesus on the Cross gave demonstration of the character of God as sheer love in action, as love that is unconquered by death. Moreover, the Cross upholds God as compassionate co-sufferer with humankind. Jesus' suffering demonstrates that God is not immune to pain, anguish, or empathy. As expressed by Hartshorne, "Jesus appears to be the supreme symbol furnished to us by history of the notion of a God genuinely and literally sympathetic (incomparably more literally than any man ever is), receiving into his own experience the suffering as well as the joys of the world."[36] In addition, the Cross shows up humanity's moral defects, namely, that people tend to be wayward, unloving, and self-willed. And finally, the Cross of Jesus gives demonstration of what human life can be when lived in freedom and love. In this regard Jesus is "a representation of what human existence can be and is meant to be."[37]

In the second place, Jesus' life and death exerted on humankind a Godward *moral influence*. In addition to the demonstration Jesus provided of the heart of God and the ideal of human life, process thinkers claim that people are lured to authenticity by an answering love. The Logos operative displayed in Jesus stimulates the person to "align himself with the dynamic movement towards growth, towards enlargement, towards sharing in love."[38] Persons are said to be spiritually renewed as they respond positively to the lure for creative advance embodied by Jesus. Wedding traditional language with process conceptualities, Ford affirms: "We are being born anew and from above as we receive novel initial aims from God originating our subjectivity from moment to moment."[39] In the process vision, salvation depends largely on the individual's own ability to actualize the novel aims God provides. In other words, God in Christ evokes from his children the best response they have to offer. Or as Griffin observes, through the divine lure presented to people, "God constantly calls us to do and become more."[40] The process schema is thus seen to be a program of salvation by self-effort. Jesus is merely the paradigm of the possibilities already latent in humankind.

Process thinkers have devoted much attention to the question of the fate of those who have never heard the name of Jesus of Nazareth. Almost unanimously Whiteheadians affirm it unthinkable that God would withhold from his loved ones the opportunity to achieve authentic existence or salvation. According to Pittenger, God is sufficiently generous in spirit that "No man can be without the hope of authentic life, no matter where he has lived or what he has come to think or believe."[41] Given the assumption that the Logos is redemptively operative in the entire world, it follows that "Men can come to life without having encountered Jesus."[42] God wills the maximal fulfillment of every person whether he be a Christian or not a Christian. What then is the church's mission? That of proclaiming the special presence and working of God in Jesus. However, the Christian church must not carry into the world the "shocking and blasphemous" idea that God threatens with hellfire the vast majority of his children who either have not heard or not responded to the message of his love in Jesus. Such a God could not be a God of consummate love.[43]

Resurrection From the Dead?

As we have seen, process theology upholds a one-order view of the universe in which reality is regarded as a single yet endless process of becomings and perishings. Since the distinction between natural and supernatural is regarded as a vestige of a prescientific world view, no 'miraculous' interruptions in the natural order are allowed. It follows from these assumptions that process theology rejects the possibility of either a personal or a bodily resurrection of believers and of Jesus himself. Hamilton insists that the notion of personal resurrection or immortality is an illusion. " Our present personality cannot be raised individually and clothed upon with a resurrection body."[44] Process thinkers appropriate the radical conclusion that the Gospel resurrection narratives, in the main, are historically unreliable. They see in the four Gospel accounts an underlying apologetic purpose, irreconcilable inconsistencies, and considerable literary imagination. They claim that the focus of concern in the New Testament is not the Resurrection itself or the empty tomb, but the *results* of the Resurrection, which somehow are profoundly revelatory. In fact, spokesmen such as Griffin claim that personal resurrection is not one of the essential elements of the Christian faith. "Because Christian faith is possible apart from belief in Jesus' resurrection in particular and life beyond death in general, and because of widespread skepticism regarding these traditional beliefs, they should be presented as optional."[45]

According to process thinkers, the disciples in the so-called resurrection appearances were confronted not with the risen Jesus, but with hallucinatory experiences. However, beneath the stories of the appearances lies the crucial truth that somehow Jesus was alive and present to his followers in the form of a dynamic that would shape their common activities. As Ford explains it:

> Peter encountered a Spirit he knew to be one with the extraordinary life of the Master he had followed, a Spirit to whom he could now fully dedicate himself in the confidence that the aims and directives it mediated served God's purposes, just as Jesus had served those purposes during his lifetime.[46]

If, according to process thinkers, Jesus' resurrection was not the elevation of his corporeal self to the heavenly realm, precisely what does his resurrection connote? Most Whiteheadians claim that Jesus' resurrection signifies the fact that God raised Jesus' concrete *experiences* into objective immortality in himself. Just as in the Incarnation God prehended or indwelt Jesus, so in the Resurrection Jesus' subjectivity was 'raised' into God to be recreated continually and afresh in God's living memory. According to Mellert, "The significance of the death and resurrection is that Jesus is immanently present in God. God has taken what is human and worldly into himself in a complete and positive way."[47] Ford defines Jesus' resurrection differently, interpreting it in terms of the formation of the church, the body of Christ, and the furtherance of the evolutionary advance.[48]

Process thought, finally, attempts to relate the significance of Jesus' resurrection to the believer. God's act of taking Jesus into his own experience means that believers likewise are continually being taken up into the divine nature and 'resurrected' into objective immortality. The fact that God has transformed Jesus' tragedy and death into resurrection possibilities, means that he will transform the believer's threats and deaths into new possibilities for the future. God is said to mediate these life-giving benefits through prayer and the sacraments.

The Whiteheadian Vision of the Trinity

Foundational Considerations

Since consideration of Jesus Christ has a direct impact on one's understanding of the Trinity, a brief explication of the process vision of the triune Godhead will now be undertaken. Given its preference of functionalism to ontology and its reluctance to discuss the inner nature of persons or things, process theology has abandoned the traditional model of three divine persons in one spirit essence. We confuse the issue, argues Suchocki, when we interpret the Trinity in terms of "the ontological understanding of the inner nature of God."[49] Moreover, a divine person experiencing his own subjectivity would be a separate actuality, and thus three such persons would constitute tritheism, which orthodoxy has always rejected. The classical model of the Trinity, process theologians argue, is not found on the pages of the New Testament and, in fact, was historically conditioned thus invalidating it as a timeless paradigm for the church. This leads Cobb to remark that "Process theology is not interested in formulating distinctions within God for the sake of conforming with traditional Trinitarian notions."[50]

In lieu of three distinct subjectivities within the reality of God process theology defines 'person' as a formally distinct principle or mode of operation of the unitary actuality that is God. Thus rather than a Trinity involving three divine persons, process thinkers uphold a triunity of principles, rooted in the actuality of God, that characterizes God's relatedness to the world. And, it is argued, this triunity of principles can be linked with the traditional symbols of Father, Word, and Spirit.

Triunity of Principles

By allegedly reflecting on the data of experience, process thinkers maintain that God the Father is not one member among several within the Godhead. Rather He is God in his own individual actuality. A principle inherent in God's primordial nature, the Father is a symbol for God as the envisagement of all temporal possibilities. The Father, moreover, is a symbol of God as he offers each actual occasion its optimal initial aim or purpose for a new and higher form of existence. Thus God as Father is the creative source and primordial envisagement of all that is.

The Logos or Word, likewise an aspect of God's primordial nature, is the instrument of God's creative expression or the power of creative transformation. The Christ, however, represents the immanence of the Word in the world. The incarnate Word, which is the Christ, lures each occasion to maximum fulfillment or to the highest level of creative transformation envisaged by the Father. It should be clear that in the process schema Christ, as the power of creative love, is not identical with Jesus. Process theologians affirm that the creative Word achieved maximal actualization *in* Jesus of Nazareth. In the words of Pittenger, Jesus is "the personalized instrument for the Self-Expressive Activity of God."[51] Since in Jesus the Word was most dynamically active, Jesus is constituted the Christ. Process thinkers underscore that Jesus was not ontologically divine. His speciality consists in the fact that he served as the human vehicle for the divine activity. Jesus of Nazareth in some special way represents the presence of God with us and for us.

The Spirit, which reflects the consequent nature of God, is the symbol of God's internal activity within the human spirit. The Spirit not only inspires creative insight, but by the Spirit persons learn to respond consciously to God. That is, the Spirit, as the power of divine love, elicits in the faithful the response of obedience, worship, and love. Thus whereas the Father is the source of novelty and the author of each initial aim and the Word is the lure that brings each occasion to maximum fulfillment, the Spirit prompts assent to the divine purpose for novelty and advance. As Pittenger puts it, the Spirit "is the 'responding,' the conforming, the returning of the 'amen' of God through the whole creation and in deity itself."[52]

In sum, process theology affirms a triunity of unconscious and impersonal principles which are said to define the divine life. Whiteheadians judge philosophical construction to be superior to the alleged heretical tri-theism of classical orthodoxy. The Father, according to Pittenger, is a symbol for God as Creative Source, the Word a symbol for God as Self-Expressive Act, and the Spirit a symbol for God as Responsive Movement in the world. Bracken formulates the patently economic Trinity in the form of God as Primal Cause, Primal Effect, and Primal Condition.[53]

Critique and Evaluation

An overall assessment of process theology's understanding of Jesus and the Trinity will now be undertaken. A former student of Whitehead reported that the master once commented that Christian orthodoxy could not be reconciled with his philosophy. Moreover, Brown, James, and Reeves acknowledge that process theology bears affinities with Theravada Buddhism, the thought of Heraclitus, the Unitarian Socinus, and the idealist philosophies of Hegel, Schelling, and T. deChardin.[54] By its own admission, then, process theology represents a departure from a theology that broadly could be called biblical and historically Christian.

Christological and Trinitarian Features

With regard to the pre-existence of Christ, we have seen that process theology regards the Logos as an impersonal principle, namely, as the totality of the divine aims. Since the Whiteheadian Logos—unconscious and impersonal—is not a discrete person within the Godhead, it hardly can be reconciled with the historic Christian explication of the eternal pre-existence of the second person of the Trinity. Biblical orthodoxy, on the contrary, claims that the Word through whom God supremely revealed Himself is an eternally pre-existent person (Isa. 9:6; John 1:1; Rev. 21:6). Similarly the process understanding of the Incarnation, the cornerstone of the Christian system, deviates fundamentally from the orthodox formulation. According to the former, the Logos is immanent as the Christ in the whole of creation. The Incarnation connotes that the impersonal Logos, as the power of creative transformation, was maximally immanent and operative in the man Jesus of Nazareth. The process view, first of all, denies the biblical assertion that the Incarnation involves the eternal second person of the Godhead entering space and time and becoming a man for us and our salvation (John 1:1, 14; 2 Cor. 8:9; Phil. 2:6-8; 1 Tim. 3:16). The process model compromises the decisiveness and singularity of the Incarnation by affirming that the Logos is immanent in all entities. It is clear that Whiteheadians have replaced the *Logos ensarkos* (the particular enfleshment of the Word in Jesus) with the *Logos spermatikos* (the general working of the Logos in the world as the principle of order and rationality). However, the process reduction of the Incarnation to the immanence of an impersonal force perverts the sense of scriptural teaching on the subject. Jesus is not so much a "routing of occasions" as the eternal Son routed from heaven by the Father's love to pursue an errand of saving mercy. So crucial is the Incarnation to the entire Christian schema that the Apostle John insists that he who denies that the Son of God has come in human flesh embodies the spirit of antichrist and forfeits the possibility of salvation (1 John 4:3; 2 John 7).

The process claim that two natures cannot relate except by displacement prompts Whiteheadians to insist that the orthodox belief in Jesus' deity necessarily vitiates his authentic humanity. Biblical Christians, however, are just as insistent as Whiteheadians upon the full humanity of Jesus Christ. Refusing to accept a Docetic Christ, orthodoxy upholds the full humanity of the carpenter from Nazareth (Matt. 8:27; 13:55; John 19:5; 1 Tim. 2:5; Heb. 2:11, 14, 17). But whereas Whiteheadians insist that Jesus was afflicted with sin that he might be like us in every respect, biblical faith declares that Jesus was the paradigm of humanity as untarnished by sin. Scripture not only states that Jesus was free from sin (Heb. 4:15; 7:26-27), it also indicates that he did not experience old age and marriage as persons commonly experience them.

Avoiding the Arian and adoptionist tendencies of Whiteheadians, historic Christianity likewise insists that while true man, Jesus is also true God. Biblical Christians take seriously the ample biblical testimony; that Jesus of Nazareth is very God in person (John 1:1, 18; 10:30-33; 20:28; Rom. 9:5; Titus 2:13; Heb. 1:8-10; 2 Peter 1:1). If Jesus be not God, then he is incapable of fully revealing the Father to people. If he be not God, then he does not have the power to save sinners. Orthodox Christians grieve over the fact that process thinkers without warrant have demoted Jesus to an inferior status. They insist, against process denials that Jesus Christ is omnipotent (Isa. 9:6; Matt. 28:18; John 10:18), omnipresent (Matt. 18:20; John 3:13; Eph. 1:23), omniscient (Matt. 9:4; John 4:16-19; 16:30; 21:17), and eternal (Isa. 9:6; John 1:1; 8:58; Col. 1:17; Heb. 1:10-12; Rev. 1:8). Biblical people stand reverently before the scriptural claim that acceptance of Jesus' divinity is a prerequisite for salvation (Rom. 10:9; 2 Peter 1:3).

Christian orthodoxy, on the basis of biblical testimony, subscribes to the truth that Jesus Christ embodies in his person both deity and humanity. It affirms, not the diluted notion that deity was operative through his humanity, but that in his very person Jesus Christ bore the characteristics essential to deity and essential to humanity (Rom. 1:3-4; Phil. 2:6-8). He was no less the second Adam than he was the first Adam (1 Cor. 15:45-49). Biblical soteriology demands that he be both true God and true man in order that he might redemptively span the gulf between heaven and earth (1 Tim. 2:5). He must be authentic man faithfully to represent us (Heb. 4:15), and he must be authentic God fully to save us (Heb. 7:24-25). Christian theology acknowledges that in the final analysis the tenet of Christ's two natures is a spiritual mystery (1 Tim. 3:16) incapable of explication by finite minds but before which faith confidently bows. Because Jesus Christ is both true God and true man, Christians do what Whiteheadians refuse to do—namely, render to the Nazarene heartfelt worship after the example of Scripture itself (Josh. 5:14-15; Matt. 2:2, 11; 14:33; Phil. 2:10-11; Heb. 1:6). Affirming a union of person as well as purpose, orthodoxy holds Jesus Christ in higher esteem than do the disciples of Whitehead.

We have seen that Whiteheadians commonly depreciate the unique character of Jesus' person and accomplishments by upholding a form of degree Christology. Jesus was a special man who well may be surpassed by another religious figure in the evolutionary future. The general tenor of Scripture, however, points in the direction of the once-happenedness of the cosmic event of Christ's enfleshment. The New Testament specifically teaches that Christ is the consummation of all previous revelations in history (Heb. 1:1-2), and as such is the absolutely final and unique agent of salvation (1 Cor. 3:11). The several "I am's" of Jesus (John 6:35; 8:12; 10:7, 9; 10:14; etc.) register the same point. Facre, who is hardly a fundamentalist, argues thusly about the process interpretation of the Incarnation: "The exemplification of a quality or process that is universal is too static and conservative a view of this revolutionary event. It is not More of the Same, not even Most of the Same, but the new."[55]

Biblical faith likewise disagrees with process theology's Pelagian rejection of human sinfulness and rebellion, both individual and social, that has provoked God's holy wrath. Moreover, the process thesis that at the critical moment when Jesus hung on the Cross,

God failed to provide him with the necessary creative lure—i.e., that in the Cross the weakness of God was revealed—contravenes the biblical claim that Christ's Cross and Resurrection represented a cosmic victory over the forces of evil (Col. 2:14-15). If God stood by powerless to comfort his beloved and failed to provide him with a saving lure, one might well conclude that the salvation of lesser mortals is tenuous at best. The biblical portrait of Christ's saving provision is much more powerful and agreeable with the human condition than the process thesis that Christ provided lures to creative advance which people actualize of their own will and power. Contrary to the process scheme of self-salvation, Scripture sets forth God's radical provision for radical human evil—namely, that on the Cross God in Christ bore the just penalty for the world's sin, satisfied God's justice, and thus made a way for rebels to be reconciled to God. The biblical teaching on this subject consists not in isolated texts, but is woven into the very fabric of the divine revelation (Isa. 53:4-12; John 3:15-17; Rom. 3:21-26; 5:6-11; Heb. 2:14-17; etc.). The process view of Jesus' work Facre discerns to be seriously deficient. "It does not assess profoundly enough the depths of human perversity or the intractability of evil in nature and history. Where these dimensions of existence are not adequately probed it regularly follows that the full meaning of the Cross and Resurrection as events which deal with sin and death is not grasped."[56]

We have noted that process theology summarily rejects the personal and bodily resurrection of Jesus and of believers in favor of the thesis that resurrection connotes God taking up into his own memory the experiences of our Lord and his followers. Since process thought denies the reality of the ego or the self, it rejects the idea that Jesus survived his death and insists only that God remembers him as so many perished occasions. This denial of Jesus' resurrection implies that there will be no personal resurrection of believers in the last day and no eternal life for anyone. One strongly suspects that the process denial of Jesus' resurrection has been reached by a priori considerations rather than by a reading of the New Testament. The hard fact is that biblical faith is resurrection faith. Christ's resurrection was fully anticipated by inspired Old Testament figures (Job 19:25; Ps. 16:11; Isa. 25:8). Our Lord himself plainly taught that he would rise from the grave after three days (Matt. 16:21; 20:19;

26:32; John 2:19; etc.). Each of the Gospels presents Jesus' resurrection as the climax and conclusion of their narratives. More extensively than the Cross, the Resurrection was the focus of the church's missionary preaching (Acts 2:24, 31-32; 3:15; 4:10; 5:30-32; etc.), teaching (Rom. 1:4; 6:4; 8:34; 1 Cor. 15:4, 20; etc.), and worship. Christians of all ages concur with B. F. Westcott that Christ's resurrection is not an accessory to the apostolic faith but is the sum of that faith itself. The Resurrection was God's decisive vindication of Jesus' divine claims and the efficacy of his atoning work. Deny the Resurrection and one must deny the remission of sins (1 Cor. 15:17) and the possibility of attaining salvation (Rom. 10:9; 1 Cor. 15:19). Rejection of Jesus' bodily resurrection means the end of all hope (1 Cor. 15:32). Since all persons, secretly at least, will admit that the survival of the self in a state of perfection is superior to the dissolution of the person, Christian resurrection faith again proves superior to the empty hope of Whiteheadian neo-classical theism.

Whitehead's identification of person with substance led him to conclude that the Christian doctrine of the Trinity involves a crude tri-theism. Therefore person, in the process schema, was viewed as an abstract or mode of activity of a single concrete subjectivity. This means that process theology upholds a triunity of abstract and impersonal principles. The subjectivity of Jesus cannot be identified with the second member of the Trinity, and likewise for the Holy Spirit. But Royce Gruenler reminds us that a triunity of abstract and impersonal principles is decidedly inferior to a dynamic society of three conscious, active, and loving persons. "Principles do not do anything: they are simply abstractions from the functions of living actualities and are ascribed to things and people as generic descriptions by conscious persons who have the power of abstraction."[57] In other words, the Whiteheadian triunity is a vacuous philosophical construct. There is nothing there that can create, reveal itself, love, or meaningfully relate to real persons. Vastly superior is the biblical model of three eternal persons bound together in one underlying reality who are dynamically related to one another and who extend themselves in loving relations to persons. The Christian doctrine of the Trinity, thus viewed as three related persons in one substantial unity, provides demonstration of the classical philosophical problems of the relation of the one to the many and of being to becoming.

The process triunity not only violates the biblical coordination of Father, Son, and Holy Spirit as three distinct and coequal persons, but its own construction is plagued with logical inconsistencies. Not the process scheme, but the historic Christian representation offers a viable basis for the salvation of persons: the Father as personal wisely devises the plan of salvation, the Son as personal executes that plan by his own death on the Cross, and the Holy Spirit applies the benefits of the salvation thus wrought to trusting persons. In the orthodox scheme salvation is wholly of God.

The entire process formulation of Christ and the Trinity diverges significantly from the historic Christian consensus. People are not seen to be fallen in sin and condemned by a just and holy God. God did not enter this world focally and bodily in Jesus Christ. Whoever Jesus was and whatever he did and said, it is claimed he was not God. Jesus' Cross did not propitiate the anger of an offended deity, and the Nazarene in no wise rose from the grave as the first fruits of those who believe. Process theology thus denies, as biblically and historically understood, Christ's eternal pre-existence, Incarnation, virgin birth, sinlessness, deity, atoning death, resurrection, ascension, and second coming, as well as the Trinity of God. In Christology and the related area of the Trinity it is difficult to say what is right and true about the process vision.

Process theology, in fact, is a classic example of what Thielicke calls the Cartesian form of theology, which begins with universal doubt of the objective character of religious truth. Cartesian theology, which Thielicke rejects as incompatible with Christian faith, identifies the autonomous person as the starting point of all knowledge and seeks to impose a system on God's Word based on supposed logic. Believing that Cartesianism transforms theology into a chapter of anthropology, Thielicke upholds a non-Cartesian model, where emphasis is placed upon the objective content of the Christian message as preserved in the classical creeds. Thielicke, who seeks a modern explication of the Christian faith, would reject as reductionistic the process explication of the Christian way.

Two Philosophical Assumptions

Process theologians have bought into several philosophical assumptions that contribute to their conclusions, two of which warrant special consideration. In the realm of epistemology it is clear that process views of Christ and the Trinity are derived not from authoritative Scripture but from the philosophy of Whitehead as refined by his followers. According to the latter company, reason working on the data of lived experience is judged competent to lead the mind into all truth. Process thought thus represents a scheme of speculative human philosophy. Assuming that an infallible revelation in history is impossible and that reason is the final arbiter of truth, process thinkers never inconsistently incorporate into their system images and language borrowed from the Bible.

Scripture teaches and experience corroborates that unaided reason working with the data of experience yields a knowledge of God that is partial and frequently in error (1 Cor. 2:6-14). Philosophy simply does not lead to an adequate knowledge of God's hidden character and purposes (1 Cor. 1:21-25). From the biblical perspective, a valid understanding of God and of His Son, Jesus Christ, is acquired by means of faith reception of intelligible special revelation. The incident of Jesus' encounter with Peter near Caesarea Philippi illustrates this truth. Jesus' contemporaries held many misconceptions about his true identity. Peter, however, rightly confessed Jesus as "the Christ, the Son of the living God" (Matt. 16:16). Jesus responded to Peter's valid confesion with the pregnant approbation, "Blessed are you, Simon son of Jonah, for this was not revealed to you by man, but by my Father in heaven" (Matt. 16:17). On another occasion Jesus remarked to skeptical Pharisees, "You have no idea where I come from or where I am going. You judge by human standards" (John 8:14-15). Who Christ is and what he accomplished are understood not on the basis of human speculation, but by the explicit teachings of God-breathed Scripture.

For this reason revelation depicts the gospel of Christ as the antithesis of schemes of human wisdom (1 Cor. 1:17, 19; Col. 2:8; 1 Tim. 6:20-21). The apostle Paul issued stern warnings against those who would corrupt the teachings of Holy Scripture (1 Tim. 1:3; 4:1; Heb. 13:9). And specifically, he cautioned against perverting the simplicity of Jesus Christ and his gospel (2 Cor. 11:3-4; Gal. 1:6-8; Jude 4). Peter solemnly predicted that false teachers would arise to corrupt the truth about Christ (2 Peter 2:1-2). Facre again directs us to the true state of affairs. Process theology, he flatly affirms, involves "a tendency toward uncritical accommodation of the Christian faith toward the trends and values of modernity."[58]

Secondly, process theology has bought into the modern embargo on ontology. All process theologians, as thoroughgoing empiricists, operate on the premise that God cannot be objectified as an existent or a substantial self. In traditional Christian thought the soul, person, or self is viewed as an entity that has its existence in itself. Following Hume and other empiricists, who argued that the idea of the self is a fiction (man being but a bundle of perceptions in flux with no identity underlying successive perceptions), Whiteheadians insist that selfhood is a mere flux or stream of energy events. Person, or *hypostasis*, is regarded as a constantly changing center of human experience. As Whitehead himself put it: "A thing *is* what a thing does." From this philosophical basis process thinkers argue that it is illegitimate to talk about ontological relations between persons as, for example, the orthodox formulations of the two natures of Christ or the Trinity. Thus Pittenger observes: "When the philosophical scheme and the terminology linked with it break down, the affirmations which were made in that terminology and in the context of that scheme are very likely to break down too. This is what happened with the classical doctrine of the triunitarian God."[59] For this reason process thinkers find the language of Nicea and Chalcedon concerning Christ and the Trinity no longer meaningful or relevant. They maintain that one's world view, with associated concepts and language, must be changed from one of substance to one of process and activity.

At the philosophical level we question whether the process denial of an enduring 'I' that undergirds the flow of momentary experiences can be sustained. Can there logically be a feeling or an experience apart from a subject, a self, or an 'I' who feels or experiences? Can there possibly be a becoming without a being that comes to be?[60] Surely it is logical to insist that the God who acts and who may be experienced is the very God who first *is*. With its denial of an 'I' that undergirds all experiences, process theology has no tool at its disposal to account for the identity of the person through the constantly changing process. Nor is there any basis whatsoever for personal responsibility or accountability if the one who speaks or acts is not the same person yesterday, today, and tomorrow. Surely it is more sound to argue, against Buddhism, Hume, Whitehead, *et al.*, that there exists an underlying immaterial and intangible reality (the self, ego, or soul) that 'has' the changing qualities, that underlies the flux of experience, and that survives the death of the body.

Process theology ostensibly argues that the classical ontology must be abandoned if we are to move from the idea of God as static and lifeless to a concept of God as active and dynamically related. The responsible choice here is not either ontology or functionalism but both rightly understood. The crude staticism of the Greeks who envisaged God as First Principle or Unmoved Mover must be avoided, as must be the sheer relativity of Heraclitus and Whitehead. The God of the Bible is both being and becoming. The living God is changeless in his being, attributes, and purposes (decrees) but dynamically operative *vis-a-vis* the created order. The triune God creates, preserves, governs, judges, calls, convicts, regenerates, gives gifts, comforts, etc.. While arguing for a balanced ontology and functionalism, let us not forget that ontological affirmations, far from being peculiarly Aristotelian, are deeply embedded in the fabric of Scripture (Exod. 3:14; Matt. 16:13; John 4:24; 10:30; Phil. 2:6; Col. 2:9; Heb. 1:3; 2:14; etc.). It is not true to the facts to argue that the ontological portrait of Christ developed late in time from the Gentile church experience. There is strong evidence to suggest that it existed in the mind of Jesus himself.

Rather than beginning one's estimate of God or Christ with an a priori philosophical scheme, it is far superior to begin with revelation and allow God's perspective on reality to judge and shape our categories. Hume, by way of example, looked for the self in his experiences, and not having found the self there, concluded that the self or 'I' as an enduring object does not exist. As we turn to Scripture we find that the category of 'being' is employed to describe the reality of God, Christ, and human persons. And likewise we find that the category of 'becoming' is used to do the same. Scripture addresses the 'What' question—Jesus Christ is both God and man—and it speaks to the 'Who' question—Christ became a man, he took upon himself sin, he loved, wept, and felt deep compassion. To claim that there cannot be an enduring self that undergirds the flux of experiences is a judgment based on a radical Humean empiricism, not on the perspective of God-breathed Scripture.

Logically process thought stands on shaky foundations. Its beloved claim that "Jesus is a man" is itself a metaphysical statement. The assertion that "one cannot legitimately do metaphysics" is not merely an epistemological claim; it is in reality a metaphysical claim. To say that "a person is an aggregate of experiences" is itself a metaphysical statement. Process thought cannot embargo a substantial metaphysics without destroying its own claims. In similar fashion the process critic of traditional ontology cannot deny there is an enduring self without somehow pointing to himself along the way.

A Final Word

In the preceding discussion, attention has been directed to philosophical considerations that have prompted process thinkers to deny Jesus' incarnation, essential deity, atoning death, resurrection, and the classical Trinity of three persons in one spiritual essence. Personally I believe that a significant moral reason lies behind the process denial of these crucial tenets of the Christian faith. A reading of Scripture and reflection on the history of human thought suggests that from the beginning of time men and women have striven to assert their own autonomy and to live their lives free from God's sovereign claim upon them. The inveterate tendency of persons under the sun is to exercise their God-given religiosity while minimizing God's superior claim as Lord and Judge of their lives. The Socinians in the Reformation era, with whom Whiteheadians claim affinity first concluded that men and women were of upright character and thus had no need to repent and to be reconciled to an offended Deity. To sustain this position they proceeded to deny the Incarnation, the deity of Jesus Christ, and the triune Godhead. Process theology, I submit, is an exercise in the same kind of futility. It offers a way of engaging in religious discussion, while limiting God's lordship and sovereignty over persons who prize their autonomy. Gruenler, who for a while aligned himself with the process movement, admits to this motivation. Process thought, he claims, is an example of "the ever recurring attempt of *homo curvus* to claim independence of the sovereign God who has revealed himself in Scripture as both Savior and Judge of the cosmic order."[61] He adds, "Its real motive, I am convinced, is to protect human freedom against the threat of a sovereign God."[62]

Process Theology

Jesus Christ, the Son of God and Savior, the second person of the blessed Trinity, offers people life. However, the life that he extends can be attained only through the experience of death—the death that comes by kneeling at the foot of the Cross, acknowledging one's sinful condition, and renouncing every element of self-sufficiency and autonomy. Today as yesterday, Jesus Christ represents the divider of persons.

NOTES

1. Emil Brunner, *The Mediator* (Philadelphia: Westminster, 1948), p. 232.
2. Norman Pittenger, *Christology Reconsidered* (London: SCM, 1970), p. 15.
3. David R. Griffin, *A Process Christology* (Philadelphia: Westminster, 1973), p. 22. See also Pittenger, *Process Thought and Christian Faith* (New York: Macmillan, 1968), p. 21.
4. *Ibid.*, p. 139. Pittenger defines special revelation as "that which is extraordinary or unusual in our experience." *The Word Incarnate: A Study in the Doctrine of the Person of Christ* (New York: Harper, 1959), p. 22.
5. John A. T. Robinson, *The Human Face of God* (Philadelphia: Westminster, 1975), p. 22. Cf. Pittenger, *Christology Reconsidered*, p. 17.
6. John B. Cobb, Jr., *Christ in a Pluralistic Age* (Philadelphia: Westminster, 1975), p. 142. Griffin adds that orthodox theology "clearly presupposes an outdated conception of the Bible, seeing it in terms of inerrant inspiration and verbal revelation." *Process Christology*, p. 143.
7. David R. Griffin, *Process Christology*, p. 24.
8. Robinson, *Human Face*, p. 148.
9. *Ibid.*, p. 203.
10. William N. Pittenger, *The Lure of Divine Love* (New York: Pilgrim, 1979), p. 11.
11. Pittenger, *Christology Reconsidered*, p. 79.
12. Pittenger, *Lure of Divine Love*, pp. 114-115.
13. Cobb, *Christ in a Pluralistic Age*, p. 76.
14. William N. Pittenger, "Meland, Process Thought, and the Significance of Christ," in Ewert H. Cousins, ed., *Process Theology: Basic Writings* (New York: Newman, 1971), p. 213.
15. Cobb, *Christ in a Pluralistic Age*, p. 170.
16. Robert B. Mellert, *What is Process Theology?* (New York: Paulist, 1975), p. 84.
17. William N. Pittenger, *Catholic Faith in a Process Perspective* (Maryknoll, New York: Orbis, 1981), p. 95.
18. Pittenger, *Word Incarnate*, p. 181.
19. *Ibid.*, p. 221.
20. Lewis S. Ford, *The Lure of God: A Biblical Background for Process Theism* (Philadelphia: Fortress, 1978), p. 88.

21. Mellert, *What is Process Theology?*, p. 78.
22. Griffin, *Process Christology*, p. 143.
23. Pittenger, *The Lure of Divine Love*, p. 107.
24. Pittenger, *Christology Reconsidered*, p. 61.
25. *Ibid.*
26. *Ibid.*, pp. 2-3.
27. *Ibid.*, p. 99.
28. Griffin, *Process Christology*, p. 227.
29. John B. Cobb, Jr., in Delwin Brown, Ralph E. James, Jr., and Gene Reeves, eds., *Process Philosophy and Christian Thought* (Indianapolis: Bobbs-Merrill, 1971), p. 383.
30. Cobb, *Christ in a Pluralistic Age*, p. 145.
31. *Ibid.*, p. 206.
32. *Ibid.*, p. 22.
33. Pittenger, *The Lure of Divine Love*, p. 118.
34. William N. Pittenger, *Unbounded Love: God and Men in Process* (New York: Seabury, 1976), p. 54.
35. Pittenger, *The Lure of Divine Love*, p. 117; cf. *Ibid.*, p. 121.
36. Charles Hartshorne, *Reality as Social Process* (New York: Collier-Macmillan, 1963), p. 24.
37. Pittenger, *Unbounded Love*, p. 11.
38. William N. Pittenger, "Process Theology: A Contemporary Trend in Theology," in Cousins, ed., *Process Theology: Basic Writings*, p. 33.
39. Ford, *The Lure of God*, p. 86.
40. Griffin, *A Process Christology*, p. 244.
41. Pittenger, *Christology Reconsidered*, p. 107.
42. *Ibid.*, p. 108.
43. *Ibid.*, pp. 105-106.
44. Peter N. Hamilton, "Some Proposals for a Modern Christology," in Brown, James and Reeves, *Process Philosophy and Christian Thought*, p. 379.
45. Griffin, *Process Christology*, p. 12.
46. Ford, *The Lure of God*, p. 78.
47. Mellert, *What is Process Theology?*, p. 85. According to Hamilton, "The resurrection of Jesus is the chief exemplification of God's raising into himself of everything compatible with his loving purpose." "Some Proposals for a Modern Christology," in Brown, James and Reeves, *Process Philosophy and Christian Thought*, p. 381.
48. Ford, *The Lure of God*, pp. 78-80.
49. Marjorie H. Suchocki, *God, Christ, Church: A Practical Guide to Process Theology* (New York: Crossroad, 1982), p. 219.
50. John B. Cobb, Jr. and David R. Griffin, *Process Theology: An Introductory Exposition* (Philadelphia: Westminster, 1976), p. 110.
51. William N. Pittenger, "The Incarnation in Process Theology," *Review and Expositor* 71 (Winter, 1974), 53.
52. William N. Pittenger, *The Holy Spirit* (Philadelphia: United Church, 1974), p. 59.

Process Theology

53. Joseph A. Bracken, "Process Philosophy and Trinitarian Theology - II," *Process Studies* 15 (1981-82), pp. 84-87.

54. Brown, James, and Reeves, *Process Philosophy and Christian Thought*, p. v.

55. Gabriel Facre, "Cobb's Christ in a Pluralistic Age: A Review Article," *Andover Newton Quarterly* 17 (Mar. 1977), p. 314.

56. *Ibid.*, p. 313. The process vision of Christ as the benign lure to creativity is incapable of explaining the fact that the mission of Jesus brought division, hostility, and conflict among people (Matt. 10:34-36; Luke 12:49-53).

57. Royce Gruenler, *The Inexhaustible God: Biblical Faith and the Challenge of Process Theism* (Grand Rapids: Baker, 1983), p. 184.

58. Facre, "Cobb's Christ in a Pluralistic Age," p. 311.

59. Pittenger, *Christology Reconsidered*, p. 16.

60. See Norman L. Geisler, "Process Theology," *Tensions in Contemporary Theology*, ed. by Stanley N. Gundry and Alan F. Johnson (Chicago: Moody, 1976), p. 280.

61. Gruenler, *The Inexhaustible God*, p. 196.

62. *Ibid.*, p. 8.

Divine Foreknowledge and Future Contingency

William Lane Craig

William Lane Craig

William Lane Craig is Associate Professor of Religious Studies at Westmont College. He previously served as Assistant Professor in Philosophy of Religion at Trinity Evangelical Divinity School. A Graduate of Wheaton College, he took two master's degrees at Trinity Evangelical Divinity School before earning his Ph.D. at the University of Birmingham (England). He is also a candidate for the D. Theol. degree at the Universität München, West Germany. Dr. Craig has published three books: *The Kalam Cosmological Argument, The Cosmological Argument from Plato to Leibniz*, and *Apologetics: An Introduction*. His articles have appeared in numerous philosophical and theological journals including: *International Journal for Philosophy of Religion, Religious Studies, British Journal for the Philosophy of Science, Australasian Journal of Philosophy, New Scholasticism, Philosophical Studies*, and *Muslim World*.

The biblical view of divine omniscience entails that God knows all past, present, and future states of affairs. In particular, He knows future contingents,* such knowledge serving to differentiate Him from all false gods who lack such foreknowledge. Any reinterpretation of omniscience which involves a denial of God's knowledge of future contingents is unbiblical and subChristian and must be rejected by the Church.

Process Theology's Denial of Divine Foreknowledge

Process theologians have been unanimous, however, in rejecting God's knowledge of future contingents. Charles Hartshorne, for example, asserts that God's foreknowledge is not clearly affirmed in the Bible, but is largely "an invention of Western thought of the Dark or Middle Ages."[1] Hartshorne affirms divine omniscience, but his understanding of that concept is such that it does not entail knowledge of future contingents. He defines the attribute of being omniscient as "to know all that exists," with the proviso that possibilities be included as part of what exists.[2] The reason that omniscience does not entail foreknowledge of future contingents is because on Hartshorne's view of time the future does not in any sense exist. He writes,

> . . . there is a highest conceivable or divine knowledge, free from error or ignorance; however, since events in time do not form a totality fixed once for all, but are an endlessly growing accumulation of additional actualities, to view all time in a changeless fashion would be an erroneous view and not at all the highest conceivable or divine form of knowledge. As the Socinians said, once for all, future events, events that have not yet happened, are not there to be known, and the claim to know them could only be false. *God does not already or eternally know what we do tomorrow, for, until we decide, there are no such entities as our tomorrow's decisions.*[3]

Since the future does not exist and is indeterminate, there is simply nothing there for God to know.

This might lead one to think that Hartshorne would therefore embrace the view of the Polish logician Ludasiewicz that future tense statements about contingent events have no truth value, that they are neither true nor false. But Hartshorne declines to take this route, since it would sacrifice the Law of Excluded Middle, a sacrifice which Hartshorne regards as a "serious inconvenience, at least."[4] As usually understood, this law holds that for any statement and its contradictory, one must be true and the other false. Hartshorne apparently understands the law in a weaker sense, however; for example, as holding that a statement and its contradictory cannot both be true. For Hartshorne's position with regard to future contingent statements is that any such statement and its contradictory are both false. Thus, for example, it is false that "There will be a sea battle tomorrow" and it is false that "There will not be a sea battle tomorrow." What is true is that "There may or may not be a sea battle tomorrow." Since the future is nonexistent and indeterminate, to assert that a future contingent will occur or that it will not occur is to assert a falsehood. While this position does sacrifice the traditional Law of Excluded Middle, it would not violate Hartshorne's weakened version, since his version does not exclude that a statement and its contradictory both be false.[5]

Since future contingent statements are all false, it is no blot on God's omniscience that He does not know what will transpire in the future. "It is not . . . true that omniscience must know details of the future, unless it can be proved . . . that the future has any details to know."[6] God cannot be said to be ignorant in any way, for He could be charged with ignorance only if it is assumed that there is something to know, that is, that events are there to be known before they happen. As the events happen, God, being omniscient, knows them.[7] Thus, though omniscient, God is increasing in knowledge with each passing moment of time. His knowledge, though growing indefinitely, is nevertheless perfect in that He knows all that there is to know: "Thus there is no reason why perfect knowledge could not change, grow in content, provided it changed only as its objects change, and added as new items to its knowledge only things that were not in being, not there to know, previously."[8] According to process theology, then, God is all-knowing and yet not aware of the denials of the future, a doctrine Hartshorne calls "temporal omniscience."

Finally, Hartshorne contends that a process view of omniscience may *still* be maintained even if it is the case that for any future contingent statement and its contradictory, one is true and the other is false.[9] For even if various future contingent statements are true, they still cannot be known to be true, since they cannot be inferred from present states of affairs. Omniscience could then be defined as "all possible knowledge," and God's failure to know the truth value of such statements would not impugn His omniscience. Hartshorne then erects one last wall of defense for the process concept of omniscience: even if one concedes that various future contingent statements are true and that they are knowable, one could still maintain that the religious idea of omniscience means only perfect knowledge of the past and present with sufficient knowledge of the future to constitute a providential plan, with enough uncertainties in the details to allow for human choice. All of these possible conceptions of omniscience must be refuted, declares Hartshorne, before it be regarded as established that religion requires the conception of an immutable Knower.

Arguments in Support of the Process View

At this point it needs to be asked what arguments support the process view of omniscience. Process thinkers do not appreciate the fact that they must shoulder the burden of proof for their positions, rather than merely criticize traditional views and present their views as a religiously appealing alternative. They do not seem to realize that the choice between traditional and process theism is not an either/or, all-or-nothing situation. In the case at hand, for example, the choice is not simply between God's timeless knowledge of all events or God's temporal knowledge of exclusively past and future events, for medieval thinkers such as Scotus and Ockham argued for God's temporal knowledge of all past, present, and future events, and many contemporary theists concur with such a view. It is therefore both naive and logically fallacious to think that in attacking God's timelessness or His immutability or impassibility that one has thereby established the process view of omniscience.

The A-Theory of Time and Truth as Correspondence

What grounds, then, may be offered for denying that God's omniscience encompasses future contingent events? As I see it, the principal argument offered in support of the process view is that divine foreknowledge of future contingents is impossible due to the unreality and indeterminacy of the future. Process thinkers hold to a view of time according to which the future is not on an ontological par with the present, that is to say, future events do not in any sense exist. From this view of time, they infer that foreknowledge of contingent events is impossible.

In order to assess this argument, a bit of background in the philosophy of time would be helpful. The Scottish philosopher J. M. E. McTaggert pointed out that the temporal series of events could be regarded in two fundamentally different ways. According to the first, which McTaggert called the A-series, events are fundamentally characterized as past, present, or future, and these properties are constantly changing: an event now present will be past, and a past event was once present. According to the second view, which McTaggert called the B-series, events are fundamentally characterized as earlier or later than other events, and these relations do not change: an event which is later than some other event is always later than that event. McTaggert's characterization of these two views of temporal series gave rise to two competing views of time: the A-theory and the B-theory. According to the first, objective becoming is essential to time; the present moment is the edge of becoming and future events are not waiting down the line, so to speak, for us to arrive at them—future events simply are not existent. According to the B-theory, past, present, and future events are all equally real and becoming is merely a subjective feature of consciousness; while future events do not exist *yet*, they still exist and their becoming present is merely a matter of our minds' becoming aware of them as present. The B-theory is especially popular among physicists, who treat time as just another axis on a space-time diagram and objects as four-dimensional entities which subsist (tenselessly) in the space-time nexus.

Now what process thinkers appear to be arguing is that the A-theory of time is correct and that a doctrine of divine foreknowledge is in some way incompatible with the A-theory. It should be noted in passing that the B-theory, with which the doctrine of God's omniscience *vis a vis* future events seems clearly compatible, enjoys a great deal of support among philosophers and scientists today, so that the A-theory can by no means simply be assumed without argument by process thinkers. Fortunately, I also happen to subscribe independently to the A-theory of time, so that we need not examine the process theologians' case for that theory at this juncture. Rather I wish to examine their claim that one cannot consistently hold to the A-theory and still support the doctrine of God's foreknowledge of future contingents.

The reason that divine foreknowledge of future contingents is said to be impossible on an A-theory of time is because future contingent statements cannot be true. But if they cannot be true, then obviously they cannot be known to be true. If they cannot be known to be true, then God cannot know future contingents. His knowledge of future events is restricted to those events which are not contingent, but are causally necessitated by events in the past and present and therefore capable of being inferred from such events.

The question then which must be raised is why future contingent statements cannot be held to be true on an A-theory of time. The assumption which seems to underlie this denial appears to be the belief that in order for a statement to be true, the reality described by the statement or at least the causal conditions sufficient for that reality must actually exist at the time at which the statement is true. Since these are lacking for future contingent statements, such statements cannot be true. But what basis is there for this assumption? It might be thought to follow from a view of truth as correspondence. According to that view, a statement is true if and only if what it asserts to be the case corresponds with what really is the case, for example, "It is snowing" is true if and only if it is snowing. A-theorists sometimes seem to presuppose a crude view of truth as correspondence which dictates that since no future reality exists to which future contingent statements could correspond, such statements cannot be true. Unfortunately, such an interpretation of truth as correspondence would require that *no* future tense statements are true, not even causally necessary ones. But typically future tense statements about causally necessitated events are regarded as true by A-theorists. An A-theorist wishing to deny the truth of future contingent statements on the basis of truth as correspondence would be more consistent to deny the truth of *all* future-tense statements. Now the A-theorist might suggest a reinterpretation of the view of truth as correspondence so as to allow that statements are true, not only if the corresponding reality exists, but also if the causal conditions for the corresponding future reality exist. But such a move would have unwelcome consequences. It would mean that a future tense statement could be true on Tuesday and false on Wednesday still prior to the existence of the corresponding reality on Saturday. For example, the causal conditions for "There will be a lunar eclipse on Saturday" could be present on Tuesday, but these might be altered by the intervention of free agents on Wednesday, say, thermonuclear testing on the moon which throws it out of orbit, so that the conditions no longer exist. But if the statement is thus false from Wednesday on, how can it be said that the statement was really true on Tuesday? It would provide no escape from this muddle to assert that the causal conditions on Tuesday include the nonintervention of free agents in the future, for then one would be referring to future contingent states of affairs, about which no true statement may be asserted. Hence, it seems that the consistent A-theorist who wishes to deny the truth of future contingent statements on the basis of truth as correspondence is bound to embrace the more radical view that *no* future tense statements are true.

In any case, the A-theorist's reasoning seems to rest upon a misinterpretation of the view of truth as correspondence. Whether or not the reality corresponding to a true statement must exist at the time of its assertion depends upon the tense of the statement. Hence, "President Reagan is being inaugurated" is true if and only if President Reagan is being inaugurated; that is to say, the reality described by the statement exists. On the other hand, "President Reagan will be inaugurated" is true if and only if President Reagan will be inaugurated; that is to say, the reality described by the statement will exist. In order for the future tense statement to be true, it is not necessary that what it describes now exist; on the contrary, if President Reagan is now being inaugurated then the future tense statement is false. Hence, only present tense statements require that the events they describe exist contemporaneously with the assertion of the statement. By their very nature, future tense statements are rendered true or false by what will be the case, as Rescher and Urquhart explain:

> . . . the issue of truth or falsity hinges entirely upon *how matters turn out at the time at issue*, so that the allocation of a truth status to future contingents is perfectly innocuous, because it prejudges nothing. No suggestion is intended that the truth status a future contingent proposition certainly *has* at times prior to the time of reference can be specified at these earlier times without any reference to 'how matters turn out'.[10]

These authors hold to an A-theory of time and a causally indeterminate future, yet they recognize that such a view does not affect the truth status of future contingent statements because such statements are true or false on the basis of how matters will turn out and not on the basis of whether present conditions can be specified which determine the statements' truth values. Hence, the claim that a view of truth as correspondence implies that future contingent statements cannot be true is simply based on a misconception.

Indeed, there are positive reasons to reject the notion that truth as correspondence requires the contemporaneous existence of the realities described in the statement. (1) The truth of a present tense statement seems to entail the prior truth of the future tense version of the same statement. As Rescher comments in another place,

> Difficulties about divine foreknowledge quite apart, it is difficult to justify granting to
> (1) 'It will rain tomorrow' (asserted on April 12) a truth status different from that of
> (2) 'It did rain yesterday' (asserted on April 14) because both make (from temporally distinct perspectives) *precisely the same claim about the facts*, viz. rain on April 13.[11]

The same reality on April 13 would seem to make the future tense version asserted on April 12, the present tense version asserted on April 13, and the past tense version asserted on April 14 all true. (2) The argument that future contingent statements cannot be true would also seem to entail that past tense statements cannot be true either. On the A-theory of time, not only future states of affairs, but also past states of affairs do not exist. But then there is no reality to which past tense statements could correspond, so that no past tense statement could be true, which is outrageous. As Baylis points out, just as the events corresponding to past tense statements no longer exist, so the events corresponding to future tense statements do not yet exist. "For the truth of propositions to the effect that certain events did occur in the past it is necessary only that the occurrence of these events was at the time specified a fact, and, similarly, for the truth of propositions to the effect that certain events will occur at a given time in the future it is necessary only that the occurrence of these events at that time will be a fact."[12] (3) The tenseless version of future contingent statements would seem to be always true or always false. One can convert a tensed statement into a tenseless one by putting the verb in the tenseless present and adding a time indicator; for example, "The Allies invaded Normandy" becomes "On June 6, 1944 the Allies *invade* Normandy." Now Talbott notes that while it is "futile" to try to translate tensed statements into their tenseless counterparts without losing some of their meaning, still the tenseless versions are always true or always false, if they are ever true or false at all.[13] But clearly, such statements are true when the realities described are past or present. But since they are tenseless, they must therefore be always true. Since a tenseless version of any future contingent statement can be formulated, it follows that such statements concerning future contingents are true or false.

Thus, the A-theory of time in no way implies that future contingent statements cannot be true; on the contrary, we have seen good reasons to think that such statements are in fact true or false depending on how the future will turn out to be. The mistake made by some A-theorists and process thinkers seems to be their confusion of the truth-status and the knowledge-status of future contingent statements. But these are not the same, for the truth of a future contingent statement does not imply our ability to know its truth. In the absence of causal conditions in the present which enable us to infer the statement, knowledge of the statement may be impossible for us; but the absence of such conditions has no relevance to the truth of future contingent statements. Hence, we can still say of some future contingent event x: "It may be that x or it may not be that x," expressing thereby either the causal indeterminacy of x or our ignorance of whether or not x will eventuate, without implying that the statement "It will be the case that x" is not true.

Moreover, the denial of the truth of future contingent statements has some absurd consequences. For example, Hartshorne's view that future contingent statements are always false has the bizarre result that future tense statements about events that do turn out as the statements predicted are still nonetheless false. For example, if one were to assert that "DeCostello will win next year's New York marathon" and in fact next year he does, then we must say that one's prediction was nevertheless *false*, which seems absurd. If we retreat to saying that future contingent statements have no truth value at all, the difficulties multiply. For statements which are disjunctions or conjunctions depend for their truth value on the truth values of their component sentences. If, then, the component sentences are future contingent statements having no truth value, the entire disjunction or conjunction will also lack a truth value. But then we should be unable to assert the truth of statements like "The Vice-President will or will not run for the Presidency," a statement which seems obviously, indeed, necessarily true. Worse still, a statement like "The President will both live out his second term and not live out his second term" cannot be said to be false, which it obviously, indeed, necessarily seems to be.

With nothing to commend it, positive arguments against it, and absurd consequences following from it, I can see no good reason to join process thinkers in adopting the view that future contingent propositions are not true. One can hold to an A-theory of time, indeterminism, and the view of truth as correspondence without thereby denying the truth of future contingent statements. Since these are the doctrines which the process thinker holds to uncompromisingly, I see no reason why he should persist in denying divine foreknowledge of future contingents, since such foreknowledge entails neither a B-theory of time, determinism, nor a noncorrespondence view of truth.

Theological Fatalism

But perhaps the process theologian would at this point demur, believing that divine foreknowledge entails fatalism.[14] That is to say, he might argue that from

> *Necessarily, whatever God foreknows comes to pass*
>
> *and*
>
> God foreknew that x would come to pass,
>
> *it follows that*
>
> Necessarily, x will come to pass.

Hence if God foreknows the future, then all things come to pass necessarily, and freedom and contingency are banished.

Now so stated, the above reasoning involves a logical fallacy. According to modal logic, the conclusion of an argument can be necessary only if both of the premises are necessary. But in the above argument, only the first step is a necessary truth; the second step is not a necessary truth, since it is not necessary that God know x— He could know y instead. Therefore, the proper conclusion to the above argument is simply:

> Therefore, x will come to pass.

From the fact that God foreknows x, we may be sure that x will come to pass; but it is not necessary that x come to pass. It is possible that x should fail to come to pass, but in fact it will not.

Theological fatalists admit that the above argument for fatalism is logically fallacious, but they have tried to remedy this defect by arguing that the second step is in a sense necessary; therefore, the conclusion does follow. The sense in which premise two is said to be necessary is the notion of temporal necessity. That is to say, the occurrence or nonoccurence of an event is said to be possible at times prior to its actual occurrence, but thereafter the event is necessary. Very often fatalists appeal to the notion of the unalterability or unpreventability of the past: while we may change the future, we have no power to change the past. Thus, events in the past are temporally necessary. If then God foreknew that x would occur, God's foreknowledge is now temporally necessary, since it is in the past and therefore x will necessarily occur. If it were possible for x not to occur, it would be possible to change the past (in this case the content of God's foreknowledge), which is absurd. Therefore, divine foreknowledge entails fatalism.

Now before we analyze this revised version, a general comment about the argument would seem to be in order. The argument must be unsound for the simple reason that fatalism is incoherent. It must be remembered that fatalism is not the same as causal determinism. According to the fatalist, future events may be indeterminate with respect to antecedent causes; indeed, they could be utterly uncaused. Yet in some mysterious way they are constrained to occur. But what can this mean? How can an event which is causally contingent in every respect be constrained to occur? To look at it another way: suppose that x will occur, but that God lacked foreknowledge and so did not know x would occur. In this case, x's occurrence is supposed to be not fated. Now suppose God does foreknow x. What has changed such that x's occurrence is now fated? How does God's simply knowing about something constrain it, when every other determining factor with regard to it remains unchanged? Or suppose that, rather than God, a psychic foreknew x would occur. How does his mere knowledge place some sort of constraint on x such that x could not fail to occur? It thus seems obvious that fatalism is itself a dubious notion; therefore, we may anticipate with a good degree of confidence that an analysis of the fatalist's reasoning will turn up a fallacy.

The moot point in the fatalist's reasoning will no doubt be the notion of temporal necessity which is said to characterize the second premise. Analysis reveals that such necessity is only obliquely temporal and does not in fact characterize statements about God's past foreknowledge. In order to see this, a few remarks may be helpful concerning the differences between the past and the future.

In the first place, there does not seem to be any sense in which the past is any more unalterable than the future. Though at first blush this sounds fatalistic, a little reflection serves to show that the idea of changing the past or future is a self-contradiction. For by definition, the past is what has occurred, so that to change the past would be to bring it about that an event which occurred did not occur, which is self-contradictory. But by the same token, the future is what will occur, so that to change the future would be to bring it about that an event which will occur will not occur, also a self-contradiction. Hence, "what has been has been" and "what will be will be," far from being fatalistic, are in fact mere tautologies.

The key difference between the past and future with respect to our abilities lies not, therefore, in the alterability of past or future, but rather in the fact that the future is causally open whereas the past is causally closed. We do not have the ability to change the future, but we do have the ability to determine the future causally by our choices and actions. By contrast, we do not, I would argue, have the ability to determine the past causally by our choices and actions. In other words, backward causation is impossible. According to the notion of backward causation, a cause does not change the past, for this is logically impossible; rather the effect simply precedes its cause in time. I would argue that backward causation is impossible because on the A-theory of time, at the time of the effect the cause in no sense exists, so that backward causation is tantamount to causation out of nothing, which is metaphysically impossible. It is, I think, our inability to causally determine the past which leads to our feeling that the past is unalterable in a sense in which the future is not. What is in fact the causal closedness of the past as opposed to the future is misexpressed in the idea that past events have an unalterability which does not characterize future events.

With respect to divine foreknowledge, then, the biblical theist wants to maintain, not that we have the power to change God's past beliefs, but rather that we have the power to act in such a way that *were* we to act in that way, God *would have* believed differently. That is to say, though God's foreknowledge is chronologically prior to our action, our action is logically prior to God's foreknowledge. We do not do *x* because God foreknows *x*; rather God foreknows *x* because we shall do *x*. Hence, there is no inconsistency in saying, "God foreknew that I shall do *x*. Therefore, I shall do *x*. But I have the power not to do *x*. If I were not to do *x*, God would not have believed that I shall do *x*." This last sentence is a contrary-to-fact or subjunctive conditional statement, and the fatalist seems to have failed to understand it. It does not express the ability to change or undo the past, but the ability to act such that the past *would* have been different than it is.

Nor is this an appeal to some metaphysically objectionable backward causation. I do not retroactively cause cognitions to spring into God's mind. Rather what I shall do determines which future tense statements about my actions are true or false, and God has the essential property of knowing only and all true statements. Thus, He foreknows my future acts.

Hence, temporal necessity is seen to be a misnomer. Temporality *per se* has little to do with the necessity of events. Rather the issue is the logical priority of one event to another. If some event *x* is logically prior to another event *y* in such a way that we can formulate a contrary-to-fact conditional:

"If it were the case that *x*, then it would be the case that *y*"

in which *y* is a consequence of *x*, then *y* is not necessary. This is so even if *y* is past and *x* is future. From the pastness of *y* we know that *x* will occur; but it would be incorrect to say *x* **must** occur. For *x* may be causally contingent and could possibly fail to occur. But if it were to fail to occur, then *y* would not have happened. The occurrence of *y* is therefore not necessary, since it is dependent upon the occurrence of a contingent event. Hence, the fatalist has failed to elucidate a sense in which his second premise—that God foreknew *x*— is necessary, and therefore his argument fails.

The failure of the argument for theological fatalism has been recognized by the vast majority, though not all, of philosophers of religion today. In addition to that fact, however, it is not often appreciated that in at least three other fields of philosophical inquiry arguments which closely parallel the reasoning of theological fatalism have been rejected by philosophers working in those fields. This tends to confirm that the reasoning of the theological fatalist is unsound. It would be instructive, therefore, to survey briefly the arguments in those fields.

The first comes from the philosophy of science and concerns the possibility of backward causation.[15] In 1954 Michael Dummett of Oxford University argued that while backward causation may be metaphysically impossible, still it is at least logically possible. The standard objection to this claim, given by Antony Flew, is closely analogous to the reasonings of the theological fatalist. According to Flew, if the effect has already occurred, then we are still at liberty to prevent the cause from happening. But if we prevent the cause from happening, then the effect would not have occurred and we would have changed the past, which is absurd. The fact that we could construct experiments using backward causes in which we prevent the cause from occurring after its effect has already occurred shows backward causation to be absurd.

Unfortunately, Flew, like the theological fatalist, fails to understand contrary-to-fact conditional statements. If we set up the experiment he envisages, then once the effect occurs, we know the cause will not be prevented. Something will go awry in our attempts to stop it. This does not mean we could not prevent it, but only that we shall not. If we were to prevent the cause, then the effect would not have occurred. Flew thinks that this claim involves the ability to change the past, but this is clearly mistaken. The claim involves a contrary-to-fact supposition: if I *were* to prevent the cause (which I shall not), then the effect *would* not have occurred (though in fact it did). Hence, one's ability to prevent the cause in no way implies the ability to alter the past, nor does the occurrence of the effect rob me of my ability to prevent the cause. If, therefore, one is to object to backward causation, he must do so, not on these logical grounds, but rather, as I have sought to do, on metaphysical grounds.

The second example comes from the field of parapsychology and concerns a phenomenon which parallels even more closely divine foreknowledge: human precognition.[16] There are some impressive experimental data which suggest that gifted persons have the ability to precognize, or know in advance, future contingent events. Now some philosophers have objected to precognition on philosophical grounds which are quite analogous to the argument against divine foreknowledge. They ask us to imagine, for example, a situation in which several psychics are on Tuesday asked to sketch a drawing of a picture which the experimenter will hang on the wall on Wednesday. Suppose the experimenter collects the drawings on Tuesday and then deliberately avoids hanging any picture on the wall on Wednesday, or perhaps hangs a different picture on the wall. This would prove that the psychics do not have precognitive powers after all.

But the error of this objection is by now, I hope, clear. If the psychics have a genuine precognition of the picture which will be hung on Wednesday, then that is only because the picture will in fact be hung. Perhaps the experimenter will change his mind or maybe the janitor will hang it up—the point is that the precognition depends on the picture's being hung the next day. If it were not to be hung, then no precognition would have been received. It is within the experimenter's power to hang the picture or not, and whether he does so or not is the condition for whether a precognition of the picture was received. He does not have the power to change the past, but he does have the power to act in such a way that were he to act in that way, an event which in fact occurred would not have occurred.

The final example parallels most closely God's foreknowledge of future contingents and concerns a puzzle in the field of decision theory called Newcomb's Paradox.[17] Imagine that you are playing a game involving a being with enormous predictive powers. You are confronted with two boxes, A and B. You may choose to take the contents of both A and B or of A alone. B contains a thousand dollars. If the being predicts that you will choose both boxes, then he will leave A empty. If he predicts that you will choose A alone, then he puts a million dollars in A. Now every time in the past, this being has been correct: everybody who picked both boxes got only a thousand dollars and everybody who picked only A got a million. So what shall you choose? On the one hand, the odds are overwhelming that if you pick A alone you will get a million dollars, whereas if you go for both you will get only a thousand. On the other hand, the money is already in the boxes; the million dollars in A will not disappear if you pick both boxes. So why not choose both?

Proponents of the two box strategy are analogous to theological fatalists. They believe that since the past is unalterable, you should choose both boxes. What you choose cannot affect the past. Sometimes two-boxers will go so far as to say that the being's prediction actually robs you of your freedom to choose; since his prediction is accurate your free choice of the boxes is illusory. You are fated to choose what the being predicts.

Unfortunately for the theological fatalist, however, if we identify the being with God and stipulate that He makes His predictions according to foreknowledge, then the debate is over. The one box strategy is then clearly correct. For one's choices condition what God foreknows and hence what He predicts and places in the box. You will choose what God predicted, not because your free will mysteriously evaporates, but because God foreknew what you would freely choose. If you were to choose otherwise, God would have predicted otherwise. True, that leaves you with the uncomfortable knowledge that in picking A alone, you are sacrificing the thousand dollars in B. But you also know that had you picked both boxes, you would not have gotten one million plus one thousand dollars, but a mere thousand. This does not mean you have the power to change the contents of the boxes; rather it means, in a contrary-to-fact manner, that you have the power to make it such that what in fact was in the boxes would not have been in the boxes. Newcomb's Paradox is paradoxical only so long as the being's predictions are made by sheer chance, but once foreknowledge is introduced into the picture, the paradox vanishes and the choice becomes clear.

The failure of the above objections to backward causation, precognition, and Newcomb's Paradox seems to indicate convincingly that the reasoning of the theological fatalist is wrong. It is a sad commentary on the state of contemporary theology that so many theologians should be convinced by reasoning which has been rejected across the board by philosophers working in many independent fields. The process theologian who is anxious to preserve free will and future contingency has nothing to fear from the biblical doctrine of divine foreknowledge.

The Basis of Divine Foreknowledge

But perhaps the process theologian might yet insist that even if future contingent statements are either true or false and even if God's knowing such statements would not entail fatalism, still it is impossible that God should know which future contingent statements are true and which false. For since future contingent events are causally indeterminate with regard to present states of affairs, they cannot be inferred from those states of affairs. But then there is no way to know them prior to their occurrence.

Now the assumption that appears to lie behind this reasoning is that all genuine knowledge is based upon either present perception or causal inference. But what justification is there for that assumption? In fact, does not our experience teach us to the contrary that much of our knowledge, say, of moral values and ethical principles, for example, is not acquired either by perception or causal inference? And how do we know that our heavy dependence upon perception and inference is not a human condition which is inapplicable to a disembodied mind? The objection seems to suffer from anthropocentrism. Why could God not possess all knowledge wholly apart from sense perception and causal inference?

Edward Khamara points out that the question of the basis of divine foreknowledge is usually approached from either of two angles: the empiricist or the rationalist.[18] The empiricist approach tends to interpret God's foreknowledge along the lines of perception, whereas the rationalist approach tends to interpret it in purely conceptual terms. Khamara contends that assimilating foreknowledge to perception tends to equate God with an omni-perceiver—perhaps the most startling example being Newton and Clarke's doctrine that just as the brain is our sensorium on which pictures are imprinted to be read by the mind, so space is, as it were, the sensorium of God. Now the process theologian seems to have clearly presupposed a perceptual model of divine foreknowledge: since the future does not exist "out there" for God to "see," He cannot foresee contingent events. Indeed, I would go so far as to say that this model underlies virtually all contemporary denials of the possibility of God's foreknowing future contingents. But as Khamara points out, the perceptual model of divine foreknowledge is simply inadequate, and it seems to be guilty of taking the metaphor of God's "foresight" of the future too literally.

On the other hand, the rationalist approach to divine foreknowledge construes God's prescience in conceptual terms. A conceptualist model of divine omniscience might hold that God possesses innately knowledge of only and all true statements. Hence, inference is out of the question; God never learned or acquired His knowledge, but has eternally believed an innate store of only and all true statements. Since future contingent statements are either true or false, God, in innately knowing all true statements, knows future contingents. Interestingly, such a model has been suggested for understanding the phenomenon of *human* precognition. Taking his cue from Jung's theory of archetypal ideas, Alan Gauld proposes that precognition be construed in terms of innate knowledge:

> The term ESP is a complete misnomer. We do not acquire the factual knowledge exhibited in so-called ESP by any quasi-perceptual or transmissive process, though sometimes we may fancy we do because of the form in which it manifests. The knowledge concerned is, from the point of view of our everyday notions of how we acquire factual information, totally anomalous. The knowledge is not 'acquired,' the information does not 'arrive.' The knowledge, so to speak,

'happens.' 'However incomprehensible it may appear,' writes Jung, 'we are finally compelled to assume that there is in the unconscious something like an apriori knowledge or immediate presence of events which lacks any causal basis.'[19]

One advantage of so construing precognition, states Gauld, is that "We could stop worrying, in connection with precognition about the problem of 'future causes' and all that goes with it."[20] Now whatever we think of this model *vis a vis* human precognition, it seems entirely appropriate for the foreknowledge of God. On this model we interpret God's knowledge of future events, not in terms of perceptions, but in terms of conceptions.

Of course, someone might persist in demanding, "*How* can God have innate knowledge of all future tense statements?" But the meaning of this demand is not altogether clear. It cannot mean, "How did God come by such knowledge?", for His knowledge is said to be innate. Nor does the demand seem to mean, "How is the concept of innate knowledge possible?", for the concept does not appear to be rationally incoherent. Perhaps the question really means, "How is it the case that God has innate knowledge of all things?" But then the demand seems to be just an expression of incredulity which could be posed of any of the divine attributes: How is it that God exists necessarily? How is it that God is perfectly good? This sort of "how" question does not seem to have any answer— God just is that way. About the only answer that could be given is that God has the essential property, of say, knowing all true statements. Since if He exists He has that property and He does in fact exist, it follows that God knows all true statements. To ask how it is that God is omniscient is therefore like asking how it is that vacuums are empty.

It seems therefore that no compelling reason has been given for rejecting God's foreknowledge of future contingents due to the absence of some inferential ground of knowledge. The assumption that all knowledge is inferential seems to be false and in any case unwarranted, and the assumption that God's knowledge of the future must be inferential seems to be based on a flawed model of divine prescience which assimilates foreknowledge to perception.

Since neither the reality of temporal becoming nor the threat of theological fatalism nor the non-inferential basis of divine foreknowledge provides any grounds for denying God's knowledge of future contingents, it would seem that there is no sound reason to embrace the process view of omniscience.

Arguments for Divine Foreknowledge

If we assume that God is omniscient, as process thinkers grant, then the argument for divine foreknowledge is simple: omniscience entails foreknowledge. Since future tense statements are, as we have seen, true or false, and since to be omniscient means to know at any time all statements which are true at that time, God must have knowledge of all true future tense statements and, hence, of future contingents. Hartshorne's retreat to the position that even if future tense statements are true or false, God's omniscience may be saved by redefining it to mean "all possible knowledge" is clearly unacceptable, for (1) this is not what omniscience means, but really asserts that it is not possible to be omniscient, and (2) this view presupposes God's knowledge must be inferential, which assumption we have seen reason to question. Hartshorne's final position that omniscience means only limited knowledge of the future seems patently inadequate as a definition of omniscience. Hence, if we are serious about preserving the truth of God's omniscience, then we must acknowledge His perfect knowledge of the future as an aspect of that omniscience.

Conclusion

If what I have argued is correct, there is no incompatibility between holding to an A-theory of time, indeterminism, a view of truth as correspondence, and the truth or falsity of future tense statements. We have seen, futhermore, good reasons for holding to the truth or falsity of such statements and have noted the absurdities which follow when this is denied. If God is omniscient, He must know all such true statements. Such foreknowledge in no way entails fatalism, a fact recognized repeatedly in various fields of philosophy. Finally, the basis of divine foreknowledge need not be inferential, but may be conceived to be innate. Therefore, I see no good reason why the process theologian should insist on denying God's foreknowledge of future contingents. Biblical theism offers him both a coherent doctrine of God as well as a view of the world which preserves becoming, freedom, and contingency.

NOTES

* A future contingent is a future state of affairs that results from a free human action.

1. Charles Hartshorne, *Omnipotence and Other Theological Mistakes* (Albany: State University of New York, 1984), p. 3.

2. Charles Hartshorne, *Man's Vision of God and the Logic of Theism* (Chicago: Wilett, Clark, & Co., 1941), p. 38.

3. Hartshorne, *Omnipotence*, pp. 38-39.

4. Hartshorne, *Vision of God*, p. 140. See also idem, "The Meaning of 'Is Going to Be'," *Mind* 74 (1965): 47.

5. In actual fact, Hartshorne's position on the Law of Excluded Middle seems to be inconsistent, for he also contends that the negation of any affirmative future tense statement, e.g. "A sea battle will occur tomorrow," is not formed simply by negating the predicate, e.g. "A sea battle will not occur tomorrow," but by conjoining to the negation a modal statement expressing the possibility of the negation, e.g. "A sea battle will not occur tomorrow or it *may not* occur tomorrow." In such a case, the tradtional Law of Excluded Middle holds, for either "A sea battle will occur tomorrow" is true or "A sea battle will not occur tomorrow" is true or "A sea battle will not occur tomorrow or it may not occur tomorrow" is true. This position of Hartshorne's is inconsistent with that explained in the text; but it is not in any case tenable, for the contradictory of any statement is clearly not formed by positing a disjunction: the contradictory of any statement "*p*" is "not-*p*," and not, as Hartshorne would have it, "not-*p* or possibly not-*p*."

6. Hartshorne, *Vision of God*, p. 14.

7. Hartshorne compromised even this doctrine of omniscience around 1960 by conceding that God cannot have knowledge of events as they happen, so that He is ignorant of the present. Indeed, it has been questioned whether Hartshorne can hold even to God's perfect knowledge of the past, in which case divine omniscience has been altogether sacrificed. For a discussion and literature, see David Diehl, "Divine Omniscience in the Thought of Charles Hartshorne and Cornelius Van Til: A Systematic Comparative Study," (Ph. D. dissertation, Hartford Seminary Foundation, 1978), pp. 295-304. In this piece, however, my object is to analyze only the process denial of divine foreknowledge.

8. Hartshorne, *Vision of God*, p. 14; cf. pp. 98, 104.

9. Ibid., p. 140.

10. Nicholas Rescher and Alasdair Urquhart, *Temporal Logic*, Library of Exact Philosophy (New York: Springer-Verlag, 1971), p. 211.

11. Nicholas Rescher, *Many-valued Logic* (New York: Mcgraw-Hill, 1969), pp. 2-3.

12. Charles A. Baylis, "Are Some Propositions Neither True nor False?" *Philosophy of Science* 3 (1936): 162. See also R. D. Bradley, "Must the Future Be What It Is Going to Be?" *Mind* 68 (1959): 204.

13. Thomas Bradley Talbott, "Fatalism and the Timelessness of Truth," (Ph. D. dissertation, University of California at Santa Barbara, 1974), pp. 153-154.

14. This is, at least, the stumbling block discerned by John C. Moskop, *Divine Omniscience and Human Freedom* (Macon, Georgia: Mercer University Press, 1984), pp. 1-28.

Divine Foreknowledge and Future Contingency

15. See A. E. Dummett and A. Flew, "Can an Effect Precede its Cause?" in *Belief and Will*, Aristotelian Society Supplementary Volume 28 (London: Harrison & Sons, 1954), pp. 27-62; Michael Scriven, "Randomness and the Causal Order," *Analysis* 17 (1956-57): 5-9; Michael Dummett, "Bringing about the Past," *Philosophical Review* 17 (1964): 338-359; Bob Brier, "Magicians, Alarm Clocks, and Backward Causation," *Southern Journal of Philosophy* 11 (1973): 359-364; Larry Dwyer, "How to Affect, but not Change the Past," *Southern Journal of Philosophy* 15 (1977): 383-385.

16. See C. D. Broad, "The Philosophical Implications of Foreknowledge," in *Knowledge and Foreknowledge*, Aristotelian Society Supplementary Volume 16 (London: Harrison & Sons, 1937), pp. 177-209; C. W. K. Mundle, "Does the Concept of Precognition Make Sense?" *International Journal of Parapsychology* 6 (1964): 179-198; *Encyclopedia of Philosophy*, sv. "Precognition," by Antony Flew; C. D. Broad, "The Notion of Precognition," *International Journal of Parapsychology* 10 (1968): 165-196; Bob Brier, *Precognition and the Philosophy of Science* (New York: Humanities Press, 1974).

17. See Robert Nozick, "Newcomb's Problem and Two Principles of Choice," in *Essays in Honor of Carl G. Hempel*, ed. Nicholas Rescher, Synthese Library (Dordrecht, Holland: D. Reidel, 1969), pp. 114-146; Maya Bar-Hillel and Avishai Margalit, "Newcomb's Paradox Revisited," *British Journal for the Philosophy of Science* 23 (1972): 295-304; G. Schlesinger, "The Unpredictability of Free Choices," *British Journal for the Philosophy of Science* 25 (1974): 209-221; James Cargile, "Newcomb's Paradox," *British Journal for the Philosophy of Science* 26 (1975): 234-239; Doris Olin, "Newcomb's Problem: Further Investigations," *American Philosophical Quarterly* 13 (1976): 129-133; Dennis M. Ahearn, "Foreknowledge: Nelson Pike and Newcomb's Problem," *Religious Studies* 75 (1979): 475-490; Terence Horgan, "Counterfactuals and Newcomb's Problem," *Journal of Philosophy* 78 (1981): 331-356; Steven J. Brams, *Superior Beings* (New York: Springer Verlag, 1983), pp. 46-52.

18. Edward J. Khamara, "Eternity and Omniscience," *Philosophical Quarterly* 24 (1974): 204-219.

19. Alan Gauld, "ESP and Attempts to Explain It," in *Philosophy and Psychical Research*, ed. Shivesh C. Thakur, Muirhead Library of Philosophy (London: George Allen & Unwin, 1976), p. 36.

20. Ibid., p. 37.

God and Evil
in Process Theology

Michael L. Peterson

Michael L. Peterson

Michael L. Peterson received his Ph.D. in philosophy from the State University of New York at Buffalo. He is Professor of Philosophy and Head of the Philosophy department at Asbury College. He is currently Managing Editor for *Faith and Philosophy: Journal of the Society of Christian Philosophers.* Dr. Peterson has published three books: *Evil and the Christian God, A Spectrum of Thought: Essays in Honor of Dennis F. Kinlaw,* and *Philosophy of Education.* His articles have appeared in *American Philosophical Quarterly, Sophia, Journal of Value Inquiry, Christianity Today,* and other journals.

The presence of evil in the world is a haunting fact which every world view must face. No philosophical or theological perspective provides a complete explanation of reality unless it offers some insight into the enigma of evil. Although dualism, pantheism, and other religious systems encounter their own versions of the problem of evil, the problem is most acute for Christianity. Since Christianity makes such strong claims about the nature and purposes of God, it must strive the hardest to account for evil.

Modern process theologians believe that traditional Christian theodicies (i.e., attempts to explain why God allows evil) are inadequate. According to these thinkers, the traditional concepts of reality, morality, power, and the meaning of existence do not allow the formulation of a viable theodicy. Process thinkers advance new metaphysical and theological concepts which entail what they believe to be a more viable explanation of evil.

The present study investigates the claims of process theodicy. The investigation begins by rehearsing the general points of comparison and contrast between classical and process theodicies. Then it examines in detail three key concepts of process theodicy which encounter philosophical difficulty. It ends with a critical overview and evaluation.

Classical and Process Theodicy

The Christian claim that God is perfect in goodness and power seems radically incongruous with the existence of suffering, catastrophe, cruelty, and a multitude of other disturbing evils. Many critics of Christian monotheism assume that if God is infinite in goodness He should want to remove the serious evils of our world. If He is unlimited in power He should be able to remove them. Yet these evils persist. The critics conclude that God does not exist. If the problem they pose is correct, then one must deny at least one of the central theological claims to escape it. They demand that the theist relinquish either the belief that a God infinite in power and goodness exists or the belief that genuine evil exists.[1] Hence, for many, the problem of evil is a major obstacle to religious faith. For some, it even provides grounds for atheism.

A theodicy aimed at vindicating belief in God is basically fashioned from the concepts already inherent in a given theological perspective. And every theological perspective rests, in turn, upon certain general assumptions about the structure of reality and the nature of values. This is why the study of theodicy quickly takes us to the very heart of a world view. As John Bowker puts it, a religion's response to evil "reveals, perhaps more than anything else, what it takes the meaning of life to be."[2]

Traditional Christian theodicies typically play upon two particular kinds of themes: the causal genesis of evil and the teleological outcome. Thus, standard Christian responses to the problem of evil assert that the world was created *ex nihilo* by a transcendent God, and that the originally flawless creation became alienated from God through man's rebellion. Such theodicies hold that God desires to protect free choice in order to allow human life moral significance. Furthermore, they affirm that God's redemptive activity will overcome evil and will include the eschatological culmination of history and personal victory over death.[3] The intent of traditional theodicies which employ these themes is to show that the existence of evil is reconcilable with the theistic claim that God is omnipotent, omniscient, and wholly good.

Modern process philosophers and theologians, on the contrary, believe that evil cannot be adequately explained within the conceptual system of theistic theology. They promise an alternative Christian theodicy which retains all of the desirable characteristics of God (e.g. goodness) while avoiding the undesirable ones. This brand of theology is quasi-theistic in that it modifies certain traditional divine attributes (e.g. omnipotence) in order to account for evil in the world. The essential themes in process theodicy can be traced from Alfred North Whitehead through his intellectual descendants, such as Charles Hartshorne, John Cobb, David Griffin, Shubert Ogden, and Lewis Ford.

According to process thinkers, the world was not created by divine fiat and endowed with its manifest structure. There has always been a world. That is, there have always been finite creatures who come into being and pass away in an ongoing process. God is not ontologically independent from these creaturely actualities. Instead God and the world are intimately and reciprocally related. Denying that this view expresses pantheism, which totally identifies God and the world, process thinkers declare that their view should be referred to as *panen-theism*, which includes the events and experiences of the world in the life of God.

God's chief goal is the realization and maximization of value within the experiences of creaturely actualities. These values include novelty, creativity, adventure, intensity, complexity, and so forth. God's program along these lines encounters one irreducible fact: the essential freedom of finite creatures. This is not a freedom which He bestowed upon creatures and thus may limit or control. Simply by virtue of being actual every creature possesses the power of self-determination. This means that human beings have the innate ability to resist God's will, i.e., they have the power to do evil. So, for God to provide opportunities for creatures to have valuable experiences is for Him to accept the risk of various kinds of evil. After all, some kinds of desirable intensity can only be generated out of discord, hardship, or pain.

Although God cannot control the free choices of creatures, He attempts to elicit His purposes through persuasive influence. In His "primordial nature" (Whitehead's term) God eternally knows all of the possible ways in which the world can advance or increase in value.[4] Out of this range of possibilities, God attempts to draw out His specific plan for the course of things. When negative experiences occur, threatening to thwart the divine aim, God simply offers new possibilities adjusted to what has already happened. So goes the evolution of the world, as God is continually creating increased order and significance out of aboriginal chaos and triviality.

Since finite actualities are always perishing, God is continually storing up their experiences in His "consequent nature". Evil as well as good experiences, negative as well as positive ones, are conserved and fittingly harmonized in God's own conscious life. As Whitehead intimates:

> The consequent nature of God is his judgment on the world. He saves the world as it passes into the immediacy of his own life. It is the

judgment of a tenderness which loses nothing that can be saved. It is also the judgment of a wisdom which uses what in the temporal world is mere wreckage.[5]

Explaining the process belief that God, in a certain sense, functions as the kingdom of heaven, Robert Mellert says, "Salvation is for all reality, because all reality has value for God. . . . Everything ultimately contributes its own reality to the reality that is God."[6]

Process philosophers and theologians believe that this scenario of God and the world adequately handles the theoretical problem of evil. Since God is no longer conceived as an omnipotent creator and thus able to control all events, He is not culpable for the presence of evil in the world. Nevertheless process theodicy projects a deity who is deeply involved in, and profoundly affected by, the experiences of finite creatures.

The Concept Of Divine Power

Process theodicy is implied by the larger conceptual system of process thought and therefore depends heavily on the extensive modification of the concepts of God and evil. No intelligent appraisal of this answer to the problem of evil can be made without careful consideration of the intricate changes which occur in these two concepts.

The process concept of God differs markedly from the classical one on the issues of divine power and goodness. Taking the matter of divine power first, the process theist rejects the classical concept of omnipotence and develops a new view of God's power. Referring to the classical concept of power as "coercive", the process thinker argues that God's power is instead "persuasive". This new position results from two convergent lines of reasoning, one regarding the metaphysics of power and the other regarding the morality of determination versus persuasion.

According to process thinkers, the classical theological concept of omnipotence is metaphysically impossible because it is conceptually incoherent. They depict the classical view as holding that God has all power. On this characterization of the classical view, God can universally bring about any logically possible state of affairs.[7] However, since process metaphysics holds that the existence of a world of finite beings is necessary and that every existing being has the inherent power of self-determination, it implies that it is impossible for God to determine completely the actions of creatures. Put simply, the process argument is that if there are other beings which have *some* power, God cannot have *all* of the power that there is. Yet His power is perfect in that He possesses all the power that it is "conceivable (possible) for a being to have", as David Griffin[8] says, or "absolutely maximal" power, as Hartshorne indicates.[9]

The direct application of this point to theodicy is not difficult to understand. It seems to many thoughtful persons that a world which contains moral good but no moral evil is certainly a logically possible state of affairs. Therefore, if the God of classical theism is thought to have the power to bring about such a desirable situation and does not do so, the conclusion that He is not wholly good would seem to be inescapable. Process theologians thus believe that they are able to avoid the dilemma which besets traditional theism, and thus to preserve the goodness of God, by developing a more adequate view of God's power.

Another aspect of the process theory of the nature of divine power relates to the morality of its employment. Process thinkers believe that limitation of God's power is required not only on metaphysical grounds but on moral grounds as well. It is not just that God *cannot* control the activities of free creatures, but that He *ought* not control them. John Cobb has declared that "the only power capable of any worthwhile result is the power of persuasion."[10] Even if God did have enough power to coerce creatures into performing all and only those actions He desires, it would be morally reprehensible for Him to do it. Divine determination of this sort would destroy the significance of creaturely action. The way for God to preserve the integrity of human choices, then, is for Him to attempt to work out His good purposes in the world through the exercise of persuasion. God must endeavor to get creatures to make right choices of their own volition. For process thought, although God's coercive power is either limited or nonexistent, His persuasive power is unlimited.[11]

A close inspection of the process view of divine power uncovers a number of difficulties. First of all, it may well be that the popular process distinction between coercive and persuasive power plays all too conveniently on an artificial distinction between, as well as a vague caricature of, the two types of power. Proponents of process philosophy and theology typically stipulate that there is a complete.

dichotomy between coercive power (commonly termed efficient causality in philosophy) and persuasive power (roughly synonymous with final causality in philosophy). Coercive power is always painted as completely determinative, even brutal and manipulative, whereas persuasive power suggests a more genteel and polite mode of power, much more fitting for a perfect deity.

Surely the either/or distinction between coercive and persuasive power is oversimplified. As Nancy Frankenberry has argued, process thinkers have ignored a whole range of power between the extremes they have erected. More profitable, she contends, would be an exploration of the more realistic modes of God's power: "productive power," or "sustaining power," or "enabling power." An investigation of these concepts would no doubt reveal that not every exercise of efficient causality is coercive in the sense that it precludes freedom of response in others. On the contrary, it often turns out that those who are endowed with great productive powers are capable of inspiring and enabling others to exercise freely their own productive powers.[12]

One reason that process thinkers polarize coercive and persuasive power is that they misunderstand the doctrine of omnipotence. They take the traditional concept of divine omnipotence to be the one represented by Leibniz and some other theists: that God can unilaterally bring about any intrinsically possible state of affairs. This same assumption has been shared by many critics of theism, resulting in demands that God create a world with moral good but no moral evil.[13] However, S. A. Grave and Alvin Plantinga have argued that God cannot straightforwardly bring about any intrinsically possible state of affairs.[14] Plantinga has made this point in his recent version of the free will defense which pays particular attention to the logic of possible states of affairs that consist in an agent's making a free choice. He demonstates that it is simply not possible *for God* to bring about possible states of affairs of this sort, for if He did the agent's choices would not really be free.[15] Thus, classical theism can preserve the goodness of God on logical grounds without having to appeal to process metaphysics.[16]

A second problem with the process view of divine power is that it seems to rely on a model of power which is inappropriate to the subject. Process thinkers typically take their cue from Charles

Hartshorne, who surprisingly argues that with respect to power ownership is exclusive.[17] With respect to property, such as apples and oranges, ownership is exclusive. If a person or group has them all, then others have none. But it is not clear that a correct paradigm of power works this way. In the physical realm, a strand of copper has the power to conduct electricity, but so does carbon. In the case of the power of human agency, this point is even more relevant to theodicy. I have the power to make my wife laugh, but so do my two sons. My possession of this power is not exclusive. Likewise, I have the power to move the fallen branch in my yard, but so does God. Actually, the traditional view of omnipotence (what process thinkers label the "monopolistic" view) has never implied otherwise. So, process thinkers may strongly criticize the monopolistic view of divine power, but they should not equate it with the classical theistic position on the subject.

Nelson Pike has stated that the "standard view" of omnipotence does not entail that beings other than God are devoid of power, but that every exercise of power on the part of finite creatures is dependent upon God's allowing it.[18] Divine permission has traditionally been interpreted not only as God's causally sustaining the created order, but also as His refraining from exercising some specific powers of His own. Thus, while it is within my power to pick up the fallen branch, the exercise of that power is contingent upon God's refraining from exercising His power to keep the branch on the ground. This is the sense in which the traditional view of omnipotence is generally thought to imply that God is capable of totally determining the activities of human beings. This is the sense of omnipotence which is usually operative when anti-theistic critics demand that God exercise whatever of His powers are necessary to prevent or eliminate tragic evils. Of course, process thinkers reject this conception of divine power, claiming that the exercise of creaturely power is not dependent upon God's permission. But the point here is that they cannot reject it on grounds that it assumes a faulty understanding of the metaphysics of power which their theory supposedly corrects.

In addition to misunderstanding the traditional concept of productive power applied to God, process thinkers have developed a concept of divine persuasive power which is not totally satisfying. Unless this concept can be salvaged from some glaring weaknesses, process thinkers have no right to claim that they have a positive alternative to the classical concept of divine power which they criticize.[19]

Whitehead's metaphysic of *becoming* is woven together with his notion that all actual entities are centers of experience. Now each entity (or "occasion" as Whitehead terms it) receives data from previous occasions and then responds in its own way. God seeks to achieve his purposes in the world by luring each occasion toward the optimum response. He does this by imparting to the elemental experience of every occasion an impetus toward the perfect outcome. Yet each actual occasion has the power to respond favorably or unfavorably to this "prehended" data. As Whitehead says, each actual occasion "derives from God its basic conceptual aim, relevant to its actual world, yet with indeterminations awaiting its own decisions."[20]

One weakness in the process concept of persuasive power, which is identified by Nancy Frankenberry, is that it is partial at best and needs to be supplemented by a concept of imparted energy. In other words, presenting to creatures purely ideal logical possibilities is a rather sterile kind of persuasive effort. In view of the massive evils in the world and what appears to be a low ebb of energy toward the good, why do process thinkers not include a concept of the transmission of divine energy into the experiential states of creatures? Frankenberry argues that representatives of process thought have not even explored whether a more dynamic conception of persuasive power is possible in terms of their own theory. She suggests two reasons for this: either they have an overly optimistic view of how creatures will respond to purely theoretical possibilities or they have not recognized the fact that power can be causally efficacious without being completely determinative.[21]

While Frankenberry exposes a serious flaw in the process concept of persuasive power, she does not go far enough. She seems prepared to settle for a more potent subliminal "nudge" as an acceptable persuasive effort. However, it is not clear that any notion which locates persuasive power in the subliminal, almost subconscious experience of creatures is fully adequate. The standard concept of moral persuasion denotes a much more conscious and rational activity than the process concept of subconscious urges, experiential nudges, or lures for feeling. Persuasion is characteristically understood as a process of argumentation in which each party attempts to find premises which the other accepts and which lead to the desired conclusion. Traditionally, the morality of persuasion has been mutual respect for the other's rational dignity and thus not seeking consent on less than reasonable grounds. Ironically, process thinkers, who loudly decry the immorality of coercion, typically describe their rendition of persuasion in terms which do not even sound remotely similar to those of classical moral persuasion.

The process doctrine of divine persuasive power not only involves severe internal problems, but also encounters serious difficulties in application to the facts of the world. The process claim is that, although God's coercive power is limited and relative to the power of creatures, His persuasive power is unlimited or infinite. However, the concept of power is an empirical one, i.e., it is verifiable in experience. Therefore critics, such as Peter Hare and Edward Madden, rightly insist that ordinary observation provides no evidence that maximum persuasive force for good is at work in the world. As they note, it can just as well be argued that the amount and distribution of actual evil suggests that a very powerful evil persuasive force is operative.[22] Lewis Ford's disclaimer that the tragic dimensions of evil are indeed "compatible with unlimited persuasive power"[23] simply renders the inherently empirical concept of power nonfalsifiable and thus meaningless.[23] Process theists will have to explain the apparently large number of people who remain unpersuaded before they can claim meaningful application for their theory.

The Concept Of Divine Goodness

Process theologians and philosophers believe that their modification of the concept of divine power allows them to retain the concept of divine goodness, and thus avoids the dilemma facing the classical view of God. However, process thought entails a view of God's goodness which is quite different from the traditional theistic conception of perfect goodness, and therefore shapes process theodicy in peculiar ways.

In process philosophy, the criteria for intrinsic goodness are harmony and intensity of experience. God's perfection is seen in His attempt to maximize both the harmony and the intensity of the experiences of finite actualities. Process thinkers indicate that it sometimes seems as if the twin goals of harmony and intensity are in tension. For example, in some situations intensity can be increased only by introducing a measure of discord or conflict. These discordant elements, however, can then be harmonized at a higher level, making the experience achieved all the more significant. God's purpose in the world is to produce an interplay of the relevant factors which make for important or "higher" experiences.

Process theodicy sees God's goodness, then, exhibited in His persistent attempts to bring the world out of discord and triviality into harmony and intensity. Hence, in the evolution of the world, God must negotiate the various trade-offs between the relevant values and disvalues. The evils of pain, suffering, injustice, catastrophe, etc. are possible in a world structured to evoke novelty, integration, adventure, and all of the other components of worthwhile experiences. According to the process world view, the complex interplay of positive and negative experiences is worth the risk of evil.

The natural criticism which arises at this point is that the process conception of divine goodness is fundamentally aesthetic rather than moral. In *The Religious Availability of Whitehead's God*, Stephen Ely argues that the divine use of aesthetic criteria in dealing with the world is morally objectionable.[24] After all, if the aims of perfect divine goodness are to increase the harmony and intensity of earthly experience, as the process scenario envisions, then many ordinary moral principles may be violated in the effort. However, in classical moral theory, which carries over into the traditional concept of divine goodness, the set of appropriate criteria develops along the lines of justice, benevolence, and so forth. Hence, in classical theology, God would not be good if He caused or allowed suffering in order to attain aesthetic aims.

David Griffin has replied to this kind of criticism by explaining the highly general character of Whitehead's concept of beauty. Griffin argues that aesthetic value is not just one dimension of human experience alongside others; instead it is a generic dimension with all others belonging to it.[25] Since aesthetic aims, in this larger sense, include moral aims, there supposedly is no essential conflict between them. But the original criticism cannot be so easily rebutted, since it calls into question the whole notion that moral values can be subordinate to aesthetic ones. If the process rebuttal were sound, then our ordinary moral principles would be illusory and God's goodness would be drastically unlike anything we are capable of recognizing as good. The presumption, then, must be in favor of our deepest moral convictions rather than the speculative constructions of a Whiteheadian theory of value.

Process thinkers hold that God's efforts to evoke beauty and importance in temporal experience are not simply for the finite actualities involved, but ultimately to provide appropriate data for His own unified and comprehensive experience. In the Whiteheadian scheme, then, the sufferings and difficulties, as well as the pleasures and achievements, of finite beings become material for God's aesthetic composition, i.e., for fitting inclusion in His consequent nature.[26] But the previous question simply recurs at another level: Is it morally permissible for deity to risk evil in order to enrich its own experience?

Along with the shift in the conception of divine goodness comes the consideration of whether the process God is worshipworthy. Moral perfection has traditionally been thought to be a necessary condition of worshipworthiness. To the extent that process thinkers make moral goodness merely instrumental to a higher aesthetic goodness in the divine life they must demonstrate that God is still worthy of our worship. It appears that such a case can only be made at the expense of our most basic moral principles.[27]

The Concept of Evil

Our understanding of the process definition of goodness can be completed by looking at the process definition of evil. Just as goodness is drained of its fundamentally moral character, so is evil. For Whitehead, the nature of evil is the phenomenon of universal perishing. He says that "The ultimate evil in the temporal world . . . lies in the fact that the past fades, that time is a 'perpetual perishing'."[28] In other words, things come to be and pass away in the ever rolling stream of time. For Whitehead, this problem is not only an inherent feature of life, but a metaphysical feature of reality.[29] Yet Whitehead provides no argument to show why this pervasive characteristic of the world is an evil, particularly from a moral point of view. As long as process philosophy makes perishing a constant structural trait in the universe, it has no resources for arguing consistently that perpetual perishing is inappropriate, unnatural, or unjust somehow. Loss and death are evil only if one presumes that something is terribly wrong in nature for such things to occur.

On Whitehead's own theory, the sheer transience of existence is simply not a sufficient condition to make life tragic. Within a more traditional moral framework, certain features of transience might be construed as tragic. It is not the passing of things which is really evil, but the premature and senseless passing of things of genuine worth. The baby who deserves to live and be fulfilled but is burned to death in a fire, the marriage which could have flourished but is destroyed by mutual misunderstanding, the well-intentioned public official who is corrupted by uncontrollable greed and whose life ends in failure and dishonor—these and innumerable other cases furnish examples of the serious evils of our world. These are the sorts of things which our concepts of moral goodness and rightness make us abhor.

The writings of Whitehead and his intellectual followers on evil in the world have a completely different tone from those which rest upon a traditional moral base. Process writers bemoan the fact that there is less adventure and novelty than there should be, not as much feeling and intensity about life. They offer a kind of romantic and optimistic hope that there are ever new possibilities for these things, that even the frustrations of life will not prevent the creative advance of the world. But such expressions seem hopelessly out of touch with the tragic and absurd elements of our existence, and certainly seem blind to what traditional theology calls sin.

It must be noted that Whitehead offers a subsidiary definition of evil. In the same passage cited above, he states: "The nature of evil is that the characters of things are mutually obstructive. Thus the depths of life require a process of selection . . . selection is at once the measure of evil and the process of its evasion."[30] Although this remark is rather enigmatic, it is probably best interpreted within the context of Whitehead's generalizatons about the aesthetic value of discords in art. Whitehead tends to see the contrasts and conflicts of existence as necessary elements which God can synthesize into a larger whole. However, this supplementary Whiteheadian comment on evil, even given an aesthetic interpretation, neither explains why the universe is built on the brute facts of obstruction and conflict nor why God's involvement with it is essentially aesthetic.[31] So, even the augmented process conception of evil still fails to account for what we ordinarily take to be its moral depth.

Whitehead constructs a vision of reality in which finitude, perishing, selection, and loss are part of the warp and woof. They are not alien factors which have somehow appeared to threaten the more fundamental nature and purpose of the cosmos. Yet Whitehead's writings are freighted with a sentimental resistance to the fact that this is the way the world is. However, since his theory of value and goodness is basically aesthetic, he has no moral grounds for the rejection. Since his system makes perishing and obstruction part of the universal process of creativity, he has no aesthetic grounds either.

The Concept of Redemption

After examining the key concepts of process thought, the question legitimately arises as to whether there are grounds for hope that evil will be decisively defeated and that good will be ultimately victorious. And, if there are any such grounds, then the important question regards the precise sense in which there can be a triumph of the good. These questions apply to three vital areas in which it is natural to hope for good to win out over evil.

The first area of concern is that of ordinary daily living, the domain of innumerable personal choices in which good and evil hang in the balance. Classical Christian theology assures us that God's activity, while not determinative of our moral choices, is supportive of the moral venture. God empowers and uplifts our human energies. Process thinkers, on the other hand, talk about God's current activity in the world in purely conceptual terms. He is always offering the sheer possibilities of good as adventurous and novel choices for creatures. The idea of God energizing the moral quest is virtually absent, and talk of His grace regenerating an individual human life is not appropriate. No doubt, process thinkers take this kind of position largely because of their fallacious dichotomy between persuasive and coercive power. Thinking that all divine activity beyond the purely conceptual is dangerously coercive, they deny that any divine agency is at work in the world.

A second vital area which classical theology has always addressed in terms of the prospects of good defeating evil is the overall framework of history. Classical Christian theism, with its view of God's omnipotent and sovereign power, provides a guarantee that evil will eventually be overcome and that good will be victorious. Process thinkers, on the other hand, do not incorporate into their system any final guarantee that such a resolution of all things will ever come to pass.[32] In process theism the future is an open risk. God is continually trying to direct the creation toward the good, attempting to persuade it to advance in the creation of positive value. But since His power is persuasive and not coercive, evil is an ever present possibility.

Process thesim offers no argument showing that we cannot resist the persuasive power of God forever, and so urges that the way is open for genuine faith in the desired outcome. Process theists criticize the counterfeit faith of classical theism which makes the triumph of good an accomplished future fact to be awaited. According to process theists, their view increases the role of ethical aspiration by proposing that the human venture is a matter of real struggle and accomplishment. God has not given absolute assurance that the good will win and so makes the moral endeavor meaningful. In effect, God has made himself vulnerable to the world. By allowing us the opportunity of moral achievement, He also leaves open the terrible risk of moral deterioration. As the process scenario goes, the world is eternal and thus the whole business of moral struggle goes on forever.

The position of classical Christian theism is that there will be a definitive resolution of all things, a time when absolute justice is meted out and a fallen creation restored. Such a scenario is not inconsistent with a doctrine of free will on the part of creatures. Within the world order which is moving toward that immanent resolution, human beings may make meaningful moral and spiritual choices. With a wisdom and power and purifying goodness that process theology does not recognize, God will establish Himself as Lord of all.

Since the orthodox Christian conception of the Fall is that it occurred within a historical context, the ultimate redemption of the world will be related to the actual historical process. Evil is essentially a moral flaw which entered creation and will be definitively eliminated from a world that was originally intended to be morally pure. It is not difficult to understand why process theology, with its impoverished conception of evil as a metaphysical feature of reality, has no logical need to postulate a historical resolution of the problem. The process deity simply does not have the power to change the metaphysical structure of a universe which eternally exists independently of His creative activity and sustenance.

Third, one might expect a theological system to provide strong grounds for redemptive hope in the matter of continued personal existence after death. Traditional Christian theism places a premium on individual human beings because they bear the image of a personal and moral God. Their salvation is conceived not only in terms of moral and spiritual renewal in temporal life, but also in terms of final transformation and everlasting life. Process theology, by way of contrast, envisions no redemption of individual persons. Redemption instead is the divine collection of all experiences of temporal creatures into His own atemporal experience. Whitehead writes: "Each actuality in the temporal world has its reception into God's nature. The corresponding element in God's nature is not temporal actuality, but is the transmutation of that temporal actuality into a living, ever-present fact."[33] Commenting on Whitehead, Elizabeth Kraus has stated that:

> The universal hunger of humanity is for redemption: redemption from loss, from partiality, from temporal limitation, from finitude; redemption through an activity which somehow weaves the threads of life into an immortal tapestry immortally self-conscious . . . . Without a redeemer, one who feels the totality of finite process into himself and gives it the immortal and perfect unity attainable only from an infinite atemporal perspective, world process, conscious process, human life, are absurd.[34]

Just as God's primordial nature contains and selects from among all initial possibilities, His consequent nature collects and harmonizes all actualized possibilities.

On the matter of ultimate personal redemption, the contrast between classical Christian theism and contemporary process theism is stark. Since, for process thought, the inexorable way of things is loss, the only kind of redemption it can offer is "transmutation."

Due to the fact that the fundamental ontological realities are *becomings*, there are no stable and enduring *beings* to experience the success of the divine program. At best, God's continual synthesizing activity will retain all incoming experiences, no matter how contrasting, and will find new ways of fitting them together. And this whole process goes on forever. Although some process thinkers can muster the motivation for religious service on this kind of scenario which projects no ultimate salvation for individuals, the more normal reaction is to say that such a scheme lacks all meaning for us.

Classical Christian theism, which rests on a richer and more adequate metaphysical understanding of being, asserts that a human being can be conceived as an enduring center of consciousness which is intimately related to a physical body.[35] Moreover, when Christian theism affirms that God will restore the creation, it implies that the persons who are redeemed will somehow be continuous with their earthly identities and that they will experience God's decisive victory. Salvation, then, both in its current progress and future culmination, is for *persons* in a most significant sense.

Summary and Evaluation

The weaknesses of process theodicy reflect deep problems within process theology itself. The attempt to interpret the Christian faith within the categories of Whiteheadian metaphysics encounters two kinds of difficulty. On the one hand, it distorts the essential meanings of major Christian doctrines. On the other hand, it becomes embroiled in numerous philosophical problems irrespective of its faithfulness to Christian orthodoxy. It is not surprising, therefore, that process theodicy fails to do justice to the historic Christian understanding of God and evil, and fails to present a philosophic answer to the problem of evil which will withstand careful scrutiny.

It must be acknowledged, however, that process thinkers have performed the salutary service of forcing the serious reconsideration of inveterate philosophical concepts and standard theological themes. Classical theists must continually be open to refining the logical and metaphysical assumptions of their system. In discussions of theodicy in particular, the process position has exposed weaknesses in the ways certain theistic ideas are presented. So, although the process response to the problem of evil faces severe difficulties, its development has forced traditional theistic thinkers to try to articulate their answer to the problem in more adequate ways.

The problem of evil is complicated and subtle,[36] but a correct understanding of classical Christian theism lays a basis for a helpful and enlightening response to it.[37] An adequate theistic theodicy must retain the classical concepts of divine power and goodness. It must also preserve the deeply personal and moral character of human choice and remain sensitive to the insidious nature of the world's evil. The complex task of showing that all of these factors are compatible has been attempted by some of the greatest theistic thinkers. They have left us a wealth of literature which eliminates the need to seek a theodicy within the process point of view and strengthens our confidence that a strong theistic theodicy for our day is indeed possible, a theodicy which is consistent with both the historic Christian faith and our best philosophical intuitions.[38]

NOTES

1. Statements of the problem of evil are abundant. Some take the problem to concern the sheer existence of evil; others take the more significant problem to concern the existence of pointless evil. Statements of the former type include: H. J. McCloskey, "The Problem of Evil," *Journal of Bible and Religion*, 30 (1962), p. 200; J. L. Mackie, "Evil and Omnipotence," *Mind*, vol. 64 (1955), p. 200. Statements of the latter type include: Walter Kaufmann, *The Faith of a Heretic* (Garden City: Doubleday, 1961), p. 139; Edward Madden and Peter Hare, *Evil and the Concept of God* (Springfield: Charles C. Thomas, 1968), p. 3.

2. John Bowker, *Problems of Suffering in Religions of the World* (London: Cambridge University, 1970), p. 2.

3. For further discussion of types of traditional theodicy, see John Hick, *Evil and the God of Love*, revised edition (New York: Harper and Row, 1975).

4. See A. N. Whitehead, *Process and Reality* (New York: Macmillan, 1929), pp. 521-22; and Charles Hartshorne, *Whitehead's Philosophy: Selected Essays, 1935-1970* (Lincoln: University of Nebraska Press, 1972), p. 139. Also see the discussion of this in Michael Peterson, "Orthodox Christianity, Wesleyanism, and Process Theology," *Wesleyan Theological Journal*, vol. 15 (Fall, 1980), pp. 47-49.

5. Whitehead, *Process and Reality*, pp. 524-25. See also Whitehead, *Religion in the Making* (New York: Macmillan, 1926), p. 98.

6. Robert Mellert, *What is Process Theology?* (New York: Paulist Press, 1975), p. 65.

7. The qualification that God can bring about only those states of affairs which are capable of being consistently described excludes questions about whether God can do the absurd. For example, God cannot create a square circle, since this is a contradiction and hence intrinsically impossible.

8. David Griffin, *God, Power, and Evil: A Process Theodicy* (Philadelphia: Westminster, 1976), p. 268.

9. Charles Hartshorne, *The Divine Relativity: A Social Conception of God* (New York: Yale University Press, 1948), p. 138.

10. John Cobb, *God and the World* (Philadelphia: Westminster Press, 1969), p. 90.

11. Lewis Ford, "Divine Persuasion and the Triumph of the Good," in Delwin Brown, *et al.*, eds., *Process Philosophy and Christian Thought* (Indianapolis: Bobbs-Merrill, 1971), pp. 288-93.

12. Nancy Frankenberry, "Some Problems in Process Theodicy," *Religious Studies*, vol. 17 (1981), pp. 180-83.

13. For example, see Mackie, "Evil and Omnipotence," p. 209. See also Anthony Flew, "Divine Omnipotence and Human Freedom," in A. Flew and A. MacIntyre, eds., *New Essays in Philosophical Theology* (New York: Macmillan, 1964; 1955), p. 149.

14. S. A. Grave, "On Evil and Omnipotence,"*Mind*, vol. 65 (1956), pp. 260-61; Alvin Plantinga, *God and Other Minds* (Ithaca: Cornell University Press, 1967), p. 137.

15. Alvin Plantinga, *The Nature of Necessity* (Oxford: Clarendon Press, 1974) ch. 9; and *God, Freedom and Evil* (Grand Rapids: Eerdmans, 1977), part A.

16. For further discussion of the differences between classical theism and process theism on the concept of divine power, see David and Randall Basinger, "Divine Omnipotence: Plantinga vs. Griffin," *Process Studies*, vol. 11 (1981), pp. 11-24.

17. Charles Hartshorne, "Omnipotence," in V. Ferm, ed., *An Encyclopedia of Religion*, (New York: Philosophical Library, 1945), p. 545ff. Also, Hartshorne calls the traditional view of omnipotence the "tyrant ideal"; see *Omnipotence and Other Theological Mistakes* (Albany: State University of New York Press, 1984), p. 11ff.

18. Nelson Pike, "Process Theodicy and the Concept of Power," *Process Studies*, vol. 12 (1982), p. 154.

19. For a more technical discussion of this issue which goes beyond the present treatment, see chapter 11 by David Basinger.

20. Whitehead, *Process and Reality*, p. 343.

21. Frankenberry, pp. 181-84.

22. Peter Hare and Edward Madden, "Evil and Persuasive Power," *Process Studies*, vol. 2 (Spring, 1972), pp. 46-47.

23. Ford, "Divine Persuasion . . . ," p. 289.

24. Stephen Ely, *The Religious Availability of Whitehead's God: A Critical Analysis* (Madison: University of Wisconsin Press, 1942), p. 52.

25. David Griffin, *God, Power, and Evil*, pp. 282-97.

26. See the discussion of this point in Ford, "Divine Persuasion . . . ," pp. 293-97.

27. Another serious consideration regarding the worshipworthiness is that, for process theology, God is not personal, but is rather an impersonal principle. See Peterson, "Orthodox Christianity . . . ," p. 50.

28. Whitehead, *Process and Reality*, corrected edition, eds. D. Griffin and D. W. Sherburne (New York: Free Press, 1978), p. 230.

29. See Arthur Holmes, "Whitehead and Ethical Monotheism," *Faith and Philosophy*, vol. 1 (1984), p. 72. Holmes argues that Whitehead essentially reduces all evil to natural evil, i.e., to the result of the natural process of things.△

30. Whitehead, *Process and Reality*, corrected edition, p. 230.

31. Frankenberry discusses this same general difficulty in "Some Problems . . . ," p. 192.

32. J. E. Barnhart, *Religion and the Challenge of Philosophy* (Totowa: Littlefield, Adams and Co., 1975), p. 151.

33. Whitehead, *Process and Reality* (1929), p. 531.

34. Elizabeth Kraus, *The Metaphysics of Experience: A Companion to Whitehead's Process and Reality* (New York: Fordham University Press, 1979), p. 162.

35. See Peterson, "Orthodox Christianity . . . ," pp. 46, 56-57.

36. See Michael Peterson, "Recent Work on the Problem of Evil," *American Philosophical Quarterly*, vol. 20 (1983), pp. 321-39.

37. See Ronald Nash, *The Concept of God: An Exploration of Contemporary Difficulties with the Attributes of God* (Grand Rapids: Zondervan, 1983). Nash discusses the attributes of God with respect to the two opposing positions of modern process theism and classical Thomistic theism.

38. See John Hick, *Evil and the God of Love*; and Michael Peterson, *Evil and the Christian God* (Grand Rapids: Baker Book House, 1982). While developing distinctive theodicies of their own, these works review much of the traditional and contemporary literature on Christian theodicy.

Creatio ex nihilo

William Lane Craig

William Lane Craig

William Lane Craig is Associate Professor of Religious Studies at Westmont College. He previously served as Assistant Professor in Philosophy of Religion at Trinity Evangelical Divinity School. A graduate of Wheaton College, he took two master's degrees at Trinity Evangelical Divinity School before earning his Ph.D. at the University of Birmingham (England). He is also a candidate for the D. Theol. degree at the Universität München, West Germany. Dr. Craig has published three books: *The Kalam Cosmological Argument, The Cosmological Argument from Plato to Leibniz*, and *Apologetics: An Introduction*. His articles have appeared in numerous philosophical and theological journals including: *International Journal for Philosophy of Religion, Religious Studies, British Journal for the Philosophy of Science, Australasian Journal of Philosophy, New Scholasticism, Philosophical Studies*, and *Muslim World*.

The biblical conception of God's relation to the world is one of Creator to creature. Dualistic conceptions of God confronted with a co-eternal, uncreated material which He fashions into a cosmos are alien to the biblical writers, who think of God as all-powerful and the source of all reality external to Himself. He speaks, and the universe springs into being, created out of nothing by His incomparable power. The biblical doctrine of creation is inextricably bound up with temporal considerations and asserts that the universe began to exist at a point in the finite past at which it sprang into being out of nothing by God's almighty Word.

Process Theology's Denial of *Creatio ex nihilo*

Process theologians diametrically oppose the biblical doctrine of creation. Nor is this denial some peripheral element in their system: their panentheism—the doctrine that the world is not ontologically distinct from God but rather constitutes a part of the divine being—entails that God did not at any time create the universe *ex nihilo* nor does He conserve it in being. The world must therefore be regarded as temporally infinite and creation reinterpreted to mean a mere refashioning of some eternal substratum.

Charles Hartshorne, for example, maintains that we should conceive of God's relation to the world on the analogy of the human mind's relation to the body.[1] The human body is a world of individual parts (its cells) and the mind is to that body like an indwelling God. Similarly, God affects the world as we affect our bodies. God's volition and knowledge are related to the world as though the objects in it function as his muscles and nerves. "God has no separate sense organs or muscles, because all the parts of the world body directly perform both functions for him. In this sense the world is God's body."[2] The body of any given mind is that portion of the world which the mind immediately knows and controls and suffers.

145

Accordingly, "God is that mind which enjoys the fullest intimacy with all things, and therefore in an undiluted sense has all the world for body."[3] It might be objected that no body can be indestructible and that therefore God cannot have a body. But Hartshorne retorts that the fact that all bodies in the universe dissolve is no proof that the universe itself is destructible. On the contrary, since the world is God's body, it follows that while no individual creature must exist, creatures in general are necessarily existent. It might also be objected that the mind/body analogy is inadequate for the God/world relation because the world, unlike one's body, contains beings which are individual minds themselves. In response to this, Hartshorne makes one of process theism's boldest moves: He claims that one's body is in fact a society of living organic cells, each of which possesses "humble forms of feeling or desire" such that the human mind both influences and is influenced by them through immediate sharing of feeling.[4] Hartshorne is thus led to a form of panpsychism, asserting that even atoms are "very simple, low-grade types of minds" which possess feeling.[5] Ultimately, everything is of the order of mind, so that God's relation to the world bears in this respect no disanalogy to the human mind's relation to its body. God is the individuality of the world and we are individuals within the world, just as we are the individualities of our respective bodies and our cells the individuals which go to make up those bodies.

Now clearly such a conception of the world entails the falsity of the biblical doctrine that the world was created by God out of nothing a finite number of years ago. God could not exist without the world. Any particular being in the universe might not have existed, but it does not follow from this that no contingent being might have existed. Without creatures, the Father, Son, and Holy Spirit would be empty formulas.[6] A disembodied mind simply cannot exist; therefore God's body is eternal. God's eternity, then, means that he has maximal duration by being ungenerated and immortal, by enduring throughout all time. The cosmos has thus had infinite time for growth, but it continues to grow: God's body, the world, is a growing infinity of individuals. And since the universe is part of God, it would not be accurate to say even that the universe is an eternal creation of God. For God does not cause the universe to exist any more than one's mind causes one's body to exist: the universe influences and is influenced by its cosmic mind, but is not created by it.

These considerations constrain Hartshorne to reinterpret the doctrine of creation. We should not, he asserts, interpret the Bible as teaching *ex nihilo* creation. "Creation" means "supreme influence upon growth," and Hartshorne sees no paradox in interpreting Genesis in this sense, which is also appropriate to Plato's notion of creation in the *Timaeus*.

> The whole present pattern of the universe doubtless had an origin, including all the elements of that pattern mentioned in Genesis or in Plato. What unimaginable earlier stage of the universe they grew out of under God's influence the Bible does not say, and why should it? To turn this reticence into an affirmation of creation *ex nihilo* is a procedure at which many well equipped scholars would protest. It seems reasonable to think that in saying simply, God 'made' the existent world, the Bible is merely saying that he somehow brought it into being, and that I am not disputing.[7]

According to Hartshorne, God formed the present universe out of an earlier universe and its potentialities for transformation. But that world was similarly made from a previous world, and that one from a yet earlier one, *ad infinitum*. Thus, the present world order is but the most recent of an infinity of prior universes in a series stretching back in time without beginning. The substratum which endures through all these transformations is something "infinitely protean and infinitely endowed with power to assimilate variety into unity"— indeed this *Urstoff* is identical with God, not a second entity.[8] This substratum is not matter, but (here one recalls Hartshorne's panpsychism) an unconscious mental stuff.[9] God is from eternity continually refashioning his body, and any stage of the cosmic body grew out of an earlier besouled stage. The process theologian may, claims Hartshorne, legitimately call God the Creator without implying *ex nihilo* creation. For to "make the world" out of a preceding world is no abuse of language; on the contrary, all the examples we have of creation are instances of transformation of something already there. Of course, God's creating is meant to be unique; but its uniqueness may be interpreted in terms of its extent. "He makes on a supreme, that is, cosmic, scale; he makes the whole, not just certain parts; and he makes not for a limited time but during infinite time. These functions are strictly unique and unrivaled, not a whit the less so because the making is still transformation, enrichment."[10]

Arguments in Support of the Process View
Religious Appeal

At this point, it needs to be asked what arguments might be offered in support of the process view of creation. Here one is surprised to discover that, for all process theology's emphasis on reason and argument, the primary grounds for affirming the process view are not rational, but religious. That is to say, the principal reason we are to regard process theology's viewpoint as true is, not because there are rational arguments demonstrating its doctrine, but because its doctrine answers more adequately to man's religious sentiments, or to put it bluntly, because it is more religiously appealing. Hartshorne asserts boldly that the disproofs of traditional theism are as conclusive as philosophical arguments can be.[11] But wherein lie such decisive disproofs? They lie in the inconsistency between the demands of the religious sentiment and the philosophical doctrines of traditional theism. The philosophical doctrines imply loosely what the religious sentiment demands: for example, it affirms that God is loving, which speaks to the ideas essential to the practice of religion. On the other hand, religious sentiment demands a God who really *is* loving, not an impassible, detached Unmoved Mover of whom love can be predicated only in a weak analogical sense. Thus, the philosophical tenets cannot be derived from the demands of religious sentiment and are in fact contradictory to it. Thus, we have a situation in which the philosophical doctrines do imply the religious ones, but the religious doctrines do not imply (and indeed imply the falsity of) the philosophical ones. Hartshorne calls this the "decisive refutation" of traditional theology: "For religious ideas claim absolute ultimacy. They must involve all ultimate truths, which must be deducible from them. Otherwise, secular truth would be more final than religious."[12] Process theology, on the other hand, is said to fulfill in its philosophical tenets all the demands of religious sentiment. It is therefore consistent, while traditional theism is not.

In the above argumentation, it seems clear that the final arbiter of truth in the contest between traditional and process theism is religious sentiment. Traditional theism is in conflict with religious sentiment, and process theism is not. Now I think one could plausibly argue that the philosophical tenets of process theology are no more deducible from religious ideas than are the tenets of traditional theism. What religious idea, after all, implies that the world is the body of God or Hartshorne's fantastic panpsychism? The demand that all ultimate truths be deducible from religious ideas seems an altogether incredible demand. Even if one softens this demand to the requirement that all ultimate truths be compatible with religious ideas, it is still not obvious that the philosophical doctrine of process theology is not in conflict with religious sentiment (e.g., the conviction that God is the source of moral value and immortality in some actual way). Or again, one might object quite plausibly that the process theologian's line of reasoning is characterized by a sort of "all or nothing," "either/or" mentality. That is to say, he makes much to-do about the religious inadequacy of an impassible, immutable deity and assumes that he has thereby falsified all the tenets of traditional theism, e.g. *creatio ex nihilo*. Impassibility and immutability become favorite whipping posts, and the falsity of these doctrines is assumed to entail the falsity of the rest. Hartshorne attempts to justify this procedure by claiming that ideas of traditional theism "belong logically together, so that there is little use in judging any of them in isolation. Either we accept them one and all, or we reject them one and all . . . ."[13] But this mutual entailment relation among the doctrines of traditional theism is far from obvious. Why could not a passible God create the world *ex nihilo*? How would the mutability of God entail the falsity of *creatio ex nihilo*? And even if the tenets of traditional theism were mutually entailing, how would the falsity of that system entail the truth of process theism? The situation confronting us is not a choice of either/or. Too often process thinkers seem to assume that in refuting traditional theism and presenting process theism as a coherent alternative, they have somehow demonstated process theism to be true. But they thereby overlook the fact that both traditional theology and process theology could be false and some third system true.

Letting all that pass, however, the main point I wish to make is that the argument from religious sentiment is strictly irrelevant to considerations of truth. In arguing that the doctrines of process theology comport more adequately with the demands of the religious sentiment, all the process theologian can hope to prove is that process theology is, well, just more religiously appealing than traditional theism. But this is irrelevant to the truth of process theology. What guarantee have we that the more religiously appealing system is in fact true? So far as I can see, we have none. Hence, Hartshorne's claims that religious sentiment does not demand that the Creator bring the universe into being *ex nihilo* and again that God as a supreme transforming influence is religiously adequate are simply irrelevant. The case for process theism is thus remarkably weak, being fundamentally a non-rational appeal to religious sentiment, a consideration which has no pertinence to the truth of the tenets of process theology.

Time and Creation

What further specific grounds, then, might be given for denying *creatio ex nihilo*? Here, fortunately, Hartshorne does give us some argumentation. He argues that the idea of a beginning of time is self-contradictory. For a beginning is a change, and change requires something as the subject of change which does not itself come to exist through that change. "The beginning of the world would have to happen *to* something other than the world, something which as the subject of happening would be in a time which did not begin with the world."[14] But as an argument against the beginning of time or the universe, this reasoning seems very unimpressive. As medieval scholars saw, creation (and annihilation) is not technically speaking a substantial change, precisely because there is no enduring substratum. An absolute beginning-to-be is not a change in the thing that begins to be, and therefore Hartshorne's argument fails. Anticipating this response, Hartshorne retreats to the position that such a beginning would at least realize a possibility which would have to co-exist with the actuality, which is self-contradictory. The first state would be an ontological lie, since it would be unlike all later states in having the appearance, but not the reality, of age. These second lines of defense, however, seem no more formidable than the first: the objection is very unclear. No contradiction is involved in the possibility of an event coexisting with the actual event, for its actuality implies its possibility. In any case, as the scholastics pointed out, the possibility of creation was not a potency in the universe itself (since it did not exist), but a potential in the active power of God in that He had the ability to create the universe. I see no contradiction in such a view. The second objection is entirely irrelevant to the truth of *creatio ex nihilo*: Why could God not create something with an appearance of age, should He so wish? In any case, an appearance of age does not seem to be a necessary correlate of *creatio ex nihilo*. Hartshorne's arguments against a beginning of creation can hardly, then, be said to be telling.

Perhaps the process theologian might object to a beginning of time on other grounds, however, arguing with Aristotle that since every moment of time is bounded by time, there can be no first moment of time. Even if this argument were sound, however, it would not suffice to refute *creatio ex nihilo*, for a theist might well hold, as Richard Swinburne does, that although the universe began to exist, time preceded God's creation of the universe and God endures throughout all time.[15] In fact, the objection seems to be unsound. If one regards any temporal interval as a potentially infinitely divisible continuum, it is not clear that any moment's being bounded by more time entails an infinite past. For could there not be, say, a first second or minute, without there being a first moment, the divisions of that first second tailing off toward a limit of infinity on the pattern of . . . , $1/4$, $1/2$, 1? It is not clear why a first instant of time must be bounded by past time as well as future time. If no physical universe existed at all and God created the universe *ex nihilo*, would not that event coincide with the first moment of time?

The process theologian might persist in arguing that there could be no first moment of time, however, contending that if time began with creation, then there must have been a time before time began, which is self contradictory. This inference, however, does not seem to follow. For on the modern relational view of time, time does not exist apart from the occurrence of events; if, therefore, there were no universe at all and no events, there would not be any time. Time arises concomitantly with the occurrence of the first event, God's creation of the universe. Any difficulty with this doctrine seems to be primarily due to our imagination. Though we can, after creation, *think* of nothingness one hour before the first event, in reality there was no such moment. Apart from God there was just nothing, and so no time existed. The idea of a "time before time" is a mental construction only, a product of the imagination. Expressions like "before creation" and "prior to the first event" represent merely a manner of speaking. God exists timelessly without creation, and with the first event time began.[16] This analysis also serves to answer the question, why did not God create the universe earlier? There simply was no "earlier," since time does not exist apart from creation. Hence, the question is meaningless, unless we take it to mean, why did not God create more events prior to the first event? But this last question does not constitute any objection to God's creating a beginning such as He freely chooses.

There seems to be no insuperable objection, then, based on the beginning of time to *creatio ex nihilo*. On a relational view of time it seems intelligible to maintain that time begins with the first event of creation. And even if we hold that time preceded creation, such a view does not as such contradict God's creation of the universe *ex nihilo*.

Analogies To Creation

Hartshorne also provides an entirely different argument against *creatio ex nihilo* and for panentheism based on analogies to human experience. God's relation to the world, he asserts, must be conceived on the analogy of relations found in human experience. Otherwise we fall into a wholly negative theology, able to say simply that God is the "cause" of the world, for the very concept of causality has a meaning only through some analogy in human experience. Hartshorne dismisses as inadequate two analogies offered on behalf of traditional theism: the father-son relation and the artisan-product relation. The first analogy fails to capture adequately God's relation to the world because it fails to express God's radical superiority to His creatures and because it throws no light on God's omnipresence in His creation. The artisan-product analogy fails to capture *creatio ex nihilo* because all our experiences of creation involve making something out of already existent materials. Comparing *creatio ex nihilo* to magic, Hartshorne asserts that there is no noncontroversial analogous phenomenon whatsoever for creation out of nothing.[17] On the other hand, the relation of one's mind to his own body does furnish an adequate analogy for God's relation to the world. For the human person is vastly superior to the cells which make up his body and yet they influence how we feel or think. Moreover, one's mind may be said to preside over the coming to be of its cells. Hartshorne even suggests that cells are sentient individuals and extrapolates this line of thought to his universal panpsychism.

Now this line of reasoning seems very unconvincing. Suppose it is the case that we find in human experience no adequate analogy for God's relation to the world. How does this prove that God did not create the universe *ex nihilo*? Is He incapable of doing something for which no analogy in human experience exists? An affirmative answer would seem anthropocentric and arrogant. Who are we to put God in a box by means of our analogies? It might be said that we should not believe in a doctrine which is incoherent. But, as we have seen, the process theologian seems to have failed to prove any incoherence in the notion of *creatio ex nihilo*. In the absence of some positive incoherence demonstrated to be entailed in this doctrine, our want of an analogy in human experience may reflect only the limits of our condition or the finitude of our minds; it does not prove the doctrine to be rationally unacceptable.

Moreover, Hartshorne mishandles the analogies he discusses. Any analogy is meant to illustrate a certain aspect of something by pointing out a similar, but not exact, feature in something else. It is easy to show other aspects of the thing which the analogy fails to capture; but this does not invalidate its illustrative value with regard to its intended purpose. Thus, the father-son analogy is meant to illustrate God's loving care for His children, and it does this very well; it is not intended to illustrate, for example, His creatorial power. Thus, it is wrongheaded to indict the analogy for failing to capture God's superiority or omnipresence—other analogies might be offered for those. If one treated Hartshorne's analogy as he handles this one, we could fault his analogy with failing to capture the parental love relation of God to His people, for we most certainly do not love our cells as we love our children, and the latter relation surely therefore serves as a better analogy of God's relation to His people than does the former. With regard to analogies of creation, the artisan-product analogy, despite its shortcomings, is still superior to the mind-body analogy, and that for a very simple reason: the former captures the crucial fact that the Creator is ontologically distinct from His creation, while the latter does not. With regard to the artisan-product analogy we need to add that God's products are not made from a pre-existent material; but to qualify the mind-body analogy by adding that the mind creates the body *ex nihilo* entirely destroys the analogy. In fact, the mind-body analogy is a helpful analogy, not for creation, but for omnipresence. If we conceive the mind-body relation dualistically, such that the mind is an immaterial entity indwelling its body, then its ability to move and control the body is somewhat analogous to God's omnipresence in the world, in that both the soul and God are nonspatial entities and yet can produce effects in the physical world. But as analogy for creation, the mind-body model fails miserably.

It seems to me that a better analogy for God's creatorial relation to the world would be my mind's ability in dreams to create and sustain a whole world of individuals and events by thinking. When I (upon awakening) cease to sustain them in thought, they vanish into nonexistence. It must be remembered that the analogy serves a limited purpose; only an uninformed or unsympathetic reader will conclude that I am saying the world is ultimately illusory or that I am an idealist. Hartshorne, in fact, dismisses a similar position that God's causing the world is like our thinking our thoughts, remarking, "But if, analogically speaking, God's causing or making of the world is similar, then the world is just God's thinking, and surely that is not the intended meaning."[18] He is right: that is not the intended meaning; therefore, his criticism is off target. God's creating and sustaining the world in being is *like* my creating and sustaining a world in thought—but this does not imply the world is God's thinking.

One final point: Why agree that analogies are necessary at all? I see no reason to think that one needs an analogy of *creatio ex nihilo* in order to understand the meaning of this phrase. Nor am I opting for negative theology: I see no reason not to assert in strong univocal terms that God created the universe from nothing. I do not thereby imply that I understand *how* He did this; but I certainly understand the meaning of the claim being made. Indeed, process theologians understand it, too, as their vigorous denials of that doctrine show. The very fact that one can find no analogy for *creatio ex nihilo* shows that one understands the concept so as to be able to search for and identify or disqualify analogies to it. So far as I can see, analogies serve an illustrative purpose only; the philosophical concept of *creatio ex nihilo* is clear and well-understood and demonstrations of its truth or falsity may be discussed wholly without reference to human analogies.

In summary, we have seen that the rational grounds for process theology's denial of *creatio ex nihilo* seem to be remarkably weak. The chief argument only serves to demonstrate that the process view is more religiously appealing (itself a moot point), not that it is true. Attempts to prove the incoherence of a beginning of the universe or a beginning of time appear to rest on misunderstandings or dubitable premises. Finally, the adequacy of analogies in human experience for God's relation to the world seems to be irrelevant and in any case not prejudicial to the truth of *creatio ex nihilo*.

Arguments for *Creatio ex Nihilo*

If there are no compelling reasons for believing that the process view of creation is true, then, it needs to be asked whether there are any rational grounds for rejecting the process view and affirming *creatio ex nihilo*. It seems to be that there are. Early Church Fathers, while heavily influenced by Greek philosophy, broke decisively with that tradition concerning one doctrine: the beginning of the universe. They recognized clearly that the Greek view of the eternity of matter was incompatible with the biblical doctrine of *creatio ex nihilo*, and they rejected the teachings of Aristotle on this head. The greatest champion of *creatio ex nihilo* in the pre-Islamic era was the Alexandrian theologian and commentator John Philoponus, who formulated a variety of arguments aimed at proving the finitude of the past series of events and thereby the beginning of the universe. His arguments were taken up and developed by medieval Islamic theologians. Jewish theologians mediated these arguments to medieval Christian Europe, where they became the subject of considerable controversy, being defended, for example, by Bonaventure, but rejected by Aquinas. Kant's first antinomy concerning time in his *Critique of Pure Reason* (1781) is perhaps one of the most famous instances of the influence of this tradition. These arguments, when reformulated in light of contemporary thought, seem to me to be cogent arguments for the beginning of the universe, a fact which also received dramatic empirical confirmation during this century.

Philosophical Arguments

To turn first to the philosophical arguments, I wish to examine two which seem persuasive: the argument based on the impossibility of an actually infinite number of things and the argument based on the impossibility of forming an actually infinite collection of things by adding one member after another.

The argument for a beginning of the universe based on the impossibility of an actually infinite number of things can be formulated in a simple three-step proof:

1. An actually infinite number of things cannot exist.
2. A beginningless series of events in time entails an actually infinite number of things.
3. Therefore, a beginningless series of events in time cannot exist.

In order to grasp the truth of the first premise, we need to understand the difference between a potential infinite and an actual infinite. A potential infinite is a collection which is increasing toward infinity as a limit, but never gets there. Such a collection is really indefinite, not infinite. The sign of this sort of infinity, which is used in calculus, is ∞. An actual infinite is a collection in which the number of members really is infinite. The collection is not growing toward infinity; it *is* infinite, it is "complete." The sign of this sort of infinity, which is used in set theory to designate sets which have an infinite number of members, such as $\{1, 2, 3, \ldots\}$, is $x°$. Now I am arguing not that a potentially infinite number of things cannot exist, but that an actually infinite number of things cannot exist. For if an actually infinite number of things could exist, this would spawn all sorts of absurdities.

Perhaps the best way to bring this home is by means of an illustration. Let me use one of my favorites, Hilbert's Hotel, a product of the mind of the great German mathematician, David Hilbert. Let us imagine a hotel with a finite number of rooms. Suppose, furthermore, that all the rooms are full. When a new guest arrives asking for a room, the proprietor apologizes, "Sorry, all the rooms are full." But now let us imagine a hotel with an infinite number of rooms and suppose once more that *all the rooms are full*. There is not a single vacant room throughout the entire infinite hotel. Now suppose a new guest shows up, asking for a room. "But of course!"

says the proprietor, and he immediately shifts the person in room #1 into room #2, the person in room #2 into room #3, the person in room #3 into room #4, and so on, out to infinity. As a result of these room changes, room #1 now becomes vacant and the new guest gratefully checks in. But remember, before he arrived, all the rooms were full! Equally curious, according to the mathematicians, there are now no more persons in the hotel than there were before: the number is just infinite. But how can this be? The proprietor just added the new guest's name to the register and gave him his keys—how can there not be one more person in the hotel than before? But the situation gets even stranger. For suppose an infinity of new guests show up at the desk, asking for a room. "Of course, of course!" says the proprietor, and he proceeds to shift the person in room #1 into room #2, the person in room #2 into room #4, the person in room #3 into room #6, and so on out to infinity, always putting each former occupant into the room number twice his own. As a result, all the odd numbered rooms become vacant, and the infinity of new guests is easily accommodated. And yet, before they came, all the rooms were full! Again, strangely enough, the number of guests in the hotel is the same after the infinity of new guests check in as before, even though there were as many new guests as old guests. In fact, the proprietor could repeat this process *infinitely more times* and yet there would never be one single person more in the hotel than before.

Hilbert's Hotel is even stranger than the German mathematician gave it out to be. For suppose some of the guests start to check out. Suppose the guest in room #1 departs. Is there not now one less person in the hotel? Not according to the mathematicians—but just ask the woman who makes the beds! Suppose the guests in rooms #1, 3, 5, . . . check out. In this case an infinite number of people have left the hotel, but according to the mathematicians there are no less people in the hotel—but don't talk to that laundry woman! In fact, we could have every other guest check out of the hotel and repeat this process infinitely many times, and yet there would never be any less people in the hotel. But suppose instead the persons in rooms #4, 5, 6, . . . check out. At a single stroke the hotel would be virtually emptied, the guest register reduced to three names, and the infinite converted to finitude. And yet it would remain true that the *same number* of guests checked out this time as when the guests in rooms #1, 3, 5, . . . checked out. Can anyone sincerely believe that such a hotel could exist in reality? These sorts of absurdities illustrate the impossibility of the existence of an actually infinite number of things.

That takes us to the second step in the argument. The truth of this premiss seems fairly obvious. If the universe never began to exist, then prior to the present event there have existed an actually infinite number of previous events. Hence, a beginningless series of events in time entails the existence of an actually infinite number of things, namely, past events.

Hartshorne, however, seems to fail to appreciate this point. After explaining God's maximality with regard to duration as enduring throughout all time, he confronts the infinite regress problem, commenting,

> My own view is that the infinite regress in quesion is an example of the 'non-vicious' type of regress, since it concerns possibilities, and these not (on one view of potentiality) as a definite multitude, whose number is infinite, but as a continuum, which in the words of Peirce is 'beyond all multitude'. . . .[19]

Hartshorne's analysis of God's duration as a potential infinite is a suitable description of God's future, but it cannot serve to characterize God's past on the process view. One only need ask, how many prior universes have existed before the present one? The answer must be, an actually infinite number. In order for the past series of events to be a potential infinite, it would have to be finite but growing indefinitely backwards toward infinity, which is absurd. The process theologian is therefore committed to maintaining that prior to the present event (or, for that matter, any given event) an actually infinite number of events have existed.

Given the truth of the two premises, the conclusion logically follows. The series of past events must be finite and have a beginning. But since the universe is not distinct from the series of events, it follows that the universe began to exist.

At this point, we might find it profitable to consider several objections that might be raised against this argument. First let us consider objections to the first premise of the argument. Wallace

Matson objects that the premiss must mean that an actually infinite number of things is *logically* impossible; but it is easy to show that such a collection is logically possible. For example, the series of negative numbers { . . . , − 3, − 2, − 1} is an actually infinite collection with no first member.[20] Matson's error here lies in thinking that the premiss means to assert the logical impossibility of an actually infinite number of things. What the premiss expresses is the real or factual impossibility of an actual infinite. To illustrate the difference between real and logical possibility: there is no logical impossibility in something's coming to exist without a cause, but such a circumstance may well be really or metaphysically impossible. In the same way, the first premiss asserts that the absurdities entailed in the real existence of an actual infinite show that such an existence is metaphysically impossible. Hence, one could grant that in the conceptual realm of mathematics one can, given certain conventions and axioms, speak consistently about infinite sets of numbers, but this in no way implies that an actually infinite number of things is really possible. One might also note that the mathematical school of intuitionism denies that even the number series is actually infinite (they take it to be potentially infinite only), so that appeal to number series as examples of actual infinites is a moot procedure.

The late J. L. Mackie also objected to the first premiss, claiming that the absurdities are resolved by noting that for infinite groups the axiom "The whole is greater than its part" does not hold, as it does for finite groups.[21] But far from being the solution, this is precisely the problem. Since this axiom is denied in infinite set theory, one gets all sorts of absurdities, like Hilbert's Hotel, when one tries to translate that theory into the real world. Moreover, not all the absurdities stem from the denial of this axiom: the absurdities illustrated by guests' checking out of the hotel stem from the self-contradictory results when the inverse operations of subtraction or division are performed using transfinite numbers. These absurdities imply that the above axiom is true and that no actually infinite collection of things exists.

William J. Wainwright suggests that we could reduce the force of these paradoxes by translating them into mathematical terms; for example, an actually infinite set itself.[22] But this amounts only to a way of *concealing* the absurdities; it was to bring out the paradoxical character of these mathematical concepts that Hilbert came up with his illustration in the first place. And the whole purpose of philosophical analysis is to bring out what is entailed by unanalyzed notions and not to leave them at face value. But would the possibility of the existence of an actual infinite entail the possiblility of such absurdities, Wainwright wonders. The answer is clearly, yes. Hilbert's illustration merely serves to bring out in a dramatic and vivid way what the mathematics necessarily implies: If an actually infinite number of things is possible, then a hotel with an actually infinite number of rooms is possible, with all its attendant absurdities.

Finally one might note the objection of Sorabji, who maintains that illustrations such as Hilbert's Hotel are not absurd. In order to understand what is wrong with the argument, he asks us to envision two parallel columns beginning at the same point and stretching away into the infinite distance. One is the column of past years and the other is the column of past days. The sense in which the column of past days is no larger than the column of past years, says Sorabji, is that the column of days will not "stick out" beyond the far end of the other column, since neither column has a far end. Now in the case of Hilbert's Hotel there is the temptation to think that some unfortunate resident at the far end will drop off into space. But there is no far end: the line of residents will not stick out beyond the far end of the line of rooms. Once this is seen, the outcome is just as explicable—even if a surprising and exhilarating—truth about infinity.[23] Now Sorabji is certainly correct, as we have seen, that Hilbert's Hotel illustrates an explicable truth about the nature of the actual infinite. If an actually infinite number of things could exist, Hilbert's Hotel would be possible. But Sorabji seems to fail to understand the heart of the paradox: I, for one, experience no temptation to think of people dropping off the far end of the hotel, for there is none, but I do have difficulty believing that a hotel in which all the rooms are occupied can accommodate more guests. Of course, the line of guests will not stick out beyond the line of rooms, but if all of those infinite rooms already have guests in them, can moving those guests about really create empty rooms? Sorabji's own illustration of the columns of past years and days is a little disquieting. If we divide the columns into foot-long segments and mark one column as the years and the other as the days, then one column is as long as the other and yet for every foot-length segment in the column of years, 365 segments of equal length are found in the column of days! These paradoxical results can be avoided only if such actually infinite collections can exist only in the imagination, not in reality. In any case, the Hilbert's Hotel illustration is not exhausted by dealing only with the addition of new guests, for the subtraction of guests results in absurdities even more intractable. Sorabji's analysis says nothing to resolve these. Hence, it seems to me at least that the objections to the first premiss are less plausible than the premiss itself.

With regard to the second premiss, the most frequent objection is that the past ought to be regarded as a potential infinite only, not an actual infinite. This was Aquinas's position versus Bonaventure, and Hartshorne seems to side with Thomas on this issue. Such a position is, however, untenable, as we have seen. The future is potentially infinite, but the past is actual in a way the future is not, as evidenced by the fact that we have traces of the past in the present, but no traces of the future. Hence, if the series of past events never began to exist, there have been an actually infinite number of past events.

The objections to either premiss therefore seem to me less compelling than the premisses themselves. Together they imply that the universe began to exist. Now if it is conceded that this argument is sound, it might be thought that God, too, cannot be actually infinite, which would be an unwelcome implication. But such an inference does not follow. The argument claims that an actually infinite number of things cannot exist; but God's infinity is not a collection of an infinite number of definite and discrete finite particulars. Typically God's infinity is a catch-all term for His necessary existence, omnipotence, omniscience, eternity, and so forth. Nothing in the argument contradicts the claim that God possesses those attributes. It would entail only that God's eternity not be interpreted in terms of infinite past duration. Hence, I conclude that this argument furnishes good reason for rejecting the process view of the eternality of the universe.

The second philosophical argument for the beginning of the universe is based on the impossibility of forming an actual infinite by successive addition. This argument is distinct from the first in that it does not deny the possibility of the existence of an actual infinite, but the possibility of its being *formed* by successive addition. This argument can also be formulated in three steps:

1. The series of past events is a collection formed by successive addition.
2. A collection formed by successive addition cannot be actually infinite.
3. Therefore, the series of past events cannot be actually infinite.

The first premiss is one which process thinkers would not dispute. They and I share a dynamic view of time according to which events are actualized in serial fashion, one after another. The series of events is not a sort of timelessly subsisting world-line along which consciousness moves. Rather becoming is real and essential to temporal process. Now this view of time is not without its challengers, but to consider their objections in this article would take us too far afield.[24] In this chapter, we must rest content with the fact that we are arguing on common ground with process theologians at this point and so proceed.

The second premiss is the crucial step. One cannot form an actually infinite collection of things by successively adding one member after another. Since one could always add one more before arriving at infinity, it is impossible to reach actual infinity. Sometimes this is called the impossibility of "counting to infinity" or "traversing the infinite." It is important to understand that this impossibility has nothing to do with the amount of time available: it belongs to the nature of infinity that it cannot be so formed.

Now someone might say that while an infinite collection cannot be formed by beginning at a point and adding members, nevertheless an infinite collection could be formed by never beginning but ending at a point, that is to say, ending at a point after having added one member after another from eternity. But this method seems even more unbelievable than the first method. If one cannot count to infinity, how can one count down from infinity? If one cannot traverse the infinite by moving in one direction, how can one traverse it by simply moving in the opposite direction?

Indeed, the idea of a beginningless series ending in the present seems to be absurd. To give just one illustration; suppose we meet

Creatio ex nihilo

a man who claims to have been counting from eternity and is now finishing: ..., -3, -2, -1, 0. We could ask, why did he not finish counting yesterday or the day before or the year before? By then an infinite time had already elapsed, so that he could already have finished by then. Thus, at no point in the infinite past could we ever find the man finishing his countdown, for by that point he should already be done! In fact, no matter how far back into the past we go, we can never find the man counting at all, for at any point we reach he will have already finished. But if at no point in the past do we find him counting, this contradicts the hypothesis that he has been counting from eternity. This illustrates the fact that the formation of an actual infinite by successive addition is equally impossible whether one proceeds to or from infinity.

Given the truth of the two premisses, the conclusion logically follows. If the universe did not begin to exist a finite time ago, then the present moment could never arrive. But obviously, it has arrived. Therefore, we know that the universe is finite in the past and began to exist.

Again, it would be profitable to consider various objections that have been offered against this reasoning. With regard to the first premiss, I have declined to consider objections based on a static theory of time, since process theologians agree in rejecting that theory. On the other hand, many thinkers have objected to the first premiss on the grounds that we need not regard the past as an infinite series with no beginning but an end in the present. Popper, for example, admits that the *set* of all past events is actually infinite, but holds that the *series* of past events is potentially infinite. This may be seen by beginning in the present and numbering the events backwards, thus forming a potential infinite. Therefore, the problem of an actual infinite's being formed by successive addition does not arise.[25] Similarly, Swinburne muses that it is dubious whether a completed infinite series with no beginning but an end makes sense, but he proposes to solve the problem by beginning in the present and regressing into the past, so that the series of past events would have no end and would therefore not be a completed infinite.[26] This objection, however, clearly confuses the *mental regress* of counting with the *real progress* of the temporal series of events itself. Numbering the series from the present backwards only shows that if there are an infinite number of past events, then we can enumerate an infinite number of past events. But the problem is, how can this infinite collection of events come to be *formed* by successive addition? How we mentally conceive the series does not in any way affect the ontological character of the series itself as a series with no beginning but an end, or in other words, as an actual infinite completed by successive addition.

As for the second premiss, Mackie objects that the argument illicitly assumes an infinitely distant starting point in the past and then pronounces it impossible to travel from that point to today. But there would in an infinite past be *no* starting point, not even an infinitely distant one. Yet from any given point in the infinite past, there is only a finite distance to the present.[27] Now it seems to me that Mackie is incorrect in his allegation about an infinitely distant starting point. The beginningless character of the series only serves to accentuate the difficulty of its being formed by successive addition. The fact that there is *no beginning at all*, not even an infinitely distant one, makes the problem more, not less, nettlesome. And the point that from any moment in the infinite past there is only a finite temporal distance to the present may be dismissed as irrelevant. The question is not how any finite portion of the temporal series can be formed, but how the whole infinite series can be formed. If Mackie thinks that because every segment of the series can be formed by successive addition therefore the whole series can be formed, then he is simply committing the fallacy of composition.

Finally, Sorabji objects that the reason that it is impossible to count down from infinity is because counting involves by nature taking a starting number, which is lacking in this case. But completing an infinite lapse of years involves no starting year and is, hence, posssible.[28] But this response is clearly inadequate, for, as we have seen, the years of an infinite past could be enumerated by the negative numbers, in which case a completed infinity of years would, indeed, entail a countdown from infinity. Sorabji anticipates this rebuttal, however, and claims that such a backwards countdown is possible in principle and therefore no logical barrier has been exhibited to the elapsing of an infinity of past years. Again, however, the question I am posing is not whether there is a logical contradiction in such a notion, but whether such a countdown is not metaphysically absurd. For we have seen that such a countdown should at any point already have been completed. But Sorabji is ready with a response: to say the countdown should at any point already be over confuses counting an *infinity* of numbers with counting *all* the numbers. At any given point in the past, the eternal counter will have already counted an infinity of negative numbers, but that does not entail that he will have counted all the negative numbers. I do not think the argument makes this alleged equivocation, and this may be clear by examining the reason why our eternal counter is supposedly able to complete a count of the negative numbers ending at zero. In order to justify the possibility of this intuitively impossible feat, the argument's opponent appeals to the so-called Principle of Correspondence used in set theory to determine whether two sets are equivalent (that is, have the same number of members). According to that principle, two sets are said to be equivalent if the members of one set can be related in a one-to-one correspondence with the members of the other set and *vice versa*. On the basis of this principle the objector argues that since the counter has lived, say, an infinite number of years and since the set of past years can be put into a one-to-one correspondence with the set of negative numbers, it follows that by counting one number a year an eternal counter could complete a countdown of the negative numbers by the present year. If we were to ask why the counter would not finish next year or in a hundred years, the objector would respond that prior to the present year an infinite number of years will have already elapsed, so that by the Principle of Correspondence, all the numbers should have been counted by now. But this reasoning backfires on the objector: for, as we have seen, on this account the counter should at any point in the past have already finished counting all the numbers, since a one-to-one correspondence exists between the years of the past and the negative numbers. Thus, there is no equivocation between counting an infinity of numbers and counting all the numbers. But at this point a deeper absurdity bursts into view: for suppose there were another counter who counted at a rate of one negative number per day. According to the Principle of Correspondence, which underlines infinite set theory and transfinite arithmetic, both of our eternal counters will finish their countdowns at the same moment, even though one is counting at a rate 365 times faster than the other! Can anyone believe that such scenarios can actually obtain in reality, but do not rather represent the outcome of an imaginary game being played in a purely conceptual realm according to adopted logical conventions and axioms?

Once again, then, the objections to the argument seem less plausible than the premises themselves. From this it logically follows that the universe began to exist. This argument, even more than the first, presses hard upon the process theologian because he conceives of God as existing in a process of development toward infinity as a limit. But if God has existed for infinite time, then his process of development should already be completed. The process theologian cannot retreat to the view that God had somehow lain fallow from eternity and had begun to develop only a finite time ago, since process and growth is deemed essential to his consequent nature. If the process theologian should respond that it is impossible for God to have completed the course of his infinite development, then it is equally impossible for the infinite series of past events to have been completed. The process thinker thus finds himself in an awkward dilemma: either hold to God's development, but abandon the infinite past or else hold to the infinite past, but abandon God's development. For if my line of reasoning is correct, the two positions are mutually incompatible.

Scientific Confirmations

These purely philosophical arguments for the beginning of the universe have received remarkable confirmation from discoveries in astronomy and astrophysics during this century. These confirmations might be summarized under two heads: the confirmation from the expansion of the universe and the confirmation from thermodynamic properties of the universe.

With regard to the first, Hubbles's discovery in 1929 of the redshift in the light from distant galaxies began a revolution in astronomy perhaps as significant as the Copernican revolution. Prior to this time the universe as a whole was conceived to be static; but the startling conclusion to which Hubble was led was that the redshift is due to the fact that the universe is in fact *expanding*. The staggering implication of this fact is that as one traces the expansion back in time, the universe becomes denser and denser until one reaches a point of infinite density from which the universe began to expand. The upshot of Hubble's discovery was that at some point in the finite past—probably around fifteen billion years ago—the entire known universe was contracted down to a single mathematical point which marked the origin of the universe. That initial explosion has come to be known as the "Big Bang." Four of the world's most prominent astronomers describe that event in these words:

> The universe began from a state of infinite density. . . .Space and time were created in that event and so was all the matter in the universe. It is not meaningful to ask what happened before the Big Bang; it is like asking what is north of the North Pole. Similarly, it is not sensible to ask where the Big Bang took place. The point-universe was not an object isolated in space; it was the entire universe, and so the answer can only be that the Big Bang happened everywhere.[29]

This event that marked the beginning of the universe becomes all the more amazing when one reflects on the fact that a state of "infinite density" is synonymous to "nothing." There can be no object that possesses infinite density, for if it had any size at all it could still be even more dense. Therefore, as Cambridge astronomer Fred Hoyle points out, the Big Bang Theory requires the creation of matter from nothing. This is because as one goes back in time, one reaches a point at which, in Hoyle's words, the universe was "shrunk down to nothing at all."[30] Thus, what the Big Bang model of the universe seems to require is that the universe began to exist and was created out of nothing.

The current standard model of the universe thus stands in a marked tension with process theism's views on the eternality of the universe. The most promising route of escape for the process theologian is to hold to an oscillating model of the universe, according to which the universe undergoes a series of expansions and contractions from eternity. Indeed, we have seen Hartshorne endorse such a cyclical view of the universe. But the problem is that such a move represents essentially an act of faith on the part of the process theologian. There seems to be no theoretical or observational grounds for affirming the oscillating model. The process thinker must therefore sheath his sword and cease his attacks upon the believer in *creatio ex nihilo* and humbly acknowledge his own view to be a faith commitment, for there can be little doubt that the standard model rests more comfortably with the doctrine of *creatio ex nihilo* as its bedfellow than with process theism.

More than that, however, there are in fact good grounds for doubting the adequacy of the oscillating model of the universe. First of all, the oscillating model appears to be physically impossible. For all the talk about such a model, the fact seems to be that such a universe is only theoretically, but not physically possible. As the late Professor Tinsley of Yale explains, in oscillating models "even though the mathematics *says* that the universe oscillates, there is no known physics to reverse the collapse and bounce back to a new expansion. The physics seems to say that those models start from the Big Bang, expand, collapse, then end."[31] More recently four other astrophysicists, who seem philosophically sympathetic to the oscillating model, feel constrained to admit, "We have nothing to contribute to the question of whether and/or how the universe bounces."[32] In order for the oscillating model to be correct, it would seem that the known laws of physics would have to be revised. Secondly, the oscillating model seems to be observationally untenable. Two facts of observational astronomy appear to run contrary to the oscillating model. First, the observed homogeneity of matter distribution throughout the universe seems unaccountable on an oscillating model. During the contraction phase of such a model, black holes begin to gobble up surrounding matter, resulting in an inhomogeneous distribution of matter. But there is no known mechanism to "iron out" these inhomogeneities during the ensuing expansion phase. Hence, the four scientists cited above confess that even if there were some mechanism that could cause the universe to bounce back to a new expansion, it is still not clear that it would prevent the inhomogeneity that would result during the contraction phase. In this case, the homogeneity of matter observed throughout the universe remains unexplained. Second, the density of the universe appears to be insufficient for the recontraction of the universe. For the oscillating model to be even possible, it is necessary that the universe be sufficiently dense such that gravity can overcome the force of the expansion and pull the universe back together again. Unfortunately the best estimates are that taking into account both luminous matter and nonluminous matter (found in galactic halos) as well as any possible contribution of neutrino particles to total mass, the density of the universe is still only about one-half that needed for recontraction. [33] Moreover, recent work on calculating the speed and deceleration of the expansion confirms that the universe is expanding at, so to speak, "escape velocity" and will not therefore recontract. According to Sandage and Tammann, "Hence, we are forced to decide that . . . it seems inevitable that the universe will expand forever." They conclude, therefore, that "the universe has happened only once." [34]

On the basis, then, of current evidence concerning the expansion of the universe, the doctrine of *creatio ex nihilo* seems more plausible than the process view of an eternal universe.

If this were not enough to warrant belief in *creatio ex nihilo*, there is a second scientific confirmation of the beginning of the universe based on the thermodynamic properties of various cosmological models. According to the second law of thermodynamics, processes taking place in a closed system always tend toward a state of equilibrium. Now our interest is in what implications this has when applied to the universe as a whole. For the universe is a gigantic closed system, since it is everything there is and no energy is being fed into it from without. The second law seems to imply that, given enough time, the universe will reach a state of thermodynamic equilibrium, known as the "heat death" of the universe. This death may be hot or cold, depending on whether the universe will expand forever or eventually recontract. On the one hand, if the density of the universe is great enough to overcome the force of the expansion, then the universe will recontract into a hot fireball. As the universe contracts, the stars burn more rapidly until they finally explode or evaporate. As the universe grows denser, the black holes begin to gobble up everything around them and begin themselves to coalesce into one gigantic black hole which is coextensive with the universe, from which it will never re-emerge. On the other hand, if the density of the universe is insufficient to halt the expansion, as seems more likely, then the galaxies will turn all their gas into stars and the stars will burn out. At 10^{30} years the universe will consist of 90 percent dead stars, 9 percent supermassive black holes, and 1 percent atomic matter. Elementary particle physics suggests that thereafter protons will decay into electrons and positrons, so that space will be filled with a rarefied gas so thin that the distance between an electron and a positron will be about the size of the present galaxy. At 10^{100} years some scientists believe that the black holes themselves will dissipate into radiation and elementary particles. Eventually all the matter in the dark, cold, ever-expanding universe will be reduced to an ultra-thin gas of elementary particles and radiation. Equilibrium will prevail throughout, and the entire universe will be in its final state, from which no change will occur.

Now the question which needs to be asked is this: If, given sufficient time, the universe will reach heat death, then why is it not now in a state of heat death if it has existed for infinite time? If the universe did not begin to exist, then it should now be in a state of equilibrium. Process thinkers would no doubt claim that the universe escapes final heat death by oscillating from eternity past to eternity future. But again, this represents a faith commitment, and we have seen that such a model seems to be physically and observationally untenable. But let us waive those considerations and suppose that the universe does oscillate. The fact is that thermodynamic properties of this model imply the very beginning of the universe which its proponents seek to avoid. For the thermodynamic properties of an oscillating model reveal that the universe expands farther and farther with each successive cycle. Therefore, as one traces the expansions back in time, they grow smaller and smaller. As one scientific team explains, "The effect of entropy production will be to enlarge the cosmic scale, from cycle to cycle. . . .Thus, looking back in time, each cycle generated less entropy, had a smaller cycle time, and had a smaller cycle expansion factor then [*sic*] the cycle that followed it."[35] Novikov and Zeldovich of the Institute of Applied Mathematics of the USSR Academy of Sciences therefore conclude, "The multicycle model has an infinite future, but only a finite past."[36] As another writer points out, the oscillating model of the universe thus still requires an origin of the universe prior to the smallest cycle.[37]

So whatever scenario one selects for the future of the universe, thermodynamics implies that the universe began to exist. According to P. C. W. Davies of the University of London, the universe must have been created a finite time ago and is in the process of winding down. Prior to the creation, the universe simply did not exist. Therefore, Davies concludes even though we may not like it, we must conclude that the universe's energy was somehow simply "put in" at the creation as an initial condition.[38]

We therefore have two scientific confirmations of the beginning of the universe. While these discoveries comport very well with *creatio ex nihilo*, they obviously run against the grain of process theism. To try to wed process theology with modern cosmology can only make us smile at the incongruity: a pitiable God, indeed, whose poor body explodes from a state of infinite density and perishes in the cold recesses of outer space! I find it ironic that philosophers and theologians should have developed such a view of God and the universe at precisely the same time that scientists were accumulating evidence that tended to confirm *creatio ex nihilo*.

We therefore have both philosophical argument and scientific confirmation for a beginning of the universe. Therefore, the process view of the world as the eternal body of God and its reinterpretation of creation in terms of a mere refashioning appear to be untenable. Rational argument and empirical evidence point instead to *creatio ex nihilo*.

Conclusion

With regard to the doctrine of creation, the biblical view of *creatio ex nihilo* appears to be more plausible than the process view of an eternal, changing universe which is the body of God. We have seen that the process arguments against a beginning of time and the universe lack cogency and that the argument for the process view based on religious sentiment is not only dubious, but irrelevant to the truth of process theism. Finally the argument for the process view based on analogies from human experience is anthropocentric and in several respects misconceived. These limited conclusions alone make the process claim to be rationally superior to the orthodox view unjustified. In addition, however, we have seen good reasons, both philosophical and empirical, for affirming a doctrine of *creatio ex nihilo*. In closing, I should like to address some remarks to the process thinker: Too often your thinking has been characterized by a sort of either/or, all-or-nothing mentality with regard to traditional theism. You seem to have difficulties with the doctrines of divine impassibility and immutabilty. But the falsity of those two doctrines does not entail the falsity of *creatio ex nihilo*. It seems to me that you could deny the philosophical understanding of those two doctrines and still remain a biblical theist. So even if you cannot embrace those doctrines, why not affirm with us *creatio ex nihilo* and return to biblical theism, rather than embrace a view of God and the universe which has little to commend it and, indeed, seems both philosophically and scientifically inadequate?

NOTES

1. Charles Hartshorne, *Man's Vision of God and the Logic of Theism* (Chicago: Willett, Clark, & Co., 1941), pp. 174-211.

2. Ibid., p. 185.

3. Ibid., p. 200.

4. Hartshorne, *Vision of God*, p. 188.

5. Ibid., p. 214.

6. Charles Hartshorne, *Omnipotence and Other Theological Mistakes* (Albany: State University of New York Press, 1984), p. 82.

7. Hartshorne, *Vision*, p. 194.

8. Ibid., p. 230.

9. Hartshorne, *Omnipresence*, p. 75.

10. Hartshorne, *Vision*, p. 231.

11. Ibid., p. 58.

12. Ibid., p. 113.

13. Ibid., p. 95.

14. Ibid., p. 233.

15. R. G. Swinburne, *Space and Time* (London: Macmillan, 1968), pp. 209, 245, 296.

16. In my opinion, with the creation of time, God enters into time and so sustains genuine relations with temporal persons and things. (William Lane Craig, "God, Time and Eternity," *Religious Studies* 14 [1978]: 497-503).

17. Hartshorne, *Omnipresence*, p. 58.

18. Ibid., p. 74.

19. Hartshorne, *Vision*, p. 37.

20. Wallace Matson, *The Existence of God* (Ithaca, NY: Cornell University Press, 1965), pp. 58-60.

21. J. L. Mackie, *The Miracle of Theism* (Oxford: Clarendon Press, 1982), p. 93.

22. William J. Wainwright, Review of *The Kalam Cosmological Argument*, by William Lane Craig, *Nous* 16 (1982): 328-334.

23. Richard Sorabji, *Time, Creation and the Continuum* (Ithaca, NY: Cornell University Press, 1983), pp. 213, 222-223.

24. G. J. Whitrow defends a form of this argument which does not presuppose a dynamical view of time, by asserting that an infinite past would still have to be "lived through" by any everlasting, conscious being, even if the series of physical events subsisted timelessly. Since process theology holds that God is such a being,

Creatio ex nihilo

Whitrow's argument would apply with special force to process theology's view of God. (G. J. Whitrow, *The Natural Philosophy of Time*, 2d ed. [Oxford: Clarendon Press, 1980], pp. 28-32).

25. K. R. Popper, "On the Possibility of an Infinite Past: a Reply to Whitrow," *British Journal for the Philosophy of Science* 29 (1978): 47-48.

26. R. G. Swinburne, "The Beginning of the Universe," *The Aristotelian Society* 40 (1966): 131-132.

27. Mackie, *Theism*, p. 93.

28. Sorabji, *Time, Creation, and the Continuum*, pp. 219-222.

29. Richard J. Gott, et. al., "Will the Universe Expand Forever?" *Scientific American* (March 1976), p. 65.

30. Fred Hoyle, *From Stonehenge to Modern Cosmology* (San Francisco: W. H. Freeman, 1972), p. 36.

31. Beatrice Tinsley, personal letter.

32. Duane Dicus, et. al., "The Future of the Universe," *Scientific American* (March 1983), p. 100.

33. David N. Schramm and Gary Steigman, "Relic Neutrinos and the Density of the Universe," *Astrophysical Journal* 243 (1981): 6.

34. Alan Sandage and G. A. Tammann, "Steps Toward the Hubble Constant VII," *Astrophysical Journal* 210 (1976): 23, 7; see also idem, "Steps Toward the Hubble Constant VIII," *Astrophysical Journal* 256 (1982): 339-345.

35. Duane Dicus, et. al., "Effects of Proton Decay on the Cosmological Future," *Astrophysical Journal* 256 (1982): 1, 8.

36. I. D. Novikov and Ya. B. Zeldovich, "Physical Processes Near Cosmological Singularities," *Annual Review of Astronomy and Astrophysics* 11 (1973): 401-402.

37. John Gribbin, "Oscillating Universe Bounces Back," *Nature* 259 (1976): 16.

38. P. C. W. Davies, *The Physics of Time Assymetry* (London: Surrey University Press, 1974), p. 104.

PART THREE

Philosophical Considerations

Why God Cannot Act

Arthur F. Holmes

Arthur F. Holmes

Arthur F. Holmes is professor of philosophy and chairman of the philosophy department at Wheaton College (Illinois). A native of England where he received his early education, Dr. Holmes received both his B. A. and M. A. degrees from Wheaton College. His Ph.D. in philosophy is from Northwestern University. He is the author or editor of eight books including *Contours of a World View*, *Ethics: Approaching Moral Decisions*, *Faith Seeks Understanding*, and *All Truth is God's Truth*. He wrote the article "Christian Philosophy" for the 13th edition of *Encyclopedia Britannica* and has contributed articles to several books of essays, as well as to philosophical and religious periodicals.

One of the most attractive features of Whitehead's philosophy, one that has made process theology particularly appealing to Christians, is that he explicity makes room for God's involvement in nature and history. Whitehead wrote against the background of mechanistic science, with its deistic corollary that the universe is closed to God's immanent activity. He wrote during the rise of positivism, with its demand for a purely empirical approach to things, an empiricism modeled on the natural sciences and excluding all metaphysics and theology. In this context, he argues for a teleological universe rather than a purposeless mechanism indifferent to all good and evil; he claims that modern science allows, even requires, that nature's processes be open to God's constant involvement.

This is a refreshing promise to hear, especially so if, as he suggests, Christianity is a religion in search of a metaphysic. He is undoubtedly on the right track in focusing on the relation between God and nature. In traditional theology, this is the framework for the entire biblical drama; every other doctrine of the faith presupposes that distinction and that relationship, whether sin or grace, revelation or the Incarnation. The God-nature relationship has consequently been the crux of theological developments since the early days of the Christian church, and it continues to be such for process theology.

Whitehead is well aware of all this. In a chapter entitled "The New Reformation" he highlights three foci in history that are crucial to his proposal.[1] The first is Plato's insight ("one of the greatest intellectual discoveries in the history of religion"[2]) that the divine element in the world is persuasive agency, not coercive force. The reference is to Plato's eternal forms, the ideal archetypes for all particular things, which the divine artificer unites with matter to make finite things. The divine immanence brings order out of chaos.

The second focus is the life of Christ, who revealed in action what Plato saw in theory:

> The Mother, the Child, and the bare manger; the lowly man, homeless and self-forgetful, with his message of peace, love, and sympathy; the suffering, the agony, the tender words as life ebbed, the final despair; and the whole with the authority of supreme victory.[3]

"The Galilean origin of Christianity," writes Whitehead elsewhere, "dwells upon the tender elements in the world, which slowly and in quietness operate by love."[4]

His third focus is the Alexandrian theologians who brought the first two together, pointing out that the divine activity is not a matter of coercive laws imposed on nature, but is rather the immanence of divine reason. Immanence is the key. As the Trinitarian debate showed the mutual immanence of three in one divine nature, and the theology of the Incarnation emphasized the direct immanence of God in the one person of Christ (dogmas about which Whitehead "makes no judgment"), so the eternal forms in the Divine mind are immanent in the creation.[5]

Immanence is a welcome corrective to the exclusion of divine activity by both deism and positivism. Whitehead plainly suggests a Logos doctrine that sees divine providence in every particular event, ordering things toward one overall goal. But it is equally plain that God gives *order, not existence*, to nature:

> . . . the doctrine of an aboriginal, eminently real, transcendent creator, at whose fiat the world came into being, and whose imposed will it obeys, is the fallacy which has infused tragedy into the histories of Christianity and Mohametanism. . . . He does not create the world, he saves it; or more accurately, he is the poet of the world, with tender patience leading it by his vision of truth, beauty and goodness.[6]

> The Semitic concept of a definite personal individual entity, whose existence is the one ultimate metaphysical fact, ultimate and underivative, and who decreed and ordered the derivative existence which we call the actual world . . . is the rationalization of the tribal gods of the earlier communal religions. It expresses the extreme doctrine of transcendence.[7]

A creator's fiat, then, would be arbitrary and coercive, violating the rule of persuasive love. But Whitehead does not stop there: other special divine acts are excluded too. The notion of imposed law can unleash violence in the name of God. "Millions have marched to battle fiercely nerved by intense faith in Law imposed by the will of inflexible Allah."[8] By the same token special grace imposed on God's elect is a degradation of love, and Paul's talk of divine judgment is odd if God is love.[9] The last book of the Bible so illustrates these barbaric elements that it would be better to have retained Pericles' speech describing the Athenian ideal instead.[10] These aspects of power awaken "every modern instinct of critical reaction." The modern world must find God through love not fear, with the help of John, not of Paul.[11]

The emphasis on persuasive love is indeed important to the biblical picture of how God works in our lives. But is it enough of the story to be asserted as exclusively as Whitehead does? His objection to coercive power is more than an irenic reaction against the fear and violence it might evoke. In *Religion in the Making*, he characterizes God in terms of purpose, knowledge, vision, wisdom, consciousness and love. The omission of action categories is obvious: God is not to be thought of as an active agent efficaciously achieving what he wants.

Yet both the biblical drama and the Apostles' Creed are about a God who acts. In the beginning he gave existence (not just order) to worlds which were not, and otherwise could never have been. He revealed himself to the patriarchs, and miraculously delivered Israel from Egyptian bondage. He gave his law, intervened again and again in Israel's history, and spoke with demanding authority through the prophets. He incarnated himself uniquely in Jesus Christ, fully God and fully man, who by his divine power quelled a storm, cured the sick, and raised the dead. Jesus himself rose from the dead, never subsequently to die, and ascended into heaven, whence he will come to judge the living and the dead. In this drama, the efficacious actions of God are plainly seen.

These mighty acts of God were not just part of the regular ordering of nature and history. So unusual are they, so evidently *acts* of God rather than natural *events*, that Christians have often called them "super-natural." And lest that word imply that God is not at work also in the ordinary and usual course of nature, we distinguish his general providence from these special acts. Had God not acted in these ways, we would have neither *ex nihilo* creation nor final judgment (both of which Whitehead explicitly rejects), neither the unique incarnation of Christ nor his miracles and his resurrection, hence neither law, prophets, nor gospel.

What then do process theologians say about this? "How Does God Act?" is the title of an article by theologian D. D. Williams. God acts, he says, by being felt by his creatures, thereby entering into the constitution of their successive moments of experience. He likens this to what depth psychology tells of the way one's feelings are absorbed by another, and then reflected back with transformed meaning.[12] But while this might lead to an explanation of religious experience and the changes it can produce in attitudes and values, we must still ask how it addresses mighty acts of God of an objective sort in history. What about the unique incarnation of Christ, his miracles and resurrection? Does God really act?

David Griffin claims that Whitehead intended his philosophy to explicate the notion that God as Holy Spirit is present in the world generally, present in each occasion as an actual datum of the experience. The world lives by its incarnation of God.[13] Jesus Christ is a symbol of this, much as he was for Hegel and the immanentistic theologians of the nineteenth century. But Griffin also asks what a *special* act of God would be: in what sense was Jesus God's *decisive* act? God's "ideal aim" for mankind, he answers, was fully actualized in Jesus, who optimally expressed God's aim (or will), and so became normative for us all, a still-valid revelation of God.[14]

But Jesus is then no more God incarnate than anyone else, but only a man who freely fulfilled his God-given initial aim without modifying it at all. Yet what more could a Whiteheadian say? The Christ of process theology is as much a corollary of the process God as the Christ of biblical theology is a corollary of the God who acts. If the process treatment of God's supreme act in Christ allows no more than divine persuasion in the natural process of a purely human life, how can other acts of God consistently be anything more? And if God is subject to the same kind of natural process as everything else, then supernatural acts of God by definition are ruled out. There can be no creation *fiat*, no special revelation, no authoritative lawgiver, no unique incarnation in Christ, no miracles, no physical resurrection from the dead, no efficacious grave, and of course no final judgment day. The sheep and the goats, the wheat and the tares, must forever live and grow together. All of the mighty acts of God must be reinterpreted as symbols of a more general divine immanence of a noncoercive sort.

Eugene Peters is explicit about this. Process philosophy is a "one-order theory of the world" as a simple structured whole.

> This means among other things that the process theologian will reject supernaturalism; he will deny that there is another—perhaps a wholly different—order or realm outside the world in which he exists. . . . Thus the process theologian will not speak of miraculous divine intervention in the world. He will try to conceive creation, incarnation, resurrection, and so forth, not as bewildering supernatural acts of God, which have little or no affinity with the structures and processes of the experienced world; rather he will conceive these as expressions, in mythical or symbolic form, of facts which, however religiously profound, are yet within the warp and woof of the world's single order.[15]

What underlies this stance, it seems, is not just a distaste for coercion, nor is it simply a matter of theological preference such that a Whiteheadian could opt either way about special divine acts. In process thought, "coercion" is impossible because it denies an irreducible measure of free self-creativity in natural events as well as in humans, The problem is not that God does not act "coercively", but could if he chose. It is rather that God cannot so act. The process rejection of special divine acts stems from an underlying metaphysic.

God and Nature

Whitehead's metaphysic is shaped by two converging lines of thought. One, arising out of his work in theoretic physics, is his claim that the concepts of matter, space and time in the mechanistic science of Newton and the eighteenth century were mistaken, unempirical abstractions and that relativity and energistic physics combine with evolutionary theory to point to a more promising direction. The basic ingredients of nature are not indivisible material atoms at fixed points in space and time, but are miniscule occurrences, little spurts of energy in an intimately interrelated field of developing events. If God is to have an effect on nature, then, it must be in the life story of a particular occurrence in relation to other events, rather than as an external force pushing bits of matter around like billiard balls on a table.

A second line of thought, fed by Whitehead's fascination with the romanticist poets and especially William Wordsworth, draws on concrete human experience. It is an unfounded abstraction to analyze an experience, as past thinkers did, into clear and distinct ideas logically related to each other in our minds. An actual experience is rather a feeling, an affective state in which cognitive awareness may arise, although some experiences involve no conscious conceptualizing at all. Whitehead extends this notion of an "experience" to biological and physical events devoid of consciousness altogether. To his mind, an analogy exists between physical, biological, psychological and mental events, whatever the degrees of consciousness, or the lack thereof. By analyzing concrete experience, then, we can see how other things influence what occurs, and see the possibilities for God to be involved as well.

These two lines of thought converge: an experience is a natural event, an actual occasion that emerges out of past events and feeds into the future. The term "actual occasion" becomes his technical term for the fundamental constituents of all reality.

We must accordingly look at the life story of an actual occasion in the light of concrete experience. The first thing to notice is that "experience" can serve as either a verb or a noun. As a verb, it denotes a feeling in itself, the experiencing of delight or satisfaction. I feel something going on within me, an inner event that is taking shape and coming to be. As a noun, it denotes an object of feeling, another happening that feeds into my experience. The same experience, moreover, can be both subject and object, for the emergent feeling (the subject) provides input (as an object) for what comes next. The life story of any occasion, then, stretches from birth to death: from its first inception conceived out of other events, to full maturation with its own subjective identity, to its dying out, biodegradably becoming, as it were, an objective datum in the emergence of other experiences that follow.

Notice also what happens in the "subjective" development of an actual occasion. It experiences, feels, and takes into account in its own growth, all the other events in its environment. "Prehension" is Whitehead's technical term for this activity, to avoid the misleading associations of a more common vocabulary. A new occasion begins, then, with a prehension of events in its past: some are prehended positively and some negatively, for the selective process has already begun to shape a specific new occasion. The past causes something to begin and contributes to the shape it takes. Past events "objectified" in a new occasion of experience are, in traditional philosophic terms, the efficient cause of what comes next.

But what guides this selectivity? The emerging occasion prehends not only its past, but also the possibilities that past now presents for its future. Consciously or not, it feels their lure, "a subjective aim" emerges as to what form it will take, and a decision cuts off what appears irrelevant or negative. The new occasion is in this regard a self-creating thing. It is never completely determined by its past. It is not completely determined either by some present future. The past establishes parameters of possibility for both its present and its future, but is never a sufficient cause of any occurrence. To some degree, every event is self-determining, self-creative. God, we shall see is one ingredient in the past (as well as the future) of every event: He too is never a sufficient cause for any occurrence.

To see how God comes into this life story of an actual occasion, we must also note Whitehead's introduction of "eternal objects." The possibilities that exist for a particular event have never actually occurred; they are not space-time events, not experiences themselves, but eternal logical possibilities. They have no subjective form, no subjective identity, no experience or feeling; they are objective ideals to be prehended conceptually, aims to consider positively or negatively as we decide. They may be attractive, persuasive, like final causes or purposes are, but they can never be efficient causes that force compliance by coercion. God influences an event by the persuasiveness of eternal objects, with their alluring possibilities for the future, not by forcing compliance.

Why then could God not coerce as well as persuade? It is the very nature of things that every actual occasion is in measure self-determining, self-creating. The effects of past events are indeed felt, but they are limited by the inner decisions that shape an occasion's subjective form. The possibilities that eternal objects present for the future provide some limitations, yet as final causes they cannot override the inner decision of an emerging occasion. God's power, like that of every other being, is limited.

The point is that God must not be treated like a being from another world. He is not an exception to the metaphysical scheme, but its chief exemplification. Like other entities, he too is in process of being and becoming, his experience is analogous to ours. He too is both subject and object, a subject assimilating the past into his own experience, an object entering into the experience of others. He too is self-creating, by his decision shaping his own subjective form in relation to the world. The main difference is that God is everlasting—he has neither beginning nor end.

Whitehead spells this out by distinguishing three aspects of God's nature: the primordial, the consequent, and the superjective. The terms "primordial" and "consequent" must not mislead us into thinking that God undergoes an extended evolution from what he was once upon a time in some distant past, to what he will eventually become in some distant future. They are not intended to indicate a temporal sequence of events at all. Rather, the three *concurrent* aspects of God's nature provide a theoretical analysis, an abstract way of conceptualizing God's role in the world at any and every point in time.

An earthly occasion, we have noted, begins with causal input from the past into the emerging subject; it involves a self-determining decision that shapes its subjective form; and it eventuates on its demise in providing causal input to the future. The first phase is a "physical prehension," the second involves a "conceptual prehension" of the relevant possibilities. In God this order must be reversed, for God has not beginning and no end. His conceptual prehension of all eternal possibilities is therefore the first aspect of his nature to consider, his primordial nature; and his experience (physical prehensions) of other events affects his consequent nature. But just as an earthly event feeds into what follows, so God's consequent nature in turn affects the world: it becomes the "superjective nature" of God.

God's primordial nature resembles what theologians have traditionally called the eternal wisdom of God, the ordered unity with which he conserves the entire range of eternal possibilities. It represents his free creative decision as to the general shape that things should take, giving order and limitation to nature's creativity. As such the primordial nature of God is unchanging, and not at all conditional on anything in particular that might occur. It defines God's aim for himself in the world, the form of satisfaction that he seeks.

This sounds like the Logos doctrine of patristic and medieval theology, which located Plato's ideal forms, the archetypes of all created things, in the mind of God. It is Whitehead's version of the Alexandrian theology, but a vast difference stands out. Their Logos, like the Logos in the prologue to John's gospel, was both the primordial source of order and the creator who imparted existence to things by the word of his power. Whitehead's God is only the source of order, like the Logos of *pre-Christian* Greek philosophy. Whitehead plainly prefers Plato and Aristotle to the Judeo-Christian revelation.[16] In his primordial nature, conceiving what kind of order will satisfy him to the full, God establishes his own subjective aim and defines the form his own experience takes. But this aspect of God can do no more than provide the world with an overall alluring ideal in which good and evil and every other contrast, however massive, are harmonized in one all inclusive whole, He is an Aristotelian final cause, rather than an efficient cause whose sovereign power effectively guarantees results. He cannot act efficaciously, or coerce; he can only persuade.

Consider now God's consequent nature. This is the aspect of God that experiences what is happening in the world. Prehending events like any other entity, God preserves and harmonizes them within his experience of the past as a whole, with a view to the satisfaction his primordial nature requires. Nothing is ever lost. Everything that ever occurs in the world is preserved, experienced, valued, and woven into the feelings of God for the harmony of the whole. In this sense, God loves and saves it all. But he does not really act on the world: rather the world acts on God.

The remaining possibility for divine action therefore resides in the superjective nature of God, whereby God's experience, including his feelings about what has occurred, feeds back into world events. The self-creative processes of nature are now affected by him. The natural creativity at work in an emerging occasion is affected by the initial subjective aim God now presents as a starting point for that entity's own process of decision. Apart from a God-given initial aim, there could be no specific actual entities and no natural order at all. He is a necessary condition of order, of individuated events harmonizing into a whole, though not a sufficient cause for anything.

The primary phase in the emergence of an actual entity is a hybrid physical feeling of God. That is to say, the consequent nature of God is one actual entity among others that contribute to the birth of novelty. God is experienced in the emerging event with particular attention to his conceptual feelings related to it, feelings that include aiming at what is best in that situation. God thus becomes immanent in things when his feelings become part of the experience which constitutes others. But it is God's conceptual feelings, his ideals that are operative, like a final and perhaps a formal cause of the new entity, but not as efficient cause actively securing his desired ends.

In effect, then, in his primordial, consequent and superjective nature, God is confined to nature's processes. His lack of efficacious power precludes the "supernatural" acts of the biblical drama. As Langdon Gilkey describes John Cobb's process theology,

> Christian notions are either radically redrawn or else dispensed with in order to fit the shape and the demands of Whitehead's system.[17]

God and Evil

If God cannot act, what assurance do we have that good will prevail, and that God's ideals are even achievable? Is persuasive love really enough without the mighty acts of God?

Whitehead's appeal to the Alexandrian theologians should remind us of the Christian response to ancient dualistic and monistic philosophies in regard to evil and the Christian hope.[18] Dualism recognized both eternal form and everlasting matter, one the source of good and the other the source of evil, one rational and the other not. It was found in Plato's cosmology, later in the Manichean heresy, and it even appears in the views which Paul opposed in his Colossian epistle. But if matter itself is uncreated, formless, and thereby the source of evil, then there is little hope that the rule of reason can triumphantly bring perfect order from such chaos, and we are left in an everlasting cosmic struggle. Christianized versions of the dualism saw Christ as less than fully God, less than the sovereign creator; it vested its hopes in the individual's own ascetic climb from physical enjoyments to the rule of reason.

The monistic alternative meanwhile came from Eastern religion and the Neo-Platonic tradition. Free acts of divine creation were replaced by necessary processes of emanation out of the divine being itself, so that the form of the divine was to some degree immanent in every existent thing. What immanence provided was rational order, and to the degree it was lacking to that degree evil prevailed. Evil was always the lack of rational form, but individuality as well meant a lack of perfect unity with being as a whole. So deliverance comes through loss of individuality: eventually the individual, who emerged in the emanation process, at her demise returned into the One whence she came. No individual immortality could occur. Christ was an emanation too, not fully God but at best (as the semi-Arians put it in this context) like God (*homoiousios*), differing in degree but not in kind from other creatures.

The early church faced these options and rejected them both, partly for biblical reasons related directly to God's acts in Christ, partly because they departed from the overall presuppositions of biblical thought on which the Christian gospel depends. In place of the God-creation distinction and relationship within which the biblical acts of God take place, dualism and pantheism respectively were being proposed. And these options could not do justice either to the acts of God or to God's ultimate triumph over evil.

Process theology confronts us with essentially the same set of options. God, for Whitehead, is not the absolute creator, but himself the prime instance of creativity, self-creativity in operation.[19] Creativity with its spontaneous, novel outbreaks of energy is not itself dependent on God at all, except for the order God offers. He limits and guides what creativity produces, but no more. This separation of creativity from God has been taken two ways. Some interpreters liken creativity to the Greek notion of prime matter, itself independent of form, and come up with a kind of dualism. Others see creativity as a mere abstraction, nothing but empty possibility apart from the limits which God's primordial envisionment of eternal objects affords. In effect, the entire creative process goes on within the being of God, his consequent nature. This is the monistic version, a panentheism characteristic of Charles Hartshorne and others.

So an ancient paradigm has returned. If process thought is a kind of Greek dualism, with creativity an unordered and chaotic spontaneity apart from the loving persuasion of God, then we must ask whether the triumph of persuasion is any more realistic a hope than was the rule of reason in fallen beings in an evil world. Are we left with an everlasting cosmic struggle? If, on the other hand, process thought is really panentheistic, monistic, with the immanence of the divine forming every individual thing, then again we are vesting our hope in rational form, the persuasive role of reason creating cosmic order.

In either case, we are offered a classical Greek means to a classical Greek end rather than biblical means to the biblical end. The Greek ideal has a harmonious balance and unity of the whole, each part playing its role under the rule of reason. This was the ideal cosmos, the ideal for art and society, and for every human being. It is the ideal of beauty which Whitehead himself adopted, and to the satisfaction of which his God aspires. To this end, loving, reasoning persuasion is the only means, rather than any forceful, efficacious act of God.

With regard to these schemes, the question that Christians posed about evil was whether reason was enough to overcome it, and make it serve the good. The process God offers us ordered beauty in a persuasive way too, with a love that touches the evildoer affectively as well as in a cognitive way. But the same question arises in new form. Is even persuasive love enough, enough to overcome all the evil in the world? Or is it an overly romanticized idealism still caught up in the evolutionary optimism that preceded the holocausts of two world wars with their threat of human extinction? Has it taken the full measure of human sin and faced its demonic dimensions? Does *all* that history brings really contribute to evolving a deeply satisfying, harmonious beauty of the whole? Or are we whistling in the dark to suppose it will all work out somehow without any special acts of God? Will the wheat and the tares feed rather than choke one another in the end? Will the tares die out of their own accord? Or must they finally be uprooted from the ground? Is persuasive love really enough? Are the immanent resources of history sufficient? Everything in the Judeo-Christian Scripture cries out against this false hope, and human history too. Hope resides in a God who really acts.

Back in the eighteenth century, the deists too rejected most of these special acts of God. Between the creation at the beginning and the judgment at the end, they saw an unbroken chain of cause and effect, a machine-like universe whose fixed laws left no room for divine intervention. Everything was natural event, a general providence with nothing "supernatural" interposing. The world we occupy runs itself, with God as the "absentee landlord." The Christian revelation, the Christian gospel and distinctively Christian experience therefore had no place in deism.

"I have no need of that hypothesis," someone is reported to have said of God to Napoleon. He spoke of the God of deism, so remote was that deity, so inactive, so unnecessary therefore to history and current experience, and so pointless if a natural evolution could explain the origin of nature and its laws. Nature, it seemed, was indeed self-explanatory, self-existent, self-sufficient, a highly developed complexity of causes and effects that precluded any God at all, let alone a God who really acts.

To make room for God, therefore, nineteenth century theologians turned from thinking of him as a transcendent being outside nature's machinery in need of some way to break in, to thinking of him as already immanent in nature, the very ground of all being that sustains and enlivens it all. They turned to romanticism's view of nature as alive, almost divine, and to German idealist philosophers like Hegel, who saw evolutionary processes as the creative activity of the divine spirit immanent in all that is. But while this made place for God in the general course of nature and history, it left no room for the "supernatural." The biblical record of God's special acts therefore had to be reinterpreted, construed as symbolic of the divine immanence in what occurs all the time. Revelation is the emergence within the human spirit of a consciousness of God and of ideas about him. Jesus emerged in the course of history, a man supremely conscious of the divine and in this sense distinctively a son of God. And the biblical drama exhibits a gradual evolution of religion from its primitive beginnings among the ancient Hebrews to Jesus' vision of a kingdom of love. With no transcendent God doing supernatural things, this "immanentistic" theology again posed the question, "Does God really act?" And the immanentist's liberal theology seemed to answer "No!"—not, that is, in the sense that the Bible and the historic creeds have affirmed.[20]

Process theology simply continues the immanentist tradition on a Whiteheadian rather than a Hegelian basis. It is not another way of expressing Christian beliefs, but an evolutionary optimism sired in the nineteenth century. Like romanticism, it reverts to pre-Christian hopes, to a Greek world view rather than the Judeo-Christian. It reverses the decision of the first four centuries of the church that Greek philosophy cannot be adopted intact, that the rule of reason will fail because in those accounts God does not really act. The same verdict was pronounced on the immanentism of nineteenth century thought, where the divine within drew the evolution of nature and history towards the light of a new day, and the rule of love was to prevail. Then came world wars, the collapse of an old order, the Holocaust, the Christian realists cried out that love alone is not enough. Coercive power there must be as well.

Process theology flies in the face of all this. But the choice is essentially the same. If persuasion is not enough, however rational and loving, then God must really act as the biblical drama declares. If process presuppositions forbid such acts of God, then by *modus tollens* something is wrong with those presuppositions. However attractive Whitehead's philosophy of nature seems, by making a God in the image of nature he has lost both the divine power and the Christian hope.

NOTES

1. Alfred North Whitehead, *Adventures of Ideas* (London: Penguin Books, 1942), chapter 10.

2. Ibid. p. 196.

3. Ibid. p. 197.

4. Alfred North Whitehead, *Process and Reality* (New York: Free Press, 1978), p. 343.

5. Whitehead, *Adventures*, p. 154, 199.

6. Whitehead, *Process*, pp. 342, 346.

7. Alfred North Whitehead, *Religion in the Making* (New York: New American Library, 1974), p. 66.

8. Whitehead, *Adventures*, p. 161.

9. Ibid., p. 155; *Religion*, p. 73.

10. Whitehead, *Adventures*, p. 201.

11. Whitehead, *Religion*, p. 73; *Science and the Modern World* (New York: Free Press, 1967), p. 191.

12. Alfred North Whitehead, *Process and Divinity*, ed. W. L. Reese and E. Freeman (La Salle, Il: Open Court, 1984), pp. 161-180.

13. David Griffin, *A Process Christology* (Philadelphia: Westminster Press, 1973), pp. 180-189, *passim*.

14. David Griffin, "Schubert Ogden's Christology and the Possibilities of Process Philosophy," in *Process Philosophy and Christian Thought*, eds. D. Brown, R. E. James and G. Reeves (Indianapolis: Bobbs-Merrill Co., 1971), pp. 347-361.

15. Eugene Peters, "A Framework for Christian Thought," *Journal of Religion*, (1967),p. 375.

16. On this contrast, see Etienne Gilson, *God and Philosophy* (New Haven: Yale University Press, 1941), ch. I-II and, with specific reference to process theology, Robert C. Neville, *Creativity and God* (New York: Seabury Press, 1980), ch. 1.

17. T. Langdon Gilkey, Review of John B. Cobb's *A Christian Natural Theology* in *Theology Today* XXII (1966), p. 532.

18. See T. Langdon Gilkey, *Maker of Heaven and Earth* (Garden City, NY: Doubleday, 1959); also this author's article "Christian Philosophy" in *Encyclopedia Britannica*, 15th ed.

19. Cf. F. H. Bradley's claim in chapter XXV of *Appearance and Reality*, that God is one appearance of the Absolute. Whitehead speaks of his own philosophy as transforming that kind of idealism on to a realistic basis (*Process and Reality*, p. xiii).

20. On nineteenth century immanentism, see C. C. J. Webb, *A Study of Religious Thought In England from 1850* (Oxford: Claredon Press, 1933).

Divine Power

*Do Process Theists Have a Better Idea?**

David Basinger

David Basinger

After receiving his Ph.D. in philosophy from the University of Nebraska at Lincoln, Basinger taught for three years at John Wesley College. He is currently associate professor of philosophy at Roberts Wesleyan College. He is the co-editor of two forthcoming books: *Divine Sovereignty and Human Freedom* and *Kerygma and Praxis*. He has authored or co-authored more than thirty-five articles in such journals as *Southern Journal of Philosophy*, *Journal of Religion*, *Faith and Philosophy*, *Sophia*, *International Journal for Philosophy of Religion*, *Religious studies*, *Evangelical Quarterly*, *Australasian Journal of Philosophy*, *The Modern Schoolman*, *Process Studies*, *Scottish Journal of Theology*, and others.

Process theists frequently claim that their understanding of God's relationship with us as humans is more adequate and satisfying than that found in classical theism. The God of classical theism, we are told, possesses and exercises coercive power. That is, he can and does at times force us to act in accordance with his will. But to conceive of God in this manner, it is argued, gives us no adequate explanation for moral evil and does not allow us to assume that anyone other than God possesses meaningful freedom or self-determination. The process God, on the other hand, is said never to coerce in this sense. He never forces us to act as he desires. He only attempts to persuade us to do that which is best. And to conceive of God in this manner, we are told, allows us to take both evil and freedom seriously.

I want to argue that this comparison is misleading. More specifically, I want to argue that the 'persuasive' God of process theism is not superior to the 'coercive' God affirmed by some types of classical theism.

God and Coercion

What exactly do process theists mean when they say that God never coerces? It is something taken to mean that the process God never brings about anything totally on his own.[1] But this is inaccurate. According to process theism, as I have said, God is continually attempting to persuade us to act in accordance with his will. Individuals may differ in their openness to such persuasion, but no one, according to process thought, can avoid such persuasion entirely. Each of us automatically becomes aware at each moment of what God desires us to do and feels some compulsion to act in accordance with his will.[2] But, of course, if God alone brings it about that we must continually consider his perspective, it cannot be said that God never brings about anything totally on his own. The process God is coercive in this sense.

In what sense then is the process God thought not to be coercive? The answer is related to the perceived strength of God's persuasive power. The crucial question, as process theists see it, is not whether God unilaterally lures each of us but whether such luring ever guarantees that we will do what God wants us to do. And to this question, process theists give an emphatic no. God cannot coerce in this sense. At every moment, as John Cobb and David Griffin put it, we "may choose to actualize [God's] initial aim; but [we] may also choose among other real possibilities open to [us]."[3]

In short, when process theists claim that God is only persuasive, they do not mean that God never unilaterally brings about anything. They mean that God never brings it about that we (or any other entity) must *act* in accordance with his will.

But why exactly does the process God never coerce in this sense? Is it that the process God could but has chosen not to coerce us? That is, is non-coercion a self-limitation? Or is it that the process God does not have the capacity to coerce us? That is, is it the case that God could not coerce us even if he desired to do so?

It appears at times that some process theists see divine noncoercion as a self-limitation. Lewis Ford, for example, tells us that:

> To the extent that God exercises [coercive] power, creaturely freedom is restricted, the reality of the world is diminished, and the divine experience is impoverished. Creaturely freedom is all important, for without it God is deprived of the one thing the world can provide which God alone cannot have: a genuine social existence. Abandoning the angelic marionettes who merely echo his thoughts as a further extension of his own being, God has elected to enter into dialogue with sinful, yet free men.[4]

What Ford has in mind here is not totally clear. But he can be read as saying that although God could have coerced us, he has chosen to use only persuasive power because only this type of power is compatible with his goals and desires.

However, the process proponent of such a self-limitation theory— if any such individual really exists—faces a problem. Many classical theists believe that God could coerce us. But a growing number— sometimes call 'free will' theists—also believe that he has chosen not to do so because a world in which there exists freedom from coercion and some evil is superior to a world containing neither. In short, a growing number of classical theists also affirm a self-limitation theory. In response to such classical theists Griffin has argued that:

> God could, on this hypothesis, occasionally violate human freedom for the sake of an overriding good or to prevent a particular horrible evil. Of course, in those moments, the apparent human beings would not really be human, if "humans" are by definition free. But this would be a small price to pay if some of the world's worst evils could be averted.[5]

But, of course, the question posed by Griffin is equally applicable to any process proponent of a self-limitation theory. Why, if God can coerce, has he not chosen in some cases to do so?

It may well be that a process theist could formulate an adequate response to Griffin at this point. But such a response would obviously also serve as an adequate counter to Griffin's criticism of the God of the classical 'free will' theist. A process proponent of a self-limitation theory could not have it both ways.

Most process theists, however, clearly believe that coercion is impossible for God. That is, most seem to agree with Griffin that divine noncoercion "is not due to a decision on God's part which could be revoked from time to time."[6] But why are we to assume that God is limited in this sense? Why are we to believe that God could not even occasionally coerce us if he desired to do so?

Griffin offers us one popular process response. To say that God could coerce us, he begins, is to say that we could be completely determined. And to say that we could be completely determined is to say that we could be "totally devoid of all power—power to determine [ourselves], even partially, and power to determine others, even partially."[7] But talk of totally powerless individuals is meaningless, Griffin argues, "since it cannot be given any experiential basis." We know it is possible for individuals to have power, but we have never experienced totally powerless individuals. Thus, he concludes, it follows that no one, including God, could totally control another individual.[8]

If Griffin is correct, then we should obviously not be able to cite any situations in which one person is being totally controlled by another person. But let us consider the case of a parent who, after trying unsuccessfully to convince a child to go to bed, finally picks up the child and takes him or her into the bedroom. Or let us consider the case of a parent who finally ends a fight between siblings by forcibly separating the children. Are not these counterexamples to Griffin's argument? Do we not here have two common cases in which one person (a parent) is unilaterally controlling another person (a child)?

Many process theists will argue that we do not. They will grant that parents do at times contol their children's behavior. But in all such cases, they will argue, the children retain some power of self-determination. They might argue, for example, that even when a parent can bring it about that a child goes to bed or stops fighting, the child retains the power to resist physically or the power to desire not to act as the parent wishes or the power to plan revenge. Moreover, they agree with Griffin's claim that a person is being totally controlled only if she or he has no power of self-determination. Thus, they will conclude that parents never really totally control their children and, accordingly, that parental control is not a valid counterexample to the claim that one person can never coerce another.

The line of reasoning, however, is problematic. Process theists have every right to claim that a person has only been coerced when he or she has lost all power of self-determination. But this is not the form of coercion with which we as humans are primarily concerned. When, for example, we put criminals in jail to protect ourselves from them, we are not attempting to remove totally their power of self-determination. We only want to insure that such individuals do not have the power to act out certain antisocial desires. In a similar fashion, those who contend that God ought to do more to control the moral evil in our world are not generally arguing that he should bring it about that those who desire to perform evil acts have no power of self-determination. They are arguing that God should at times bring it about that potential evildoers are unable to act out certain antisocial, dehumanizing desires.

Accordingly, for process theists to argue that behavioral control is not really coercion is in a very real sense for them to 'win the battle but lose the war'. If for the sake of argument we grant the process theist the definition of coercion, then no one—including God—can coerce. But unless process theists can also demonstrate that God cannot effectively control human behavior, their claim that God cannot coerce becomes rather insignificant. For if God can 'coercively' control human behavior, then process theists must explain why the process God does not control human behavior in a 'noncoercive' manner more frequently. They must explain why God does not, for example, 'noncoercively' stop people like Hitler from performing extremely antisocial actions.

Moreover, it is not clear that humans cannot in fact be coerced in the sense intended by process theists. It may be true that the children cited in the previous examples retained some meaningful sense of self-determination. But let us consider the case of the parent who kills his or her child out of fear, anger or frustration. The parent in this situation is not simply controlling one aspect of a self-determining individual's behavior. The parent in this case makes sure that the child no longer has the power of self-determination in any sense.

In response, it might be argued that a parent who kills his or her child is not really controlling the child's actions. The parent is only bringing it about that the child can perform no action at all. But this will not do. If it is not truly coercive for one individual to insure that another individual can no longer act at all, then Griffin's challenge to the classical free will theist again appears in a modified form. If it would not be coercive for the process God to bring it about that certain humans no longer exist, why does he not do so occasionally? Why, for example, did he not bring it about that Hitler no longer existed?

Perhaps, however, there is a way in which the process theist can circumvent this general line of criticism. Humans, it might be granted, can control the behavior of other humans and maybe even coerce them. But this is only possible because we as humans possess 'bodies' which have the ability to control unilaterally the 'bodies' of other humans. God has no body. Thus such control or coercion is not within his power.

Or, stated differently, it might be argued that we as humans can only be controlled or coerced by the use of threat of physical force. Thus, since God cannot use physical force, it still holds that he can only persuade.

But why should we grant that humans can only be controlled by the use of physical force? Let us assume, for example, that someone discovers that a certain woman is having an extramarital affair and threatens to tell the unsuspecting spouse if not paid ten thousand dollars. And let us further assume that the consequences of discovery are so undesirable for our adulteress that she sees no option but to pay the blackmailer. It appears in this case that our adulteress has in a very real sense been *forced* to act against her will. But the force in question is psychological, not physical.

Or let us consider a more 'positive' form of psychological manipulation. Let us assume that a parent knows that his child wants desperately to be a sports hero. And let us further assume that the parent convinces the child that she cannot fulfill this dream unless she learns to obey orders and gets a great deal of sleep and that the child, therefore, willingly goes to bed whenever the parent tells her to. In this case the child has not been forced to act against her will, but the control is no less real. The parent has, by the use of standard manipulative techniques, insured that the child will act as he wishes.

It might be argued that the 'control' in these cases is not really total or complete since our adulteress still retains the power to refuse to meet the blackmailer's demands and our child still retains the power to disobey the parent. In one sense this is true. Psychological manipulation, unlike some physical manipulation, does not make it impossible for an individual to refuse to act in accordance with the wishes of the manipulator. But given the value system of our adulteress, it is not clear that she would *in fact* seriously consider not paying the money. And given the value system of our aspiring sports hero, it is not clear that he/she would *in fact* seriously consider not going to bed. In short, it is not obvious that individuals can in fact always resist psychological manipulation. Such manipulation does appear in some cases to result in very successful behavioral control.

But is such psychological manipulation widespread? It seems to me that it is. With proper training some of us might be able to recognize and resist even the most subtle manipulative techniques. It is a well-documented fact that advertizers can very successfully manipulate consumer activities. And it is also a well-documented fact that the media can successfully manipulate our social and political perspectives. Such examples bear witness to the fact that the attitudes and thus behavior of the general public can on the whole quite consistently and effectively be controlled apart from the use of physical force.

But what of the process God? Could he use psychological 'manipulation' to control human behavior? Could he, for example, make our adulteress experience enough guilt or fear of exposure to insure that she stopped her illicit affair? Or could he, like the parent, play upon the desires of the child to insure a reasonable bedtime? It seems to me that the answer to such questions is yes. Process theists, we have seen, believe that God has the ability to make each of us aware of his perspective at each moment. Thus I see no reason to deny that the process God has the power to bring it about that an adulterous woman becomes aware of the real possibility of exposure or that a child becomes aware of the fact that going to bed is consistent with long-term goals. And process theists also believe, we have seen, that God has the power to bring it about that we feel some compulsion to act in accordance with his wishes. Thus, I see no reason to deny that the process God could cause our adulteress or child to feel some compulsion to do the right thing.

But could the process God ever insure that individuals would act in accordance with his wishes? It might be argued that he could not. God, we might be told, has enough power to insure that certain motivating factors will be considered, but not enough power to insure that such factors will determine behavior. Such reasoning, however, is not convincing. First, effective psychological manipulation is not normally based on some quantitative sense of manipulative power. It is normally based on a thorough understanding of the values and personality traits of those being manipulated. Thus, for example, a person who knows his spouse or child well can frequently control or modify the behavior of either quite easily with a simple glance or short utterance. There is, accordingly, little reason to believe that a being who understands us better than we understand ourselves and has the power to make us feel some compulsion to act in accordance with his wishes *could not* manipulate our behavior upon occasion.

Secondly, according to process thought, God has the ability to influence to some extent even those individuals who are consciously choosing to live lives which are not in keeping with his general aims or who tend not to be easily influenced by others. But if this is so, is it not reasonable to believe that God at least has the *ability* to 'overwhelm' those who consciously choose to live lives compatible with his basic aims or who are very easily influenced by others?

In short, while there may well be good reasons why the process God *would* never control our behavior through psychological manipulation, I see no reason to deny that such control is possible. And if such behavioral control is possible in even some cases, then the process theist is again open to a version of Griffin's challenge to the classical free will theist. If the process God could prevent (or minimize) some particularly horrible evils by the use of psychological manipulation, why does he not do so?

It appears then that process theists such as Griffin face a dilemma. We as humans seem at times to possess the ability to control the *behavior* of other humans. If process theists argue that such control is not really coercive because those humans controlled retain some power of self-determination, their point becomes trivial. For the crucial question which the existence of evil requires all theists to answer is not whether God could take away all our power of self-determination. The crucial question is whether God could, in a manner analogous to a parent controlling a child, control our behavior in some cases. If, on the other hand, process theists grant that humans can at times control other humans but argue that God cannot do so, then their position appears less than convincing or satisfying. For as we have seen, it appears that the process God does possess the ability to control human behavior through psychological manipulation in at least some contexts. And if this is so, then the process theist must explain why God does not control human behavior at least occasionally.

But perhaps I have missed something. In *Process Theology: An Introductory Exposition*, Griffin argues that to have the power of self-determination in a meaningful human sense means that we have the ability to "disregard the initial aim proffered by God in favor of some other real possibility for that moment of existence."[9] In other words, as Griffin sees it, to have meaningful human freedom means that we can choose not to act in accordance with God's will for our lives. The truth of this principle, he maintains, is "not dependent upon a choice, even a divine choice." Rather, "any development which God can promote will have to conform to [it]."[10] Moreover, Griffin adds, God's persuasive action has fortunately brought it about that we are at this time truly free in a meaningful human sense. Thus, he concludes, it follows that God does not have the option of coercing us, even if he so desires. Since we are truly free and since even God's behavior must conform to the principle which stipulates that truly free activity cannot be controlled, God can only use persuasive power.

This is an interesting line of reasoning. But it is inadequate in the present context. It may be true that we can be considered truly human only in those contexts in which we have the power to reject God's wishes. But it does not follow from this that God could, in fact, never unilaterally control our behavior. For example, it does not follow from the assumption that Hitler only acted in a truly human fashion in those instances in which he was not controlled by God that God *could not* have unilaterally controlled Hitler occasionally. To establish that God could never control us, Griffin must do more than establish that we are only truly human when we have the power to reject God's wishes. He must establish that God must always allow us to be truly human. And this he has not done.

But there remains yet another way in which process theists might attempt to defend their belief that God could never totally control our behavior. The process view of reality is based on the assumption that we as humans are functioning as self-determining beings at every moment. At every moment, it is held, we as humans must decide how we wish to intergrate what has happened in the past, what God desires and what we desire into a "unified experience".[11] Accordingly, it might be argued, it can make no sense to ask whether the process God could coerce if he desired to do so. It may be that another being with the capabilities of the process God could totally control us. But to be a process theist is to accept a view of reality which automatically rules out such coercive activity. Within the process system, the possibility of total control does not arise.

In one sense this is a satisfactory response. If the belief that God cannot totally control us is one of the foundational beliefs within the process system, then the process theist need not attempt to justify it. For the foundational beliefs in any system of thought are not based on or inferred from any other beliefs. They are rather the assumed truths upon which all other acceptable, nonfoundational beliefs must be based (or with which they must be consistent).

However, the process theist must pay a price for approaching the issue in this manner. If there are good sound arguments supporting the belief that God could never totally control us, then process theists can justifiably maintain that those who disagree with them are wrong. But no objective argumentation exists for foundational beliefs. Thus, if the process belief in divine noncoercion is foundational, then it no longer necessarily follows from this belief that the classical belief in the possibility of total divine control is not justifiable. For the classical theist has as much right to assume as a foundational belief that God can control us, as process theists do to assume that God cannot. And, of course, if the belief that God is noncoercive is rendered immune from attack by categorizing it as foundational, the same is true for the belief that God is 'coercive'.

Or let me state this important point in more neutral terms. If process and classical theists both declare their beliefs on the question of divine control to be unchallenged assumptions within their systems of thought, then both groups can justifiably accept their beliefs as true. But neither can then justifiably claim that its opponent's beliefs are false.

Perhaps, however, this seeming stalemate will not bother all process theists. It is true, some might acknowledge, that the classical theist's position cannot conclusively be proven false. But surely, they might argue, to think of God as a being who cannot totally control us is much more reasonable and personally satisfying than to conceive of God as the classical theists do. If God can unilaterally bring it about that we must act in accordance with his will, then we must assume that nothing happens which God does not desire to happen. But if this is so, we must either make the dubious assumption that all evil is desired by God as a means to some greater good or acknowledge that some evil is unnecessary and thus that God is not perfectly good. Moreover, to maintain that God can totally control us makes a mockery of the claim that we possess meaningful freedom or self-determinism.

On the other hand, such process theists might continue, if God cannot totally control us, we can admit both that some evil is unnecessary and that God is perfectly good. For, given this perspective, some evil can be seen as the undesired, but unavoidable, by-product of meaningful, but misused, human freedom.

There are two basic problems with this line of reasoning. First, there is no reason for classical theists in the 'free will' tradition to grant that belief in a God who has the ability to coerce makes a mockery of human freedom, trivializes evil, or leaves the seeming absence of useful divine intervention unexplained. The classical free will theist, as we have seen, believes that a world in which individuals have the power of self-determination, and thus the potential for generating evil, is a better world than one in which God unilaterally controls everything.

Accordingly, the classical free will theist need not grant that simply because God has the capacity to control us, he could justifiably do so at any time. As I have argued elsewhere, it may well be incompatible with a meaningful sense of human freedom for God to intervene in human affairs on a continual or widespread basis.[12] Nor need classical free will theists grant that a God with coercive powers would have intervened more frequently than he has. They can simply maintain that God has already intervened to the extent compatible with meaningful freedom. And, thus, such classical theists can also deny that nothing happens which God does not desire to happen. That is, they can acknowledge that some evil is unnecessary. Such evil can be viewed as the undesired, but unavoidable by-product of the type of universe God has chosen to create.

Also, there is a strange irony in the process contention that the 'noncoercive God' of process theism is in some way morally superior to the 'coercive God' of classical theism. Process theists claim that coercion is impossible for the process God. He can only persuade us. But if God has not chosen to persuade, rather than coerce us, it would appear that he cannot be praised or commended for acting as he does. Or, stated differently, if God only has the power to persuade us, the fact that he doesn't totally control us would appear to tell us nothing about his character or moral nature.

This does not mean that the process theist cannot agree with Ford that divine coercion, "whether limited or unlimited, is incompatible with divine perfection." And the process theist can still agree with Cobb that "the only power of any worthwhile result is the power of persuasion."[13] But unless the God of process theism has the power to control us, he cannot be considered morally superior to the classical God *because* he in fact only persuades us.

It might be argued in response that since divine coercion is incompatible with divine perfection and doesn't produce "worthwhile results," the process God wouldn't coerce even if he could. Thus, he can at least be praised for his intentions if not his actions. But such a response generates a serious problem of its own. Griffin, remember, argues against the classical free will theist that if God could coerce, it would surely be better if he did so occasionally. If Griffin is correct, then process theists cannot justifiably argue that "limited or unlimited divine coercion is incompatible with divine perfection." They must assume rather that the process God would coerce occasionally if he could. And they must conclude, accordingly, that the fact that God only persuades stands not as a sign of divine perfection, but as an unfortunate, unavoidable limitation of his activity.

On the other hand, if even limited coercion is incompatible with divine perfection, then it follows that the process God would not control us even if he could. But then the fact that the process God cannot control us becomes irrelevant when comparing him to the God of the classical free will theist. If the process God can be praised because he would not control us even if he could, then the God of the classical free will theist must also be praised for not controlling us even though he can. The process theist cannot have it both ways.

In Conclusion

We must conclude then, I believe, that the process perspective on divine power is not in any obvious sense superior to the perspective affirmed by classical free will theists. Process theists have every right to view divine noncoercion as a foundational assumption within their system. But they have not produced any convincing arguments to support their belief. Thus classical theists retain the right to belief that God does, in fact, have the power to control us.

NOTES

* A somewhat different version of this chapter was published in the *Journal of Religion* (vol. 64, July 1983) under the title, "Divine Persuasion: Could the Process God Do More?". The version that appears in this book is published with the permission of the University of Chicago Press.

Divine Power: Do Process Theists Have a Better Idea?

1. See, for example, Barry Whitney, "Process Theism: Does a Persuasive God Coerce?" *The Southern Journal of Philosophy* 17 (1979), pp. 133-141.

2. Lewis Ford, "Divine Persuasion and the Triumph of Good," in *Process Philosophy and Christian Thought*, ed. D. Brown, R. James, O. Reeves (New York: The Bobbs-Merrill Company, Inc., 1971), pp. 291, 295; and John Cobb and David Griffin, *Process Theology: An Introductory Exposition* (Philadelphia: The Westminster Press, 1976), p. 91; John Cobb, *God and the World* (Philadelphia: The Westminster Press, 1969), pp. 91, 125.

3. Cobb and Griffin, p. 53.

4. Ford, p. 289.

5. David Griffin, *God, Power and Evil: A Process Theodicy* (Philadelphia: The Westminster Press, 1976), p. 271.

6. Ibid., p. 281.

7. Ibid., p. 266.

8. Ibid., p. 267.

9. Cobb and Griffin, p. 73.

10. Ibid., p. 72.

11. Griffin, p. 76.

12. David Basinger, "Human Freedom and Divine Providence: Some New Thoughts on an Old Problem," *Religious Studies* 15 (December, 1979), pp. 491-510.

13. Ford, p. 284; Cobb, p. 90.

Christian Theism and Whiteheadian Process Philosophy

*Are They Compatible?**

W. Norris Clarke, S. J.

W. Norris Clarke, S. J.

W. Norris Clarke, S. J. received his Ph.D. from Louvain University in 1950. He has been a professor of philosophy at Fordham University since 1955. Dr. Clarke was the co-founder of the *International Philosophical Quarterly* which he also served as editor from 1961 to 1985, Dr. Clarke is a past president of the American Catholic Philosophical Association, the Metaphysical Society of America and the Jesuit Philosophical Association of America. He received the Aquinas Medal for distinguished contribution to Christian Philosophy from the American Catholic Philosophical Association. He is the author of *A Philosophical Approach to God* and some fifty articles or chapters in books.

There is little doubt that during the last few years the principal challenge to traditional Christian theism has come from process philosophy and theology, which has continued to show itself as one of the most lively and creative movements in contemporary philosophical and religious thought.[1] A growing number of Catholic thinkers have also been drawing inspiration from the writings of this school.[2] But I have the impression that some of the latter, especially theologians, are a little incautious in speaking of themselves as "process theologians," or as "using process philosophy," taking the latter rather vaguely and generally as thinking about God in dynamic terms, without fully realizing all the implications involved in taking over the whole process philosophical system as such. Hence it seems timely to propose some initial and tentative reflections on just how far process philosophy and traditional Christian theism—especially as found in the Catholic tradition—are really compatible, or whether there are still some irreducible differences between the two.

Let me begin by summing up briefly the general position I intend to develop here. On the one hand, process thought contains a number of *basic insights* that can and should be fruitfully assimilated by Christian theism. On the other hand, process thought *as a system*, at least in its principal presently established forms—the systems of Alfred North Whitehead and Charles Hartshorne—is still in serious tension, if not incompatibility, with traditional Christian theism on several key points, both philosophical and theological, with respect to the nature of God and His relationship to the world. It would be unwise, however, to lay down any unbridgeable incompatibilities of principle with future possible developments of the process stream of thought, since it itself is in full process of evolution, to which it is committed in principle.[3]

A very significant evolution has in fact already taken place. With some notable exceptions, such as Charles Hartshorne, the early Whiteheadian disciples tended to form a closed school interested mainly in the internal working and clarification of the system rather than in creative adaptations. When confronted with oppositions between the system and traditional Christian teaching, many Whiteheadians tended to bend their theology to fit their philosophy rather than adapt their philosophy to their theology, as has always been the hallmark of the great orthodox Christian theologians of the past. Now that the main lines of the system have been tied down with some general consensus, this "scholastic period," as some have called it, is for the most part over. Neo-Whiteheadians are springing up everywhere, especially among Christian theologians and philosophers, who exhibit a new spirit of creative adaptation, even significant revision, of the system where they feel it necessary to fit their Christian belief or human experience. Christian thinkers can only welcome this trend, since it promises a much more open and creative context for fruitful dialogue to the enrichment of both parties. All that we say hereafter must be understood in this open-ended context of development among sincere Christians whose faith is seeking understanding.

Is God Creator of the Universe? Whitehead's Position

God is not, in the original Whiteheadian system, the Creator of the universe out of nothing—i. e., out of no pre-existing material or subject.[4] The universe is an ongoing system which has always been and always will be. God does indeed play an indispensable role in this world system, in four ways: (1) as source of the "eternal objects," the possible intelligible forms or structures which He holds eternally in His mind and presents at the appropriate time for integration by the momentary "actual occasions" or events (also called "actual entities"), which alone are real outside God Himself; (2) as providing the initial "subjective aim" or ideal goal of each newly arising actual occasion; (3) as providentially guiding the universe toward the greatest possible realizable value, not by determining or coercing creatures through efficient causality, but by "luring" them with the persuasive power of the good; (4) as eternally preserving in His memory the objectified values achieved by the successively perishing actual entities.

But God is not the ultimate source of the very being of the universe, or even, it seems, of its universal built-in character of self-creativity, for two reasons. In the first place, God's activity always presupposes the universe as somehow already present, at least in inchoate form, as subject of His action, as something He can lure to the good by presenting form and goal but of which He is not the ultimate source and hence over which He does not possess absolute control. The situation is close to that of the Platonic Demiurge, which injects forms into pre-existing chaotic matter and which Whitehead explicitly recalls as his basic model. Thus he excludes any theory of the absolute beginning of the universe or of any one ultimate source for all reality.[5]

Elsewhere Whitehead adds that we should not pay God the dubious "metaphysical compliment" of being "the foundation for the metaphysical situation with its ultimate activity." For if this were the case, "there can be no alternative except to discern in Him the origin of all evil as well as of all good. He is then the supreme author of the play, and to Him must therefore be ascribed its shortcomings as well as its successes."[6] Thus God is not the ultimate initiator of the cosmic drama with all its players, nor, especially, does He initiate and carry it on by an act of free volition. God and the world are necessary mutual collaborators forever, by the very nature of each: ". . . metaphysics requires that the relationships of God to the world should lie beyond the accidents of will, and that they be founded upon the necessities of the nature of the world."[7]

The *second reason* why Whitehead cannot accept the strict interpretation of creation out of nothing is closely linked with the first. It is because each actual occasion (or actual entity) is a *self-creative act*—not entirely out of nothing, but as a novel autonomous integration of the prior actual occasions in its environment which present themselves to it for selective prehension (these data for decision include God's own presentation of ideal form and goal). "Creativity," which is really self-creativity, is a universal attribute of all actual entities, of which God is the supreme but not the only instance. This concrete act of self-creative integration, which constitutes the very subjective being of each actual occasion, must, insofar as it is a concrete existential act, be *its own* act and not received from another. At best God might be called "co-creator" of each actual occasion in that he provides the initial subjective aim to guide the entity's own self-creative act. Creativity is not concentrated in God alone, nor does it seem to derive from Him alone (as we shall see, this point might be open to a different interpretation or at least adaptation of Whitehead), but is shared among all actual entities, from the lowest to the highest, and necessarily from the very nature of things, not from any free volition of God's part. As Whitehead puts it:

> In this way an actual entity satisfies Spinoza's notion of substance: it is *causa sui*. The creativity is not an external agency with its own ulterior purposes. All actual entities share with God this characteristic of self-causation. For this reason every actual entity also shares with God the characteristic of transcending all other actual entities, including God.[8]

And Lewis Ford comments:

> From the standpoint of Christian concerns Whitehead's metaphysics is most distinctive in that it is a philosophy of creation which does not identify creative power exclusively with God. Instead of distinguishing between a creator who is uncreated and creatures who do not create, Whitehead conceives of all actualities, including God, as self-created. . . .Creativity is the underlying dynamic activity enabling each actuality to create itself, but this creativity is not actual in and of itself, only in its particular instantiations. The role of God is not to supply this creativity but the actuality's ideal of itself (the initial subjective aim) which functions as the principle of selective appropriation of past causes.[9]

Lewis Ford goes on to explain elsewhere, very perceptively, why, according to his mind, Whitehead cannot accept a strict doctrine of divine creation.[10] Take, for example, a free act. It would make sense—say, in a Thomistic system—for God to create a *free agent* which then produced its own free act from within by its own power (supported, if need be, but not determined by God). But this would imply a distinction between subject or agent and act which a Whiteheadian could not accept without going back to the old substance-accident doctrine. For him there is no distinction between the agent and its act. There is no other being of the free agent save the momentary free act itself. The agent is its act. On the other hand, it would not make sense to say that God created the *free act itself* of another being, for then He Himself would be responsible for the act and it would no longer be the free act of another. Hence, just as the act of any agent must be its own act, if it is free, and cannot be given to it ready-made by God or anyone else, so the very being of the free agent for Whitehead, since its being is identical with its act, must be *causa sui* and not given by anyone else, even God— though God can contribute to it and cooperate with it. It follows that in the Whiteheadian system it is impossible for God to create any free agent.

Furthermore, we can push the argument all the way to include all actual entities. For since every actual occasion for Whitehead is a novel, not entirely predetermined act of self-integration, it contains something analogous to freedom within it. Hence none of them could have been created by God. In a word, if all actual entities are *nothing but their acts*, one actual entity for each act, and even God cannot directly create the act, let alone the free act, of another being, then God cannot create any actual entities at all. If God were a creator, He could directly create only agents, not acts. (As we shall see later, there may be another alternative to this neat and tight argument against the possibility of creation for Whitehead, in that he himself carefully limits the meaning of self-creation and distinguishes it from the prior initial constitution of the new subject by the inflow of God and the surrounding world, from which point the creative self-integrating act of the subject then takes off.)

Conflict with the Traditional Christian Notion of Creation

It seems evident enough from all these texts, especially the first set, that Whitehead is quite explicitly and self-consciously rejecting what he understands to be the traditional Christian concept of God as radical ultimate source of the universe, bringing it into being out of nothing in an absolute beginning, by His own free creative act of will. In so doing he is returning to an older Platonic primal dualism of God and the world, in its aspect of primal raw material of multiplicity to be brought from chaos to order—neither of these two poles being ultimately responsible for the origin or total being of the other. The only ultimate source of unity in the universe—if there is one at all—seems to be pushed back even beyond God to an inscrutable, necessary, and eternal amorphous force of "creativity" or self-creativity (of which God is the primary and highest instance, but not, it seems, the ultimate source): a force which carries strong overtones of the ancient Greek *ananke* of necessity, which Plato himself appeals to. We shall see later how the implicit resources of Whitehead's own system will allow contemporary Neo-Whiteheadians to take quite a different position on this point.

This conception of God's relation to the world falls short of the traditional Judaeo-Christian belief in God as the radical Creator or ultimate source of the very being of the universe with all its components—a belief professed clearly by all major Christian creeds: "I believe in one God, the Father almighty, Creator of heaven and earth . . .". From the early Church Fathers down to the present, this has always been interpreted as meaning creation out of nothing (*creatio ex nihilo*)—i.e., initiating the being of the world out of no pre-existing subject matter. It is true that the biblical texts themselves contain no explicit metaphysical statements such as "creation out of nothing." But the early Fathers, from the second century on, quickly agreed on this interpretation as what distinguished their doctrine from that of the pagans.[11] Thus St. Theophilus of Antioch, writing as early as 181 A. D., explicitly repudiates the doctrine of the "Platonists" that matter itself was not created by God but is eternally coeval with Him as that out of which He made the world:

> But if both God and matter are ungenerated, then God is no longer the creator of all things, according to the Platonists. . . .But the power of God is shown forth in this, that he made out of nothing whatsoever he wished. . . .And so in the first place all the prophets have taught with complete consensus that God created all things out of nothing.[12]

This doctrine was agreed upon so unanimously by all, heretics included, that the early church councils, directed primarily against Trinitarian and Christological heresies, found no need to explain and define the point explicitly. But in the thirteenth century the resurgence of new forms of Manicheanism brought about a formal definition of the doctrine, in 1215, in the Fourth Lateran Council—an ecumenical one—where God is defined as "Creator of all things, visible and invisible, spiritual and corporeal, who, by his almighty power, from the beginning of time has created both orders in the same way out of nothing, the spiritual or angelic world and the corporeal or visible universe."[13] The same teaching was repeated in later councils, down to the First Vatican Council in our own century.[14] Thus the doctrine of the initial creation of all things out of nothing is not merely one theological interpretation put forward by some particular theological school or schools, but a basic pillar of orthodox Christian faith, in both Eastern and Western Churches, for all who accept the teaching authority of the Church, unanimous on this point from its earliest days, in both East and West. It should be carefully noted, however, that in no fully authoritative document of the Church (decrees of councils, for example) is there any further determination of what is meant by "from the beginning of time." Whether this positively excludes interpretation in all possible Whiteheadian senses *might* still be open for theological and philosophical discussion.

Metaphysical Difficulties

In addition to being incompatible with traditional Christian belief in God as creator, Whitehead's rejection of an initial creation of the world out of nothing runs into serious metaphysical difficulties. On the one hand, as we have said above, it brings us back to an older Platonic primal dualism of God over against the world (in the latter's aspect of primal raw material or multiplicity to be brought from chaos into order), where neither of these two primal poles is ultimately responsible for the other. What then is the ultimate source or explanation of the unity of the universe, of why its two correlative poles, God and the multiplicity of the world, are attuned to each other so as to make up a single system, since neither one ultimately derives all its being from the other? If there is to be any ultimate source of unity in the universe at all—which is dubious, just as it was for Plato—it seems to be pushed back beyond even God to an inscrutable, faceless, amorphous force of creativity which is just *there*, everywhere in the universe, as a primal fact with no further explanation possible—a kind of generalized necessity of nature, with striking similarities to the ancient Greek *ananke*. It should be remembered, too, that creativity for Whitehead is not an actuality in and for itself, but only a generalized abstract description of what is as a matter of fact instantiated in every actual occasion of the universe. Creativity seems to be an ultimate primordial *many*, with no unifying source.

But not only is this doctrine in any of its forms not Christian; it also suffers from all the irreparable deficiencies of any ultimate dualism or multiplicity not rooted in the prior unity of creative mind. This lacuna in Plato was quickly recognized by the post-Platonic schools of Neo-Platonism culminating in the great synthesis of Plotinus, who considered himself as only completing the unfinished business of Plato by his doctrine of emanation of all reality from the One, including matter itself. Whitehead has turned our metaphysical clocks back not only to a pre-Christian but to a pre-Neoplatonic position, thus cancelling out one of the most decisive metaphysical steps forward in Western thought.

Even aside from the question of how to ground the unity of the system of the universe, with its two intrinsically correlated poles, God and the world, there remains another difficulty. If all creativity does not ultimately derive from God, why does this creativity continue to spring forth endlessly and inexhaustibly, all over the universe, in each new actual occasion, from no actually existing source. For creativity is not, as Lewis Ford insists, an actuality in and of itself, but merely a generalized description of the primal fact that it does spring up in each new actual occasion. It is not itself a source because it is not in itself an already existing concrete actuality. Hence the individual bursts of self-creativity which characterize each newly arising actual entity, and which are the only ground or referent for the term "creativity," seem literally to emerge out of nothing insofar as their actual existence (*becoming*) is concerned, with no prior ground for their actuality whatsoever—though there is prior ground for their formal elements. Why this creativity should bubble up unfailingly and inexhaustibly all over the universe through endless time, with no active causal influx or gift of actuality from another already existing actual entity, remains a total enigma—one that is not simply a mystery to us at present, but in principle rebuffs any further penetration by intelligence, since there is no more ultimate ground.[15]

Lewis Ford, one of the most representative process thinkers in America, has responded to this objection that once this first step is granted, everything else falls into place, and that this is the most one can ask of an initial metaphysical principle. It seems to me, however, that the price of this initial enigma is too high. The doctrine of creativity is admittedly obscure and underdeveloped in Whitehead. But until this difficulty is cleared up, the process theory of God remains both theologically and philosophically inadequate to express either the traditional Christian conception of God as creator—i.e., Ultimate Source of the very existence of the universe, as well as of its intelligible structures—or the metaphysical exigencies of an ultimate ground for the unity of the universe. An infinitely fragmented force of creativity cannot be an authentic ultimate, precisely because it is *actually* a many, and only abstractly one.

We find ourselves here in the presence of what seems to many of us *the* most radical metaphysical opposition between Whitehead and St. Thomas—and, it seems to me, on St. Thomas's side, most of the great metaphysicians in history, both Eastern and Western. In St. Thomas there is an absolute priority of the One over the many, so that the many is unqualifiedly derivative from and dependent on the One, in an asymmetrical relation. In Whitehead, there is in the last analysis an *original priority of the many over the One.*[16] No matter how much Whiteheadians may insist that the One brings into unity the many—that the One and the many are intrinsically correlative to each other, so that neither is prior to the other—it remains unalterable that the unity of synthesis is a *later or secondary ontological moment*, not necessarily temporal.

The original or primordial ontological contribution of each side of the correlation of God and world is radically and ultimately *independent of each other*. God is not responsible for there being a many at all—i.e., the basic "raw material" for a world to be brought into order at all. He is not even responsible for its primordial potentiality to be ordered; nor, obviously, is the world responsible for there being a God with the power to order it. This is true even in the primordial nature of God with respect to the infinite set of "eternal objects" or formal pattern—models of order and value which He eternally envisages and draws upon to lure the world into harmony, like the Platonic Demiurge which Whitehead takes as his explicit inspiration. Though the determinate ordering of these pure formal ideal possibilities is due to His creative initiative, still the primordial presence of some quasi-indeterminate reservoir of not yet integrated formal possibilities is not itself generated by the divine creative act but—vague and obscure as its status is in Whitehead— remains an ultimate given of independent origin even for the divine mind and power.[17]

Though this ultimate reservoir of the many in the order of forms does not possess full actual existence as actual entities, still they possess *some* kind of primordial being of their own as their own con- tribution of raw material for the act of divine ordering into a deter- minate world of possibilities. Again the many has radical priority, since the duality of God *and* world, God *and* possibles, is itself an ultimate original many. Thus there is no explanation finally of why both sides of this correlation are originally present at all, nor (another serious difficulty often overlooked) is there any reason given why there should be a positive *affinity* of one for the other—i.e., a positive *aptitude or intrinsic capacity* in one to be ordered by the other. Thus neither the *original presence* or giveness of the two sides of the cor- relation One/many (God/world) nor their *intrinsic tendency and capacity* to mutual correlation is given any explanation or ground. The many—at least in the sense of this initial duality of component terms—retains absolute priority, grounded in no prior or deeper unity.

But practically all of the great metaphysicians of the past, East and West (except Plato and Aristotle) have agreed on at least this: that *every* many must ultimately be grounded in some more primor- dial and ultimate One. A many makes no sense at all unless there is some common ground or property (existence, goodness, actuality, creativity) shared by each, without which they could not be com- pared or correlated at all. Nor can any many be intrinsically oriented toward order and synthesis unless some ultimate unitary/ordering mind first creatively thought up within itself this primordial correla- tion and affinity and implanted it in the many from one source. Not only all actual order, but all ultimate possibility of order must be grounded in a One, and in a Mind. As St. Thomas often puts it, following the ancient "Platonic way" (*via Platonica*), "Wherever there is a many possessing some one real common property, there must be some one ultimate source for what the many hold in com- mon for it cannot be because things are many (not one) that they share something one.''[18] Thus either we leave the many and its correlation with the One ultimately ungrounded, with no attempt at intelligible explanation at all, or else we must have recourse to some further hidden ultimate principle of unity. But this would require for Whitehead recourse either to some ultimate inscrutable principle of blind necessity or to some further God hidden behind his God—hardly Whitehead's cup of tea.

In sum, despite Lewis Ford's insistence that the primordiality of the many as co-equal with the One is one of Whitehead's unique new contributions to modern metaphysics the fact that it is new does not make it viable.[19] In the last analysis, what is missing from Whiteheadean metaphysics is that it remains content with Plato's Demiurge without pushing on to the underlying doctrine of the One or the Good, which Plato himself finally saw had to be the last word and which Plotinus carried all the way to its implicit consequences— the origin of matter from the One.

The Response of the Whiteheadians

Process philosophers, especially theologians, are by no means unaware of these difficulties.[20] They are generally willing to admit that the Whiteheadian conception of God as ''co-creator'' or collaborator with the universe differs significantly from the traditional Christian interpretation. Some conclude that the latter, especially as it includes the notion of an absolute beginning, is a mythological image which should be dropped. Such a response, however, simply wipes out a large part of the unanimous Christian tradition on this point and can hardly be acceptable for orthodox Christians. Others, like John Cobb, wish to push the process of conception closer to the tradition by drawing out the implications of the Whiteheadian doctrine that God alone gives the initial subjective aim to each new actual occasion Since this constitutes the initial phase of the latter's being/becoming, it might be likened to an initial gift of being, as an overflow from the divine creativity.[21] At least it makes God the indispensable primary initiator of every new entity, the One without whom the universe would not be.

Why could this not be a somewhat new but still orthodox interpretation of the biblical datum of creation? If it meant that giving the initial subjective aim to each new actual entity includes giving the dynamic thrust or energy to pursue this goal, we might have a more acceptable interpretation. In this case the self-creativity of the created actual occasion would consist only in how it would *use* the creative energy given it by God to integrate in its own novel way the environment presented it to pursue its subjective aim. But if it meant that God gave only the formal determination of the subjective aim and its drawing power as a final cause or good, but not the actual energy to pursue it, we would still be faced with the emergence out of nothing of the entity's actuality or actual power.

There is, however, another, much more promising line of approach now being advanced by a number of younger Neo-Whiteheadian Christian philosophers and theologians, who propose that there is a positive overflow, an actual causal influx, both from God and from the neighboring perishing actual entities, by which the living current of creativity is passed on before or just as the immediately preceding actual entities pass away. To back this up, appeal is made to Whitehead's too little exploited terms such as "transitional creativity," "transference of energy," and "transmission of energy." The "self-creativity" or *causa sui* aspect of the newly arising actual occasion so stressed by Whitehead is in fact limited to what it does with this influx of transitional creativity, how it selects subjectively its own ways of prehending its past. It is here that the transitional creativity, not yet fully subjectivized, passes into concrescent subjective creativity. When this phase is completed and turns into objectification, the concrescent creativity turns again into transitional creativity and is passed on to the next occasion, or rather actively evokes it.

Many of what we might call the more "classical" Whiteheadian interpreters insist that the denial of active causal influx from one actual entity to another is such a central piece in the Whiteheadian system that it cannot be given up without radically transforming the system into something else. Yet it seems to me—and to many others, including a growing number of Neo-Whiteheadians—that this is precisely one of the two or three weakest points in the whole Whiteheadian metaphysical system, that this is precisely where Whitehead must be adapted, expanded—transformed, if necessary. Dr. Suchocki seems to me entirely on the right track here. It is simply impossible to render intelligible a dynamic universe without a strong role being given to active causal influx—what an Aristotelian or Thomist would call "efficient causality." Perhaps all that Whitehead really meant, or should have meant, is that one actual entity does not actively determine the inner *part* or core of another actual entity that is the latter's own subjective dealing with the creative energy that has been actively given to it by another. This would not preclude, indeed would require, a genuine active influx into the first phase of the new entity—not merely a presentation of form and lure to the good—and from something actually present, not past. A similar interpretation, stressing the transition from the perishing universe to the newly concrescing actual entities as an active energy evoking the first phase of the new, has been brilliantly presented by Jorge Nobo.[22]

Divine Infinity

The second point of tension between the Whiteheadian process concept and the traditional Christian conception of God is the question of divine infinity. Is the divine perfection truly infinite, and in what respects? As far as the traditional Christian position is concerned, the doctrine of the positive infinity of the divine perfection has been solidly established and universally recognized since at least the fourth century. The term "infinite" itself occurs nowhere explicitly in the Scriptures or in the very early church fathers, since it had not yet worked its way into either ordinary or philosophical vocabulary as a positive concept. In classical Greek thought, including both Plato and Aristotle, perfection was habitually identified with the finished, the well-defined or determinate—i.e., the finite or limited—typified by intelligible form. The infinite was identified with the indeterminate, the unfinished, the chaotic, the unintelligible, typified by unformed matter. Even the linguistic term in Greek for perfection came from the limit, end (*teleios*, "perfect," from *telos*, "end" or "limit"). It is only with Plotinus and Neo-Platonism, as foreshadowed by Philo Judaeus, that the notion of a positive infinity, indicating an excess of perfection *above* all form and not below it, is finally worked out with clear conceptual and metaphysical precision.[23] The first Greek fathers trained in the Neo-Platonic schools at once took it over as the only adequate expression of their belief, and from then on it became the common doctrine of all

Christians. It was finally, solemnly defined in the First Vatican Council (1869-1870) that God is "infinite in intellect and will and in every perfection."[24]

When we turn to the Whiteheadian God, we must first distinguish between the primordial nature of God, as He is in Himself independently of His relations with the created world, and the consequent nature of God, as He is in terms of the mutual ongoing interchange between Himself and the world. Most of our trouble will concern the primordial nature of God. The finitude of the consequent nature of God can, I think, be given both sufficiently orthodox and metaphysically acceptable interpretation, though the language would certainly not be Thomistic. As regards the primordial nature, we shall follow mostly the interpretation of Lewis Ford.[25]

The primordial nature of God, Whitehead says, is infinite. But when the concept is pressed hard, what it finally seems to come down to is only an infinity by extrinsic denomination—i.e., in terms of the *infinite number* of all intelligible possibilities, each of which is of course finite in itself, which the divine mind thinks up in a single act of primordial envisagement from all eternity. The infinity lies thus on the side of the products of the divine mind, and even here only in their number. But nothing seems to be said of any *intrinsic* infinite fullness of perfection within God's own being in itself. In fact, the primordial nature in itself is said by Whitehead to be "deficient in actuality and unconscious." The reason is that for him all actuality involves a definite, determinate decision, finished off and completed; hence all actuality as such is finite. Whitehead still remains here under the domination of the ancient Platonic notion of the finite as the finished, the perfect—already decisively surpassed by Plotinus. The primordial nature is also "unconscious," because the special meaning of consciousness for Whitehead involves the actual prehending of another actuality. God thus becomes properly conscious only by His actual interchange with the world. It seems, then, that the entire satisfaction and conscious fulfillment of God is an *extroverted* one, absorbed entirely in guiding the world toward intelligibility and value and in treasuring up within Himself the values actually achieved by it in an endlessly ongoing process of mutual enrichment. Here we have a world-dependent God as well as a God-dependent world. And since God is not seen as the actual fullness of all perfection, which He communicates as ultimate source to all creatures in varying degrees of participation, His enrichment in the actual order by what He receives from the world is to be taken in a literal and quite strong sense.

If we leave this conception of God undeveloped, as stated above, it is clear that there is quite a gap between it and the traditional Christian theological and metaphysical one of an infinite fullness of God's own intrinsic perfection, of His own inner self-conscious life, quite independently of the world, which He then shares graciously and freely with the world out of the superabundance of His own goodness. Here is where the Christian theological notion of God as Trinity of Persons takes on sharp philosophical relevance. For it illumines how God's own inner life is already rich in infinite self-expression by the Father's total gift of His own being to the Son and the procession of the Holy Spirit from both as their mutual act of love. It is then quite freely—although one might well say inevitably, according to the natural "logic" of love—without any need or desire for further self-enrichment, but purely out of the joy of giving, that this divine inner life can pour over to share itself with creatures.[26] However, if we admit the creative expansion of the Whiteheadian notion of God to make room for a doctrine of creation as suggested above, I see no insuperable reason why the richness of the traditional notion of the divine infinity cannot also be poured into the admittedly undeveloped Whiteheadian conception of the primordial nature of God. But in order to pull this off successfully, a theory of participation would have to be injected into Whiteheadian metaphysics, according to which the unlimited fullness of an ultimate source is shared diversely in limited degrees by varying finite participants. The apparent absence of such a doctrine casts a puzzling ambiguity over the world of the Whiteheadian metaphysics of God in relation to the world.

With respect to the finitude of the *consequent nature* of God and its constant ongoing enrichment by the response and value-achievements of the world, I would like to treat it in the following section, since it is inseparable from the question of the divine relativity and mutability.

God's Real Relatedness to the World, Mutability, and Enrichment by the World

In this section I shall deal with the questions of God's relatedness to the world, His mutability, and the resulting finitude of His "consequent nature" (according to Whitehead), since all three are inextricably linked. What I shall say is a follow-up of my previous paper, "A New Look at the Immutability of God," published in 1972.[27] Continued reflection and discussion with process thinkers on these problems have led me to a significant rethinking of some of my positions there and a notable emendation of one of them in particular—namely, the real relatedness of God to the world.

There is no doubt that the primary positive contribution of process thinkers to the philosophical elucidation of the Christian (and any personalist) conception of God has been their notion of God as profoundly involved in and personally responsive to the ongoing events of His creation, in particular to the conscious life of created persons as expressed in the mutability, the mutual giving and receiving, proper to interpersonal relations. All metaphysical explanations must make room for these exigencies in any form of personalist theism. From this Whitehead drew three main consequences: (1) God is *really related* to the world, especially to persons; (2) since what happens in the world makes a real difference to the conscious life of God (for Whitehead, His consequent nature) and since He is constantly experiencing new joy from the growth of value in the world and the personal loving response of His creatures (as well as new compassion for its dis-values) and newly responding to this, God is constantly changing *in time* as the world goes on; (3) because of this, *His consequent nature is finite in perfection.* As Hartshorne puts it, at any one moment God is the supremely perfect Being, surpassed by no other, yet constantly surpassing Himself as He both gives and receives more from the world. God is *truly enriched* by the genuine novelty of the ongoing world.

These three conclusions run into headlong opposition to the traditional Thomistic position that there are no real relations on the part of God toward the world (though there are, of course, on the part of the world toward God, because of its dependence on Him); that God is totally immutable, and not finite in any way in his real perfection or being. In my earlier article, I tried to mitigate this opposition by distinguishing between two orders in God: the order of *real being* (*esse naturale*)—i.e., His own intrinsic, real perfection, which remains always an Infinite Plenitude—and the order of *intentional being* (*esse intentionale*)—i.e., the contents of the divine field of consciousness as related to creatures. With respect to the latter—even for St. Thomas, as I tried to show—God's consciousness is certainly contingently *different* in content (in the order of both knowledge and love), corresponding to His decision to create this world rather than that, and also corresponding to what actually happens contingently in the created world, especially the free responses of rational creatures. Thus the world clearly makes a highly significant difference to the conscious, hence personal life of God. And since the divine consciousness as knowing and loving is truly related, by distinct and determinate relations in the intentional order, to creatures—relations based on His distinct ideas of them—it follows, even for St. Thomas, that it is both correct and necessary to say that God is *truly personally* related to the world. Relations in the intentional order are not simply nothing; they are true and authentic relations. But it is also true that in his strict technical terminology and theoretical framework such relations cannot be called "real relations," since all "real" relations for him require as their foundations some change or difference in the real intrinsic ("absolute") being of the subject related—which would not be compatible with the divine infinity, allowing, as it does, for no increase or diminution of its intrinsic plenitude of real perfection. Thus, for St. Thomas, the *difference* in the divine consciousness as intentionally related to creatures does not thereby entail any *change* in the divine consciousness, let alone the intrinsic real being of God. For these relations are not first absent at one moment of time and later present at another, but simply present without change in the eternal Now of God present to all points of time. This eternal Now is itself outside the flow of our motion-dependent time, but present in its own unique time-transcending way to all points of time without internal succession in God. Difference (*this* rather than *that*) does not logically imply *change* (this *after* that).

God as Really Related to the World

I would now like to make a significant emendation in the above position, with respect to the lack of real relations between God and the world. On the one hand, I think it is still theoretically possible to defend this position, understood in its strict technical sense as found in St. Thomas. Yet the price of doing so has become so high, and the returns so diminishing, that I think it is wiser strategy for Thomistic metaphysicians today to shift frameworks and simply drop this doctrine. The reason is that the doctrine is in itself so highly technical and narrow in the meaning it allows to "real relations"—a much narrower meaning than the one intuitively held by most people (including philosophers) today—and leaves so much else that is important *unsaid* as a result, that it is simply too difficult to explain convincingly to most people. The effort is no longer worth the increasingly meager returns. To tell people that God is "truly personally related" to the world but still "not really related," that the tremendously important personal relations of God's love toward us and joy in our responses are not "real," strikes them at first blush as so counterintuitive, so in conflict with the surface meaning of religious language and the language of revelation, that they are simply not disposed to make the austere effort to enter into a difficult technical doctrine that opens such a chasm between technical and ordinary language, between the assertions of metaphysics and those of religious devotion. Metaphysical discourse is not a timeless essence but an ongoing, historically rooted process; and when the metaphysician realizes he has reached a certain threshold of diminishing returns in the rhetorical effectiveness of his discourse, he should be ready to cut his losses and shift to a new, more effective conceptual-linguistic framework.

I think this point has now been reached for the Thomistic doctrine that "God is not really related to the world." I am willing to go on record as saying that it should be quietly dropped, and that we should without hesitation say that "God is really and truly related to the world in the order of His personal consciousness." For the consolation of those Thomists who are not willing to make such a "framework-decision," it should be noted that this does not mean that the older doctrine is thereby declared false, *as understood in its own context* or framework. It is simply to declare that this context is now judged too narrow and restrictive to do justice to the problem for our time and that a new, much broader and looser meaning of "real relation" now serves the purpose more effectively. This move also involves a shift in the primary, often unconsciously governing *models* from which to draw metaphysical concepts: a shift from the physical and biological world, which was the prime analogate of metaphysical concepts for Aristotle and St. Thomas following him (though significant expansion has already begun in the later, to the order of the person and interpersonal relations as the prime analogates for such concepts for the contemporary Western metaphysician).[28]

Once one has conceded that God can and should be said to be really related to the world, there follows at once what Hartshorne has felicitiously called the "surrelativity" of God: If God is related at all, then He must be the *most related* of all beings, related to absolutely everything without exception. I might add that when I recently told Professor Hartshorne in private conversation of my shift in position on the real relatedness of God to the world, he was delighted, and added that this he considers to be the single greatest obstacle blocking further dialogue with Thomists, that with this long-closed door open a new chapter of fruitful discussion was possible. I now wish formally to open this door.

Does this real relatedness of God to the world imply that God is "affected" by what happens in the world, in particular by the response of love of created persons, so that the personal relation of love between God and man can properly be called a mutual relation, with not only giving but receiving on *both* sides? This is one of the points that process thinkers insist on most strongly, as alone being able to do justice to the implications of Christian (or any personalist) religious language and to the very nature of interpersonal relations as we understand them more reflectively today.

I would answer—in my stance as "creative Neo-Thomist" (or if you prefer, as I do, "Thomistically inspired metaphysician")—that our metaphysics of God must certainly allow us to say that in some real and genuine way God is affected positively by what we do, that He receives love from us and experiences joy *precisely because* of our responses. In a word, His consciousness is contingently and qualitatively *different* because of what we do.[29] All this difference remains, however, on the level of God's *relational consciousness* and therefore does not involve increase or decrease in the Infinite Plenitude of God's *intrinsic inner being* and perfection—what

St. Thomas would call the "absolute" (non-relative) aspect of His perfection. God does not become a more or less perfect being because of the love we return to Him and the joy He experiences thereat (or its absence).

The mutual giving and receiving that is part of God's relational consciousness as knowing and loving what is other than Himself is merely the *appropriate expression* or living out of the intrinsic perfection proper to a perfect, hence perfectly loving *personal being*, the expression of the kind of being He already is. To receive love as a person, as we better understand the unique logic of interpersonal relations today, is not at all an imperfection, but precisely a dimension of the *perfection of personal being* as lovingly responsive. What remains fixed as the constant point of reference in our concept of God is *Infinite Perfection*. But just what such perfection in fact entails, especially when applied to God as personal, is something that can slowly evolve, even change, in *our* consciousness—as the latter itself slowly evolves and deepens in both experience and understanding. Our concept of God is bound to be open to partial evolution as our own understanding evolves as to what it means to be a person, drawn from reflection on our own experience of what it means to be a *human* person, both in relation to other human persons and to God.

Following up on this point, let me make a further concession to my Whiteheadian friends. It has long been a special claim made by Lewis Ford and other Whiteheadians that in the Whiteheadian conception of God, He is not just the supreme *Cause* of the world, but equally if not more so the supreme *Effect*, in the sense of being the supreme Receiver from all things that exist, more than any other being. This is not an imperfection but one of His supreme perfections.

Such language is certainly quite foreign to Thomistic and other traditional ways of speaking about God, and would seem, understood in *their* sense, to imply the direct negation of the divine infinity. But understanding what is being said in terms of what we have just conceded above—that God in His consciousness can be said to be different and so affected because of whatever creatures do—we can indeed say (and I am willing to do so) that God is the *supreme Receiver*, gathering together in His consiousness all that creatures do and responding appropriately to it. This is indeed part of His supreme perfection. I would prefer the term "Receiver," however, to "Effect," since the language of strict efficient causality, as though creatures acted physically on God, does not seem appropriate or needed here (how would a worm act physically on God as pure Spirit?), as we will show later in attempting to explain how God knows the acts of creatures—i.e., by acting along with them, not by being acted on by them.

God as Changing in Time

Does this mean, then, that God undergoes change—is mutable, properly speaking? Does contingent difference in God's relational consciousness necessarily imply change—i.e., temporally successive states in that consciousness? Process thinkers insist on this as one of the key innovations in their concept of God as compared with the traditional Thomistic one, and as necessarily following from the admission that God is really related to the changing world and positively affected by what happens in it.

My answer here is two-fold. First, it is not at all clear that contingent *difference* in the divine relational consciousness of the world necessarily involves *temporally successive* states *in God*. I have the impression that process thinkers tend to move too quickly here, and take for granted without sufficient exploration of other hypotheses, that the only way to register in consciousness differences deriving from a changing world is by being immersed in the same kind of time-flow. I do not see how they have ruled out the possibility that the divine consciousness is present to the contingent changing world in a mode of presence that transcends our time-succession.[30] Just because we cannot *imagine* what it would be like to know thus is not a reason why it cannot be *thought* and affirmed for metaphysical reasons.

Our kind of time-succession is based principally on the *continuous physical motion* going on in our world and in ourselves which serves as a point of reference for asserting change, a continuous flow of *before* and *after*, subject in principle to measurement. It is therefore based not principally on the pure succession of contents of consciousness, of "intentional being," but in changes in our underlying real, physical, and psychic being. In God, however, there is only the succession in the order of relational consciousness, of intentional being, without any "moving around" or physical motion inside His own intrinsic being. What kind of time would be generated by such a pure flow of consciousness in an otherwise motionless being? We have no clear idea and should be more willing than process thinkers seem to be to leave this as a mystery, not prematurely closing off any metaphysical options.

I have the distinct impression that the process thinkers I know have never clearly grasped the extremely austere and metaphysically spare meaning of the eternal Now of God's presence to all time-events as proposed by St. Thomas.[31] They tend to conceive of the divine eternal Now as some kind of continuously ongoing time-flow, existing long before—and perhaps after—the present and responding to it *from* all eternity—i.e., long before it happened. Such a concept would indeed be open to the severe criticism advanced by process thought. But a Thomist would rather say that God knows and responds to the world not *from* all eternity, but in His eternal Now, simply present to each event as it actually takes place. The key point usually overlooked is that our "nows" *exclude* each other, whereas the divine Now *includes* all others. Hence an equivocation or category mistake is always involved if we attempt to answer questions such as this: "Does God know *now* (i.e., at 10:00 a.m., August 3, 1978) what will happen on August 3, 1980?" The proper answer should be either "no," or "The question is meaningless, or at least badly put." What we can and should say is simply this: "God *knows* what happens on September 5, 1980 as it happens." But *no time adverb at all*, none of our "nows" or "thens," can be applied to situate His knowledge anywhere in *our* time-sequence. The relationship between his Now and our nows is not expressible in any of our "nows" or time-language. The "No" answer would also be appropriate, since any of our nows *excludes* a future one; hence even God could not know in *one* now *another* now excluded by the first!

It follows in St. Thomas's austere logic of the divine eternity, as pure Presence to that which is, that all questions about divine *foreknowledge, predestination*, and so forth are, properly speaking, false problems, misplaced questions if taken to refer to temporal priority in God. The *mode* of the divine presence is left entirely mysterious. In other words, it is impossible for us ever to *say* in our language *when* God knows anything. Any translation from the all-inclusive Now of God into any of our exclusive "nows" or "whens" is irremediably equivocal. God simply *knows*—period! The consistent overlooking of this key point of the logic of Thomistic God-language by process thinkers seems to me to vitiate most of their objections to this part of the Thomistic doctrine of God. To see the point can lead to a sudden metaphysical illumination of the Wittgensteinian type: "Whereof one cannot speak, thereof one must be silent."

Granted all the above, that a nontemporal view of the divine relational consciousness is *one* viable metaphysical option which we should be willing at least to tolerate, let me now go on to say that I think it is also possible to adopt a version of the process view of God as changing, as an orthodox Christian view—though not a traditional one—and one acceptable even to a creative Neo-Thomist like myself. Change is repugnant in God only if it involves some imperfection in God's real being, some lack of perfection in God's inner plenitude. But if change is restricted to the rational dimension of God's consciousness, we can rethink the concept of change so that it is seen to involve no imperfection at all. The giving and receiving in a mutual relation of interpersonal love is not an imperfection for a person, but an integral part of the very perfection proper to a person, as we understand this theoretically today so much more fully than the Greeks. Hence it is quite possible, it seems to me—without compromising any really essential Thomistic principles—simply to give up the whole, so often sterile, battle over change in God and simply say that some kinds of both mutability and immutability are appropriate to a perfect person and some are not.[32]

What must certainly be held onto, however, is that God's "time," if one wishes to use the expression, is of an incomprehensibly different modality than ours. It is important for process thinkers to add this qualification in order to avoid getting caught in the serious paradoxes they have been charged with because of the implications of the Einstein relativity theory of time—which to my mind they have not yet adequately addressed.[33] For if, according to Einstein, there is no one time-framework for the whole cosmos—there is no one "now" for the whole cosmos at once, but many different "nows," according to one's perspective from within the physical system—

then which time-framework is God in? If one says that He is present to each thing or even in its own immediate time-framework, then how does He coordinate them all into a unity of consciousness, as He must clearly do? Would not such a coordination be precisely in some sense a knowledge *transcending* at least all forms of our time, since the latter by nature simply cannot be synthesized in its own terms but is intrinsically and irremediably multiple? The recent date of the last quantum mechanics and of parapsychology—controversial as such data still is—plus the fascinating new hypotheses now being put forward to explain them, should also give pause to any facile application of time-sequence to God.[34] As Karl Pribram the brain researcher, David Bohm the physicist, and others are suggesting, there may be two faces to the universe, one of the "explicate" face spread out in space and time, the other its "implicate" face—all together in an interior unity all at once, in the mode of a hologram transformation into a nonspatial, nontemporal frequency code—and it is possible for the human psyche under special conditions to penetrate into this inner dimension momentarily and experience telepathy, precognition, and the rest. If this is so, then why should we be surprised that an infinite pure Spirit such as God could do all the time what even the human psyche can do occasionally? There may be far more surprises hidden in the depths of our human world, not to speak of the divine world, than have yet been dreamed of by our philosophies.

In conclusion, let us leave *both options* open for describing the relational consciousness of God: either as a time-transcending eternal Now of pure presence, or as involved in His own unique mode of time-succession correlated with ours.

God's Way of Knowing

I have thus made two important concessions to my many respected friends among process thinkers: (1) it is *better* to say that God is really related to the world in the order of His intentional consciousness; (2) one *can* say that God changes in a certain sense in His relational, world-oriented consciousness. I must now add an important codicil: that this does not prejudice the *way* God receives knowledge, joy, and love from his creatures. It does not follow that the way God knows and receives from creatures is by being acted upon physically by them. It is not clear that this even makes any sense in the case of material beings acting on a pure Spirit. The explanation of the way God knows what is done by creatures as I outlined it in the previous pages still, I believe, holds good. It is that God is constantly working in and through us with His supportive and collaborative power, supporting both the being and action of every creature. But He allows this power to be determinately channeled by the respective natures, especially the free-will decisions of creatures. Thus God knows what we are doing by how we allow His power, in itself indeterminate, to flow through us; by how we determinately channel this flow of power, according to our own free initiatives. Thus He knows not by being acted on, but through His own action in us. He knows what we are doing by *doing with us* whatever we are doing, except that it is we who supply the determinations to specify the in-itself-transcendent (and thus indeterminate) fullness of His power. To receive these determinations from creatures is not to be acted upon by them in any proper sense, though the result is determinate new knowledge in the divine consciousness.[35]

God as Finite

We come now to a more difficult question. Does my admission of real relatedness in God toward the world, even change in His relational consciousness, imply that God is truly *growing, increasing* in the sum of His perfection and thus in some significant way *finite* in his perfection at any one moment—finite in His "consequent nature," not His "primordial nature," as Whitehead would put it? Since for Whitehead all actuality must be determinate, and all determination implies limit and finitude, must we then say that the actuality of God is, as actuality, finite (the infinite primordial nature remains for Him, as noted earlier, still partly indeterminate, "unconscious," hence not fully actual); or, to use Charles Hartshorne's felicitous expression, that God's perfection is *unsurpassed by any other* at any given moment, but *constantly surpassing itself*—really growing, increasing, but ever finite?

My answer must be complex. First, I think it can be admitted that the divine *relational consciousness*, precisely in its content of *intentional being* (*esse intentionale*) *as related to the world*, can be called finite and, if you wish, growing. Here I agree with one of the basic

demands of Lewis Ford in his remarkable article on my position—
namely, that in a personalist interpretation of infinite perfection we
must say that the infinite, remaining infinite, can still be "enriched"
by the finite.[36] The old correlation, *infinite = no enrichment whatsoever*, is too simplistic and not suited to the unique characteristics
of personal being as truly loving. This is paradoxical, but, as I shall
try to show, not contradictory.

I still insist, as I did in my earlier paper, that all such "novelty"
and "enrichment" in God (new joy and so forth), authentically new
as they are, can only be new *determinate modalities of expression*
of the already infinite intensity of actual interior joy in God, and
hence can never rise higher in qualitative intensity of perfection than
the already infinite source of which all finite modalities are only
limited participations. In this sense, and in this sense only, it is
impossible to add to or enrich the infinite, in the sense of raising
the infinite to a *qualitatively higher level of intensity* of perfection
than it had before. In this sense, too, it could be said (to do justice
to Aristotle and St. Thomas) that therefore there is no real "change"
in God, though such statements can be misleading by saying too little.

But the important point for our present discussion is that a refined
concept of "infinite Person" (or "personal being," to allow for the
Trinity of Persons in the Christian concept of God) not only does
not exclude but in fact invites an immense flowering of true novelty
and enrichment, within the *relational field* of the divine consciousness, in the form of *new determinate modalities* of the already
infinite, hence indeterminate (= *beyond all determinations as limits*)
intensity of the interior divine perfection. The infinite, contrary to
an all too common misunderstanding, does not exclude all other
being than itself, as though it were a single motionless block already
including in itself actually all possible real being. It excludes not other
beings but only a *higher level* of being, of intensive qualitative perfection, than itself. In the old Scholastic terminology this was expressed
in the classic adage that after creation there are *plura entia, non plus
entis*—i.e., *numerically* more beings, but not more (a *qualitatively*
higher level) of *being* itself (the perfection of being). Such is the logic
of the infinite.

One of the main objections Lewis Ford raises against the Thomistic
and my own position is phrased in terms of his sharp opposition

of "two logics" in speaking about God: the *logic of enrichment*, which he and Whitehead defend and according to which the infinite can be enriched by genuine finite novelty, and the *logic of delimitation* which St. Thomas and I are supposed to be committed to, according to which anything new is only delimitation, hence a partial negation of what is already in God, hence *not really new at all*. The terminology is neat and partially illuminating, because it sharpens up the issues beautifully. But it is too neat. My logic of delimitation allows for genuine finite novelty and enrichment, in God as well as in the world, but not one that is *higher* than the original Source. The enrichment is distinctly *new*, has never existed before in actuality, but is not higher than what existed before.

This is the key point that Ford has missed, and I admit that it is not easy to catch hold of until one has really penetrated the logic of *participation metaphysics*, the lack of which seems to me such a serious gap in Whitehead. Ford's conception of God as infinite actuality seems to be that it excludes all genuine novelty, that it must include *all possible determinate actualities already in act within it*.[37] In such a case, of course, there could indeed be no genuine novelty. But the actual infinity of a Source in participation metaphysics is precisely an indeterminate plenitude—i.e., beyond all forms or determinations; indeterminacy by *excess* rather than defect, as is the case with the indeterminacy of matter—and hence does *not* contain in an actual state of real being any finite determinations or entities at all. When it is said to contain "all being" or "all perfection" within it, this means only a *qualitative intensity* of perfection that contains *equivalency* in a higher and quite different though analogous way at least as much and more comparative perfection as in any possible finite.

Thus God's infinite love contains all the intensive perfection of loving, and far more than in any finite love. But it does not mean that it already contains actually the unique new determinate *existential* mode of every finite love. It does not. Such, when created—and known by God—are definitely *new* limited editions, participating modalities, of the Primal Perfection, hitherto unpublished in the history of reality. God welcomes them and rejoices in them precisely because they are genuinely new, unique, and (especially if personal) irreplaceable expressions of His own infinite but in itself formless ocean of perfection—just as it gives joy to a father to see his son growing in a new personal sharing of the knowledge the father already has. It is part of the ancient logic of the Platonic Good—transformed by Christian personalism into love—that God is "by nature" self-diffusive and takes delight in sharing his goodness with *genuinely new existential* participants. When a new finite self comes into being and enters into loving dialogue with the infinite Self (or Selves) of God, there is genuine novelty and enrichment both in the total horizon of being and within the relational consciousness of God ("it is better for this to be than not"), but without raising God to a *higher level* of perfection. In sum, I accept Ford's "logic of enrichment." But my "logic of delimitation" is not in opposition to it; it is intrinsically complementary to it.

We have admitted that God can be affected by new modalities of joy resulting from our responses to Him. This immediately raises the correlative question whether God can also be affected by sorrow or suffering because of what happens among us. This is indeed a difficult and delicate question, involving a profoundly mysterious dimension of the divine life. However, I think we must have the courage to be consistent, and should therefore admit in the divine consciousness something corresponding to what we would call compassion (suffering-with-us, wounded love, etc.) but purified of all that would be genuine imperfection (whatever this might be in this case; we must be careful not to judge too quickly what would be imperfection in compassion or even sorrow). Thus for God to be compassionate would not entail that He is also thereby unhappy. This is true even among highly developed human persons, although to explain how the two can be coexistent is a psychological mystery difficult if not impossible to express, though it can certainly be lived.

I myself have been very cautious in venturing into this area, since I did not see my way clear to unravelling the paradoxes. But I am happy to say that the issue has been taken up very competently recently and this position persuasively defended by a well-known Catholic theologian, Jean Galot, S. J., of the Gregorian University of Rome. Father Galot bases his stand on exactly the same distinction that I have used, between the relational dimension of the divine consciousness and God's intrinsic absolute perfection, though he has followed its implications farther than I have hitherto dared to do.[38]

Conclusion

In sum, I have made important concessions to process thinkers in regard to the core of their valuable contribution to religious-metaphysical thought and language about God: that God can be said in some significant though carefully qualified way to be both (1) *really related* to the world in His intentional consciousness and (2) contingently *different*, even *mutable* (though not necessarily so, since the "eternal Now" view of God is still viable), *because of* what happens in the created world (hence truly affected, *enriched* by new modalities of joy due to our responses)—but all this only in His relational, intentional consciousness.

I have insisted, on the other hand, that process thought both can and should adapt to assimilate the notion (1) an *active causal influx* of God on all finite actual entities, such as He can radically constitute their whole initial being in a first radical beginning needing any independent primordial multiplicity to work on—in a word, a truly creative God from whom all creativity and other perfections flow as from a single ultimate unitary Source, so to be freely shared by loving participation with creatures, which then truly have their own intrinsic (though received) power to exercise by their own initiative (this implies the radical and absolute priority of the One over the many, though not the swallowing up of the many in the One); and (2) the *actual infinity of the intrinsic reality* of God, already present in His own inner life—made specific by the Christian doctrine of the Trinity of Persons within the divine nature—and not an infinity merely potential or by extrinsic denomination resulting only from thinking up an *infinite number of finite* possibilities. This actual divine infinity can indeed be enriched by creatures in the order of determinate modalities of intentional consciousness, but can never be raised to a higher qualitative level of intensity than the original Source.

May new light flow in both directions through this sincerely and hopefully opened door!

NOTES

* This paper has been excerpted by Prof. Clarke from a fuller version which appears in his *Philosophical Approach To God: A Contemporary Neo-Thomist Perspective* (Winston-Salem: Wake Forest University Publications, 1979).

Process Theology

1. This chapter is a follow-up to my previous essay, both broadening its scope and taking into account some recent developments in process philosophy. Cf. "A New Look at the Immutability of God," in Robert Roth, ed., *God Knowable and Unknowable* (New York: Fordham University, 1973), pp. 43-72.

2. Cf. Robert Mellert, *What Is Process Theology?* (New York: Paulist, 1975); Ewert Cousins, ed., *Process Theology* (New York: Paulist, 1971); David Brown, Richard James, and Gene Reeves, eds., *Process Philosophy And Christian Thought* (Indianapolis: Bobbs-Merrill, 1971).

3. Cf. the excellent historical survey by Gene Reeves in the collection cited in footnote 2.

4. Cf. the various essays in the collections cited in footnote 2. See also the standard studies such as Ivor Leclerc, *Whitehead's Metaphysics* (Bloomington: Indiana University, 1958); William Christian, *An Interpretation Of Whitehead's Metaphysics* (New Haven: Yale University, 1959). To me the fullest and most enlightening discussion of creation in Whitehead is Kenneth Thompson's *Whitehead's Philosophy of Religion* (Hague: Mouton, 1971), chapter 4, where the author defends Whitehead as far as possible, while objectively pointing out lacunae.

5. See Alfred North Whitehead, *Process and Reality* (New York: Harper and Row, 1960) pp. 146-147, 519, 343-344.

6. Alfred North Whitehead, *Science and the Modern World* (New York: Macmillan, 1926), p. 258.

7. Whitehead, *Adventures in Ideas* (New York: Macmillan, 1933), p. 215.

8. Whitehead, *Process and Reality*, p. 339.

9. Lewis Ford, "The Immutable God and Fr. Clarke," *New Scholasticism*, 49 (1975), p. 191.

10. Lewis Ford, "Can Freedom Be Created?", *Horizons*, 4 (1977), pp. 183-188.

11. Rouet de Journal, *Enchiridion Patristicum*, twenty-first ed., (Rome: Herder, 1951), at the *Index Theologicus*. Number 783, for some thirty-eight references on *creatio ex nihilo* and the non-eternity of the world and matter.

12. Theophilus of Antioch, *Ad Autolycum*, 2, 4 (*Patrologia Graeca, VI,* 1029; Rouet de Journal, number 178). Cf. also Irenaeus, *Adversus Haereses*. I, 22, 1 (*Patrologia Graeca, VII,* 669; Rouet de Journel, Number 194): "We hold the rule of truth, i.e., that there is one omnipotent God who constituted all things through the Word and made them out of what was not." Also the very early text of *Hermas Pastor*. Mandatum 1, 1, (*Patrologia Graeca,* 11, 913; Rouet de Journel, Number 85): "First of all believe that there is one God, who made all things from nothing into being (*ek tou me ontos eis to einai*)." Nothing could be clearer than the later text of St. Augustine, *De Genesi Contra Manichaeos*, 1, 6, 10 (*Patrologia Latina,* XXXIV, 178; Rouet de Journel, Number 1540): "God is rightly believed to have made all things from nothing, because although all things formed have been made out of matter, this matter itself has been made entirely out of nothing (*de nihilo omnino*). . . . For we should not be like those who do not believe that the omnipotent God could have made anything out of nothing since they consider that artisans and other workers cannot fabricate anything unless they have something from which to make it."

13. *The Church Teaches: Documents of the Church* (St. Louis: Herder, 1955), p. 146.

14. E. G., the Council of Florence (*The Church Teaches*, 148) and the First Vatican Council (*The Church Teaches*, 152). For a similar Protestant Christian View, see Langdon Gilkey, *Maker of Heaven and Earth* (New York: Doubleday, 1965), 42-43: "Almost the entire Christian tradition is in substantial agreement that God brought the finite world into being out of nothing by a 'purposeful' act of His free will."

15. Cf. Edward Pols, *Whitehead's Metaphysics: A Critical Assessment* (Carbondale: Southern Illinois University, 1967), p. 131.

16. Cf. David Schindler, "Creativity as Ultimate: Reflections on Actuality in Whitehead, Aquinas, Aristotle," *International Philosophy Quarterly*, 13 (1973), 161-171; and "Whitehead's Challenge to Thomism on the Problem of God: The Metaphysical Issues," *International Philosophical Quarterly*, 19 (1979). The point of the latter article is that for St. Thomas the ultimate common attribute that unites all things, the act of existence (*esse*), is grounded in one actual, concrete source (God), in which it is found subsistent in all its purity and plenitude and from which it flows by participation to all other instances, whereas for Whitehead the ultimate unifying property, creativity, is never found condensed and concretized in one ultimate source, but remains always radically multiple, dispersed among many. See also the important article of Robert Neville, "Whitehead on the One and the Many," *Southern Journal of Philosophy*, 7 (1969-1970), pp. 387-393.

17. Whitehead, *Process and Reality*, p. 392: "God does not create eternal objects; for his nature requires them in the same degree that they require him. . . .This is an exemplification of the coherence of the categoreal types of existence" Cf. Leclerc, *Whitehead's Metaphysics*, 199; cf. also Kenneth Thompson, *Whitehead's Philosophy of Religion*, 127: "God does not bring creativity into being. . . .Neither does God bring pure possibilities into being. Pure possibilities are named 'eternal objects' precisely because they are uncreated."

18. *On the Power of God*, Queston 3, Article 5, cf. *Summa Theologiae*, Part I, Question 44, Article 1, Part 1, Question 65, Article 1.

19. Lewis Ford, loc. cit., in footnote 9.

20. Cf. Gene Reeves and David Brown, "The Historical Development of Process Theology," chapter 2 in *Process Philosophy and Christian Thought*, op. cit., in footnote 2.

21. Cf. John Cobb, *A Christian Natural Theology* (Philadelphia: Westminster, 1965). See also the careful discussion in chapter 4 of Kenneth Thompson's *Whitehead's Philosophy of Religion*.

22. See his article, "Transition in Whitehead: A Creative Process Distinct from Concrescence," *International Philosophical Quarterly*, 19 (1979), 265-285. See also Nancy Frankenberry, "The Power of the Past," *Process Studies*, 13 (1983), pp. 132-142.

23. For a brief history, see my article, "The Limitation of Act by Potency in St. Thomas: Aristotelianism or Neoplatonism?" *New Scholasticism*, 26 (1952), 167-194; also "Infinity in Plotinus," *Gregorianum*, 40 (1959), 75-98.

24. *The Church Teaches*, 355.

25. See the important dialogue between Lewis Ford and William Hill, O. P., "In What Sense Is God Infinite?" *Thomist*, 42 (1978), pp. 1-27.

26. Ewert Cousins makes this point cogently in his "God as Dynamic in Bonaventure and Contemporary Thought," *Proceedings of the American Catholic Philosophical Association*, 48 (1974), 136-148. See also Anthony Kelly, "Trinity and Process: The Relevance of the Christian Confession," *Theological Studies*, 31 (1970). 383-414.

27. See footnote 1.

28. There has been a remarkable convergence among recent Thomists toward toning down St. Thomas's doctrine on the real relation between God and the world. Most do not go quite as far as I go here, but try to show how, while not denying the strict words of St. Thomas, one can loosen their interpretation and enrich his doctrine by saying much more than he does—for example, that God is "truly personally related" to the world. See Anthony Kelly, "God: How Near a Relation?" *Thomist*, 34 (1970), 191-229; William Hill, "Does the World Make a Difference to God?" *Thomist*, 38 (1974), pp. 148-164; idem, "Does God know the Future? Aquinas and Some Modern Theologians," *Theological Studies*, 36 (1975), pp. 3-18; idem, and the superb scholarly study of John Wright, "Divine Knowledge and Human Freedom: The God Who Dialogues," *Theological Studies*, 38 (1977), 450-477. See also his "The Historicity of God," ibid., 45 (1984), pp. 320-333.

29. Hence I formally reject Lewis Ford's interpretation of my position in "The Immutable God and Fr. Clarke," *New Scholasticism*, 49 (1975), 194, where he says, "First, it is clear that the contents of God's intentional consciousness are not derived from the external world." In my original essay, and again in this one, I assert exactly the opposite—namely, that God's knowledge of the actions of creatures, especially their free actions, is due to them, determined by them, hence derived from them. This occurs, however, not by their physically acting on God, but rather by His acting with them. This special mode of His knowing will be discussed presently.

30. See on this point the penetrating critique of Hartshorne by Merold Westphal, "Temporality and Finitude in Hartshorne's Theism," *Review of Metaphysics*, 19 (1966), 550-564, and the discussion of it in *Process Philosophy and Christian Thought*, op. cit., pp. 44-46.

31. Cf. John Wright, art. cit., in footnote 37.

32. After finishing this article my attention was called to a book by a distinguished German Catholic theologian on the mutability of God as background for a future Christology. The author develops the same point that the immutability attributed to God must be that proper to a perfect personal being—i.e., an immutable intention to love and save us, which intention then includes all the adaptations and responses necessary to carry this intention through in personal dialogue with us. Thus personal immutability includes relational mutability. See Herbert Muhlen, *Die Veranderlichkeit Gottes Als Horizont Einer Zukunftigen Christologie* (Munster: Aschendorff, 1969).

33. Paul Fitzgerald, "Relativity Physics and the God of Process Philosophy," *Process Studies*, 2 (1971), pp. 251-266.

34. Cf. Robert Anderson, "Quandaries of Mind, Brain, Cosmos," *International Philosophical Quarterly*, 18 (1978), pp. 215-222; and Lawrence Beynam, "The Emergent Paradigm of Science," *Revision*, 1 (1978), pp. 56-70.

35. Article cited in footnote 1, pp. 67-70, and the admirable textual study of St. Thomas by John Wright, article cited in footnote 37.

36. "The Immutable God and Fr. Clarke," art. cit., 193ff.

37. Cf. art. cit., 193: "The logic of delimitation seems to imply that all these determinations . . . are already fully present in the initial indeterminate abundance of power, and that all that has happened is the singling out of one for its appearance on the temporal stage of the world." See also 194: "For there can be no difference in content between God's intentional knowledge of the creature and His knowledge of the creature as part of His own infinite being. Since He always knows the creature as part of Himself, how can that intentional content in any way be new?" My answer is that between God's knowledge of a creature merely as a possible mode of imitation of His own essence and the knowledge of the same as actually existing and freely acting there is most certainly a dramatically new addition: precisely the real act of existence and the real action of the creature, which is not present at all in the knowledge of it as a possible.

38. See Jean Galot, S. J., "La realite de la souffrance de Dieu," *Nouvelle Revue Theologique*, 101 (1979), 224-244. In it he sums up the growing literature on the suffering of God and answers objections to his own book on the subject, *Dieu Souffre-f-il?* (Paris: Lethielleux, 1975).

Is God an Exception
to Whitehead's Metaphysics?

James Mannoia, Jr.

James Mannoia, Jr.

James Mannoia, Jr. is Associate Professor of Philosophy and Chairman of the Division of Humanities at Westmont College. Prior to going to Westmont, Dr. Mannoia taught at Grove City College. He received his B.S. degree in physics at the Massachusetts Institute of Technology and his M.A. and Ph.D. degrees in philosophy from Washington University in St. Louis. His published work includes a book, *What is Science: An Introduction to the Structure and Methodology of Science*, as well as articles and reviews in such journals as *Process Studies*, *Modern Schoolman*, and *Christian Scholars' Review*.

The attractiveness of the process metaphysics as a framework for Christian theology derives in large measure from its purportedly superior coherence over the metaphysics of "substance" in which theology is traditionally expressed. According to Whitehead, *coherence* means "that the fundamental ideas, in terms of which the scheme is developed, presuppose each other so that in isolation they are meaningless" (PR 3; cf. PR 9).* Coherence presupposes consistency, the lack of contradiction. Incoherence in a metaphysical system produces a corresponding incoherence in any theological doctrines expressed in terms of that metaphysic. Therefore it is important to ascertain if the process metaphysics is coherent *before* investigating its adequacy for expressing Christian doctrine. A fundamentally flawed, even internally contradictory, framework could *never* provide an acceptable foundational metaphysics for Christian theology. Questions of coherence are what I call *internal* questions and are more properly within the domain of the philosopher than the theologian.

Internal Versus External Questions

Most discussions of process theology do *not* focus on internal questions of coherence but on *external* questions of adequacy. The adequacy of a theory is the degree to which the theory can successfully explain the non-negotiable "givens" of experience. For example, a scientific theory which cannot explain or find room for certain everyday empirical observations is inadequate. For a Christian, there are certain non-negotiable "givens" of religious experience (doctrines) which must be accommodated by any metaphysical theory Christians might use to express their beliefs. These "givens" vary from theology to theology, and in some cases are open to widely differing interpretations. These differences in what are non-negotiable givens and what are not, together with disputes about whether process metaphysics can adequately accommodate certain givens, provide the grist for most debates about process theology.[1]

In this chapter we will focus on the *internal* question of metaphysical coherence. I will show that God is an exception to the requirements of Whitehead's own system (he calls these requirements his *categoreal scheme*) and that this makes the process metaphysics radically incoherent and therefore unsatisfactory as a basis for Christian theology.

Philosophical incoherence is fatal to any theory. To some persons, philosophical coherence is more important than theological adequacy, and for other persons theological adequacy is more precious than philosophical coherence. Ideally, a reasonable faith is both philosophically coherent and theologically adequate. In practice, however, inconsistencies in a metaphysical theory may make the theory seem theologically *more* adequate. Alternatively, a metaphysical theory's theological inadequacies may make it easier for the metaphysics to be philosophically coherent.[2] Therefore valid criticisms of the philosophical coherence of process metaphysics may actually be inconsistent with other valid criticisms of its theological adequacy. My criticisms of process metaphysics' philosophical incoherence and those of its theological adequacy in other chapters of this book cannot necessarily be used *together* to make a stronger case against process theology than either *alone* would afford.

In Defense of Process Metaphysics: Evidence for Its Coherence

There is considerable evidence to support the claim that process metaphysics is more coherent than the "substantival" and "dualistic" metaphysics that orthodox theology has traditionally employed.[3]

In a substantival metaphysics, the basic entities which are real are entities which endure through time; they are "things." In process metaphysics, however, the basic entities are "events" which do not so much occur and endure in time but instead actually define time by their succession.

In a dualistic, substantival metaphysics, the basic entities are of two fundamentally different kinds. These two kinds are usually called "mental" and "physical" to account adequately for what appear to be fundamentally different dimensions of reality. The views of Aristotle and Descartes are substantival and dualistic or pluralistic.

Both have significantly shaped the way in which traditional theology has been expressed and interpreted.

But within such metaphysics there are major dichotomies which the process metaphysics appears to remedy. A 'dichotomy' is a gap or separation between the fundamental concepts in the system. It is a gap which leaves them isolated and disconnected from one another, conceivable in abstraction from one another. Put more simply, dichotomies in a metaphysics mean that the system has more than one starting point, with multiple assumptions which cannot be tied to one another by any unifying principle. One can always ask: "Why are there these two or several assumptions instead of only one?" This is incoherence.

One such notorious dichotomy in substantival dualism is that between the object and subject in the context of knowing. What you "see" is not what you "get." There may be significant distortions or misrepresentations introduced into the knowing process when the object known is separated from the knowing subject. Substantival metaphysics separates the object of knowledge from the knowing subject because by definition different substances are always "outside" of one another. 'Substance' is defined, in Aristotle's words, as "that which is neither predicable of nor present in another". Process metaphysics attempts to overcome this dichotomy and to gain coherence, by denying "Aristotle's definition of a primary substance as always a subject and never a predicate" (PR 157) and affirming that the objects known actually enter into the real constitution of the knowing subject.

A second dichotomy in substantival dualism is that between fact and value. Values are external to facts and are imposed on them from outside. This forces one either to give up the objectivity of value, or to give up at least the possibility of deriving that value from fact itself.[4] One can turn instead to God, whose commands bridge the fact-value gap, and nature can thereby receive value, But this only makes God an exception to the fact-value separation. Process metaphysics seeks to avoid the dichotomy altogether by affirming the subjectivity (broadly defined) of *all* facts. Since *all* facts are no more and no less than experiential processes (not to be confused with the narrower idea of conscious experience) all facts will have an associated value which Whitehead calls its subjective form. This universality of value provides for the development of a naturalistic basis for value, and this provides a foundation for ecology. While most theists may find such a legitimization of naturalism unnecessary, they should re-evaluate both the price in coherence they pay for getting value only by divine command and the associated practical problems of determining what those values are. Such a Christian naturalism may be undesirable because it seems theologically inadequate, but it may be philosophically more coherent.

A third dichotomy in substantival dualism is that between mental and physical substances. While not all substance metaphysics are dualistic on this issue, those variations in which orthodox theology is often expressed frequently are. The categorical separation of mental and physical substances has produced an incoherence in the metaphysics illustrated by the longstanding mind/body debates. Do bodies affect minds and do minds affect bodies or are these relationships merely illusory? In Whitehead's metaphysics, mentality and physicality are understood as opposite ends of a continuum on which everything in the universe (called 'actual entities' or 'actual occasions') can be placed. Because everything consists fundamentally of experience (broadly defined), the difference between that which is "mental" and that which is "physical" derives merely from the quality of that experience. Simple repetitive experience is physical whereas complex novel experience is mental. For Whitehead, the dichotomy disappears.

Besides avoiding such dichotomies, with alleged gain in coherence, process metaphysics also claims increased adequacy for accommodating modern empiricism in general and modern physics in particular.

To some, Whitehead appears to *oppose* empiricism because he *rejects* the primacy of what he calls 'experience in the mode of presentational immediacy' (PR 121ff). This refers to the high-level sensory experience of colors, sounds, tastes and so on. Because they were preoccupied with basing all knowledge on just such experience, many modern empiricists were trapped in the dead end of positivism. There they faced problems of how to use sense experience to tell which statements are meaningful (verification), how to generalize from particulars of sense experience (induction), and how to be certain of the existence of anything or anyone outside one's own internal experience (solipsism).

But the truth is that Whitehead *affirms* a reformed variety of empiricism. He broadens the notion of experience to include a kind which is deeper and much more fundamental than the traditional empiricist's high-level sensory experience. Whitehead calls this deeper type of experience "experience in the mode of causal efficacy" (PR 121ff). This kind of experience, though less "clear and distinct" than that of presentational immediacy (high-level sensory experience), includes not only all everyday perception, but also *all* causal interaction in the world. Therefore, in good empiricist style, many concerns of epistemology and physics overlap.

Whitehead's "reformed empiricism" is said to give process metaphysics an advantage over traditional empiricism on those troublesome problems of induction and solipsism.

Insofar as experience in the mode of causal efficacy allegedly transmits causal efficacy, it provides process metaphysics with a connection between past and present. The lack of such a systematic connection has been the Achille's Heel of induction since the time of David Hume.

This same broadened experience in the mode of causal efficacy is the means whereby Whitehead's Principle of Relativity functions (PR 22). Such "experience" transmits causal influence from every cause to every effect, but in so doing also organically interrelates everything in the world. "Every*thing*" is a bit misleading because 'thing' suggests a substantival metaphysics. Instead, Whitehead calls them 'events', 'actual entities', 'actual occasions', or 'drops of experience' (PR 18).

Organic or internal interrelation, in contrast to external relation, is the view that *what* the event/entity *is* depends on *how* it is related to other event/entities (cf. PR 56). In short, the relationships make an internal difference to the very nature of the things related; they are not externally imposed or "tacked on." Consequently, for process metaphysics, the solipsistic danger of being alone in the universe is simply impossible.

An important additional advantage to such a system is the superior way in which it reflects the thinking of contemporary physics. According to field theory and the general theory of relativity, everyday physical objects exert a subtle yet important influence on everything else in the universe. In fact, these objects may turn out to be no more than "lattice". According to quantum theory, action occurs in discrete pieces, not continously. These two views of modern physics seem to be more compatible respectively with the organicism and discrete event/entities of process metaphysics than with the traditional substantival metaphysics used for example by Newton.

If process metaphysics' claims to superior philosophical coherence and adequacy for empiricist concern can be supported, then the Christian's ambivalence towards process thinking is only heightened. On the one hand is the alleged theological inadequacy of the process metaphysics. This constitutes the usual criticism of process theology and many of the other chapters of this book raise precisely these criticisms. On the other hand the apparent philosophical coherence and empirical adequacy of the process metaphysics make it very attractive when compared to the dichotomous substantival dualisms in which theology is often traditionally expressed. But if it can be shown that the process metaphysics is *not* coherent, it loses much of its attractiveness for Christian and non-Christian alike!

Interlude: The Two Areas of Incoherence Introduced

Is God an exception to Whitehead's metaphysics? If so, this would constitute an incoherence of exactly the kind Whitehead himself sought to avoid (PR 3). This sort of incoherence would seriously discourage using Whitehead's metaphysics to interpret Christian doctrines.

Whitehead said that "metaphysical first principles can never fail of exemplification. We can never catch the actual world taking a holiday from their sway" (PR 4 cf. PR 42).[6] Therefore if Whitehead's concept of God can be shown to violate metaphysical first principles, then an "arbitrary disconnection" (PR 6) has been introduced and this would amount to incoherence within his system. Since Whitehead had the great virtue of making his metaphysical first principles explicit in what he called his "categoreal scheme" (PR Chap 11), the task of detecting incoherence is made that much easier.

One such first principle Whitehead called the "Ontological Principle" (Category of Explanation XVIII, PR 24). According to this principle, everything requires a reason for its existence. But for Whitehead, *only the fundamental event/entities (he called them 'actual entities'), can ever serve as such a reason. "The ontological principle means that to search for a *reason* is to search for one or more actual entities" (PR 24). In short, all explanations must go back finally to some actual entity; "no actual entity then no reason" (PR 19).

I wish to examine two ways in which Whitehead applied this Ontological Principle in his system. Both involve Whitehead's concept of God. The first application has to do with giving reasons to explain how the past affects the present. Whitehead called this process 'causal objectification'. The second application has to do with giving reasons for God's own existence.

In the first case, (explaining how the past affects the present), to satisfy the ontological principle in explaining causal objectification, one must appeal either to natural or to divine reasons. As I will show, a naturalistic approach makes Whitehead's metaphysics incoherent because it allows for two different kinds of fundamental reality, becoming and being, either of which can provide adequate reasons for things. A theistic approach requires that God has a status and a way of relating to the world that are different from anything else in a system (Whitehead's in which God is supposed to be just another instance of all "things", or events PR 343).

I will show that incoherence arises in the second case because the explanation for God's own existence openly violates the ontological principle and makes God "the ultimate irrationality".[7]

Incoherence in How the Past Affects the Present

According Whitehead, the objects of everyday life, tables, trees, and turkeys, are actually collections ('societies') of more fundamental realities called 'actual entities'. Each actual entity itself actually *consists* of experience called 'concrescence'. In concrescence, the diverse experiences of the past (both distant and immediate) are brought together in a new synthesizing experience. Although this synthesizing process comprises every single actuality in the universe, they are rarely conscious.[8] This Whiteheadian conception of reality is difficult to grasp because Whitehead does not mean that every thing (substance) *has* such experience, he means that every "thing" (event/entity) *is* just such experience. Hence the fundamental actualities in the world are not beings but becomings; they are "drops of experience" (PR 18).

The broadest generalization that can be made about this universal process of concrescence is that it is creative. Creativity characterizes each drop of experience (concrescent actual entity) because the diverse experiences of its past are synthesized into a new unity which itself then becomes past for another subsequent drop of experience. "The many become one and are increased by one" (PR 21). But creativity (Whitehead's Category of the Ultimate) is merely an abstraction from what is actual. Therefore creativity is not actual. And so, according to the ontological principle, creativity is not an acceptable *reason* for anything.

I wish to focus on Whitehead's explanation of *how* past experiences are made available to the present "drop of experience". Whitehead calls this process 'causal objectification' (PR 23, 58). The key question is "Why is the past available for, or given to, the present?"

Earlier I said that according to the ontological principle, only actual entities may legitimately be used as reasons to explain anything. But this raises two difficulties. First, exactly what did Whitehead mean by 'actual' in specifying that actual entities are the sole legitimate reasons for anything? And second, is such an entity available as a reason for the givenness of the past?

What does 'actual' mean? Did Whitehead mean to restrict reasons to actual entities which were *still experiencing*; i.e., are in concrescence? Or can actual entities still function as reasons though they have creased to become and have as Whitehead puts it, "perished" (PR 29).

In some places Whitehead appeared to mean that an actual entity continues to exist beyond the completion (called 'satisfaction' or 'perishing') of its concrescence. "Actuality in perishing *acquires objectivity*, while it loses subjective immediacy. It loses . . . final causation . . . and it acquires effic̶i̶e̶n̶t̶ ̶c̶a̶u̶s̶a̶t̶i̶o̶n̶" (PR29, emphasis added).

In other places, Whitehead adamantly affirmed "that apart from the experiences of subjects there is nothing, nothing, nothing, bare nothingness" (PR 167; cf. PR 32). The satisfaction which marks the completion of the concrescence "never really is, losing the actuality of the atomic entity" (PR 84).

But in still other places there is ambiguity. In stating "that *how* an actual entity *becomes* constitutes *what* that actual entity *is*'' and that ''its *being* is constituted by its *becoming*'' (PR 23), Whitehead unfortunately introduces ambiguity by his use of the verb ''to constitute''. Jorge Nobo has argued that Whitehead used ''to constitute'' in these crucial passages ''either transitively or reflexively, in the sense of 'to create' or 'to form' ''.[9] But I have argued elsewhere that Whitehead uses the verb ''to constitute'' as a copula, i.e., as an alternate form of the verb ''to be''.[10] In other words, I have argued that in these crucial statements of what makes an actual entity actual, (what he calls the Principle of Process [Category of ExplanationIX]), Whitehead does not mean that the process *creates* the actual entity but that the process *is* the actual entity.[11]

Although this may appear to be hair-splitting, the stakes are high. How do we explain the availability of the past for the present? Causal efficacy—that broadened kind of experience that allegedly gives process metaphysics superior coherence to the dualistic substance views—is only possible if one can relate the past to the present. Not only is the availability of the past to the present essential to Whitehead's explanation of how we know and perceive, it is important for all physical science—since science presupposed causality— and for metaphysics in general. How can the ''many become one'' if the many (past) are unavailable to the present? If the past has been completed and has perished and ceased to exist, how can it have any effect on the present experiences of new entities?

The second difficulty (Is an entity available as a reason for the givenness of the past?) turns on the first. Those who believe that the completed actual entity has a kind of actuality sufficient to satisfy the ontological principle will propose a naturalistic account for the givenness of the past. In this case, the past will provide its *own* reason for being available to the present. But those who insist that the kind of actuality required by the ontological principle must be the subjective immediacy of a present becoming will *deny* that the past can be the reason for its own availability to the present and will turn to God to explain causal objectification. These two alternatives, the naturalistic (appealing to the *past* as its own reason) and the theistic (appealing to *God* as the reason), appear to be the only serious possibilities for connecting the past and the present. No other actual entity seems readily available.[12]

I would like to show two things. First, the *naturalistic* approach is not the one Whitehead followed and makes the process metaphysics incoherent by maintaining two rather than one fundamental kind of reality, becoming *and* being. Second, the *theistic* interpretation requires an appeal to God that makes God an exception to the metaphysics and the system consequently again incoherent.

The Naturalistic Approach

The naturalistic approach is expressed in the thinking of D. Sherbourne, W. Christian (in certain places), C. Johnson, and to a lesser degree L. Ford.[13] The basic problem with adopting a naturalistic approach is that to do so fails to take seriously Whitehead's doctrine of satisfaction and perishing. Each of these men suggest that the "satisfied" or finished entity lingers, allowing the entity to make itself available to the present before it perishes completely. Christian calls it "a pause in the midst of flux",[14] Johnson says it is "dead but not gone",[15] and Ford uses Whitehead's own term "being".[16]

According to Whitehead, the "satisfaction" of an entity is the "closing up" (PR 84) of the subjective experience of the entity. Until the entity is satisfied it is *not* determinate and therefore cannot contribute to the experience of another entity (PR 25). But Whitehead goes on to say that the satisfaction is just an abstraction.

> The notion of "satisfaction" is the notion of the "entity of concrete" *abstracted* from the "process of concrescence"; it is the outcome separated from the process, thereby *losing the actuality* of the atomic entity" (PR 84).
>
> Completion is the perishing of immediacy; "it never really is" (PR 84).
>
> In the organic philosophy, an actual entity has perished' when it is complete (PR 81).

Here is the dilemma for the naturalistic approach. If an actual entity cannot be given until it is complete (satisfied), but *has* perished when it is complete (it never really *is*), then how can the entity be the reason for its own availability (givenness) for the present?

Although he generally adopts a theistic approach, elsewhere W. Christian states that "the satisfaction represents a pause in the midst of flux. . . . It is not in 'becoming'. It *is*".[17] This pause permits the entity that is satisfied and past to be its own reason for its givenness to the present. However such a pause makes the entity simultaneously the subject of its own experiences and the object for the experiences of another. But according to Whitehead, this cannot be (eg. PR 85). No entity can enjoy another's experiences as they happen without the two entities collapsing into one. Furthermore, why does this pause end? Why can't the *distant* past linger as well? Christian's "pause" contradicts his own affirmation of the seriousness of perishing. He says "there is nothing in the universe which is not in process, except abstraction".[18]

According to Johnson,

> If an occasion cannot be prehended the instant *before* it completes itself (since it is not yet a determinate prehendable reality) nor the instant *after* (since it then has perished and disappeared) it must be prehended *at the same instant* it attains satisfaction. . . . The end of the old *is* the beginning of the new.[19]

But this approach also appears to make the satisfaction simultaneously both object and subject, to give to what is only an abstraction, a kind of reality status Whitehead seemed to deny it. Johnson understands this danger of overlapping past and present. As he says, it would be a leap out of Hume's frying pan (a view that past and present have no necessary connection) into Spinoza's monistic fire (a metaphysics where no such connection problem exists because all beings are really *one* being). To try to avoid both horns of this dilemma, Johnson describes the satisfaction as dead but not gone.[20] This suggests that actual entities lose their actuality in two stages. But such a two-stage theory of perishing is inconsistent with Whitehead and with what Johnson himself says. According to Johnson, "Being just a little past is like being just a little pregnant".[21] But the idea of being dead but not gone is equally inconsistent.

Of course, being dead but not gone would *not* be meaningless in a substantival metaphysics like Aristotle's or Descartes', because in those systems, the lack of change (becoming, experience, con- crescence) does not mean that an entity has less being. That brings me to a way of restating the criticism that none of the naturalistic approaches takes Whitehead's doctrine of perishing seriously.

The distinctive intuition of Whitehead's system in contrast to substantival metaphysics seems to be the affirmation of the primacy of becoming over being. That intuition is what makes it possible to say that causal efficacy works at all; it allows the past cause actually to be "present in" the present effect in a way impossible in traditional substantival metaphysics. Therefore to affirm a kind of persistent being beyond becoming in order to make causal objectification work without God is self-defeating. And such a theory is incoherent because it maintains two, not one, kinds of fundamental reality, becoming the being.[22]

Theistic Approaches

To reconcile the centrality of subjective *becoming* and the seriousness of perishing, and to satisfy the demands of the ontological principle (which requires a reason for the givenness of the past) one must turn from the past and all naturalistic grounds to God.[23] In other words, *God*, must become the actuality that satisfies the ontological principle and that is the reason for the availability of the past for the present. *God* provides the ground for the givenness of the past for the present. *God* is the intermediary through whom all causal interaction is effected. Although such a position certainly keeps God "busy", God's degree of involvement is no problem for a theist who wants to affirm God's role as sustainer of the universe. D. Sherburne, L. Eslick, and L. Ford have pointed out the incoherence of such theistic interpretations of Whitehead's doctrine of causality.[24]

If God is the entity through whom causality is mediated, then the past must first be available (given) for God before it can be available (given) for the present. But this seems only to beg the question. What is the ground or reason for the availability (givenness) of the past to *God*? As Sherburne points out,

> The key problem concerns how God gets to perceive occasions in the first place . . . But now all the problems that clustered about the ontological ground of X [the past] when we thought of A [the present] prehending X come back to haunt us".
>
> Any way that this problem is approached is going to make God an exception to principles governing and limiting normal, temporal, actual entites.[25]

Whitehead viewed God as a single actual entity, which because of its unlimited potential, both pure (subjective aim) and real (the whole world), is *never* complete ('satisfied') but always in concrescence. But if God is the entity to which the past is first given, then what is the ground or reason for *this* availability? Either the past provides its own reasons, or God is the reason, or there *is* no reason.

But the past cannot be its own reason, as we have seen above, because while it was concrescing it was incomplete and could not yet be given; and once it is complete and satisfied, it is dead and gone. If the past could be its own reason for its givenness to God, it could be its own reason for its givenness to the present directly, and God's intermediate involvement would be unnecessary.

But suppose that God is the reason for the availability of the past to God? Or, to say the same thing in another way, suppose the past can be its own reason for givenness to God because God prehends it while the past occasion is still in concrescence? In the first place this violates Whitehead's restrictions about the objectification of incomplete entites, i.e., his refusal to allow an entity to affect another entity *before* it is complete. To allow such an overlap of feelings would collapse the two entities into one as pointed out above. But second, this makes God an exception to Whitehead's prohibition or causal interaction among contemporaries, an exception invoked to save the system from collapse (eg. PR 123).

But finally, to say that there is *no* reason for the givenness of the past to God is to introduce a mode of interaction between the past and an actual entity (God) that is completely different from that of causal objectification. This even more clearly makes God an exception to the metaphysical categories. Sherburne concludes that this demonstrates that "Whitehead's system *with* God is incoherent".[26]

Eslick agrees with Sherburne that divine mediation introduces incoherence. Eslick points out that for Whitehead, enough *causal* interaction among contemporaries is ruled out for entities which are temporal, there may be an entirely different *non-causal* mode of interaction for God who is not temporal. By virtue of his unlimited potential, God is never completed (satisfied), and since for Whitehead time is *derived* from the succession of *completed* occasions, God is not temporal. He is what Whitehead called 'everlasting' (PR 346).[27] Whitehead used the expression, 'unison of becoming' to describe the way in which God received the world to himself (PR 345-346,

350-51, 340). In Eslick's words, "God prehends temporal entities as contemporaries with them in a 'unison of becoming' ".[28]

But this version of the divine mediation view reduces Whitehead's entire system to a kind of panentheism, where the whole world is nothing more than an aspect or extension of God's own experience. That not only makes the system inadequate to express most Christian theologies, but it also reveals a fatal internal incoherence. Such a mode of divine interaction with the world cannot, as Eslick puts it, "be subject to the categoreal descriptions of *Process and Reality*."[29] Eslick's point is that if the basis for God's privileged interaction with the world is his everlastingness, which in turn derives from His unique eternal incompletion, then this seems inconsistent with Whitehead's claim that God is not an exception to the metaphysics but its chief exemplification. In Eslick's words, "God in Whitehead's metaphysics, is the descending God in the Basket, *deus ex machina*."[30] Such a view is incoherent.[31]

Because of this and other difficulties, years ago Charles Hartshorne proposed his major modification to Whitehead's system. While Hartshorne's modifications did bring improved coherence in some areas, it leaves unanswered the question we have raised here.[32]

As Ford puts it:

> There are not very many alternatives . . . The everlasting concrescence model [Whitehead] conceives of God as a present activity in causal independence of other activities. The societal alternative [Hartshorne] sees god as past, insofar as past divine occasions causally affect occasions.[33]

Ford proposes that God's interaction with the world "must be conceived in terms of some activity of the future."[34] Ford uses this divine activity of the future to vindicate, among other things, Whitehead's allowance for *direct* prehension of the *distant* past (PR 226, 284), though not to vindicate prehension of the immediate past, because for Ford this poses no problem for a naturalistic account.[35]

> Thus from each future standpoint, God directly prehends each actuality once it comes into being. Since [God's] concrescence is everlasting, including every prehending in the immediacy of [God's] becoming, [God] can bequeath that direct prehending of that entire past to the nascent occasion. Thus the nascent occasion takes over

a prehensive activity directly prehending the entire actual world, including the distantly past.[36]

Ford's view, like the version of divine mediation that I criticized above, seems to involve two stages. In the first stage God "directly prehends" each actuality, i.e., the world is somehow available to God. In the second stage God "bequeaths" that direct prehension to a new occasion, i.e., God is somehow available to the world. But there are problems with both stages.

The second stage seems devised to avoid the problem of God's availability to the world, the problem which had moved Hartshorne to propose the societal model. Unfortunately, though Ford talks of "bequeathing" and "pluralizing" and "transferring", he does not tell us how this works, or how it avoids the panentheism and incoherence he himself ascribes to the unmodified Whiteheadian view. Clearly it is not a case of causal objectification. And if it is not, then once again God is an exception to the system because he has His own mode of influencing the world.

The problem with the first stage is that Ford again does not tell us how it works. He assumes that God's prehension of the immediate past (i.e., the availability of the immediately past world to God) presents no problem. Although in one case he says that "God prehends every actual occasion as it becomes" he does not seem to mean either that God shares its immediacy or that prehension can occur before the occasion is completed.[37] He seems to mean that because God is immediately future to *all* occasions, the first stage of God's activity is always just a case of causal objectification of the immediate past. But though Ford would disagree, we are right back where we started with our criticism of the unmodified Whiteheadian problem. How is even the immediate past made available to the present occasion (whether divine or otherwise)? Ford's first stage begs the question of causal objectification. Of course, this assumes that when he says God "prehends" the past he is indicating a case of causal objectification. But if he is not, he must explain what kind of interaction he is referring to. Then he must explain how it avoids the problem of panentheism wherein God and the world overlap in common experience and reality. Finally, he must show how this mode of interaction satisfies the requirements of the ontological principle. Unless it does, Ford is open to the now familiar

271

charge that by making God an exception to its categories, process metaphysics is incoherent.

In summary, process metaphysics stumbles on the fundamental question of the causal connection between the past and present. To fulfill the requirements of the ontological principle, a reason must be given for the availability or givenness of the past for the present. But if one also takes seriously the principle of process (that concrescence is the fundamental kind of actuality) and the doctrine of perishing (that completed entities are no longer concrescent and cannot be reasons) then naturalistic accounts break down. The past is dead and gone, unable by any *natural* process coherent with these principles to give itself to the present. If on the other hand, appeal is made to God to mediate all causal interaction, then God is an exception to the metaphysics and again incoherence is introduced; not to mention panentheism. Hartshorne's attempts to modify Whitehead seem to beg the question and to introduce new problems as well.

Incoherence in the Reasons for God's Own Existence

Whitehead's view of God's role is incoherent in a second way, and this can be seen when the ontological principle is applied not to the justification of causality, but to the question of the reasons for God's existence.

Although he rejected the idea of proving God's existence (PR 343), Whitehead's radical empiricism (expressed in the ontological principle) requires that to assert God's existence in the metaphysical system requires a reason or ground for God in the character of immediate experience. No ontological argument which begins with concepts alone could ever work for Whitehead, and neither could any traditional cosmological argument which concludes with an utterly transcendent God. But there is a kind of hybrid argument that goes back to the demands both of Whitehead's categoreal scheme and of experience.

According to the principle of relativity (Category of Explanation IV, PR 22), everything makes a difference to everything (within the limits of physics). This principle makes Whitehead's metaphysics a philosophy of organism as well as a philosophy of process. In other words, this principle tells us it is a characteristic of *all* entities that they function as possibilities for other entities.

Yet for possibility to function at all, it must be made relevant to the actual entities in which it will be realized. Put simply, not all possibilities are *real* for a given entity. Becoming a prince is not a real possibility for the frog. Therefore, there must be some explanation in Whitehead's system for the ordering of possibilities which makes them real for some entities but not for others. That is to say, there must be an *explanation* for the determination of relevance of what would otherwise be pure possibility (eternal objects) and not real possibility.

As we have already seen, the ontological principle requires that all explanations or reasons must be grounded in the experience (real togetherness) of some actual entity. And so the stage is set for an argument for God's existence. As Whitehead himself concludes:

> The ontological principle can be expressed as all real togetherness is togetherness in the formal constitution of an actuality. So if there be a relevance of what in the temporal world is unrealized, the relevance must express a fact of togetherness in a formal constitution of a non-temporal actuality (PR 32). This actuality is what Whitehead calls God in his Primoridal Nature (PNG).[38]

The incoherence in Whitehead's system emerges clearly here in the form of either an exception or circularity. The argument in this passage for God's primordial nature appeals to the ontological principle. The primordial nature of God is itself deficiently actual because it is only the divine subjective aim, it lacks concrescence of its own. Therefore, because it is not itself an actual entity, God's primordial nature cannot be its own reason for existence. But neither can the world be the reason for God's primordial nature, because the world presupposes it, as I have shown above, as the reason for the ordering of possibilities. Therefore, the appeal to the world is circular. Nor, finally, can a reason be found in God's consequent nature. The consequent nature of God (CNG) is normally viewed as God's own concrescence. But this again is circular since CNG presupposed the world, (It *is* just God's reception of and presentation of the world in Himself), and the world presupposes the primordial nature as we saw above for the ordering of possibility.[39]

So if all attempts to provide a reason for the primordial nature of God turn out to be circular, then the doctrine of God's primordial nature has no explanation. It is an exception to the ontological principle whose preservation originally necessitated its assertion.

The fact that Whitehead seemed to be aware of this problem in no way eliminates it. Referring to the primordial nature of God, Whitehead said, "The particularities of the actual world presupposes *it*; while *it* merely presupposes the general metaphysical character of creative advance, of which it is the primordial exemplification" (PR 344). This is an admission that God is an exception in his metaphysics to the ontological principle. In another place Whitehead says, "The nontemporal act of all-inclusive unfettered valuation [PNG] is at once a creature of Creativity and a condition for Creativity" (PR31). No wonder, as Eslick points out, that Whitehead himself in *Science and the Modern World*, refers to PNG as "the ultimate irrationality".[40]

Conclusion

I have attempted to illustrate the incoherence of Whitehead's metaphysics by pointing out that God is an exception to his categoreal principles.

First we examined God's role in causality in general (causal objectification). The ontological principle, the principle of process, and the doctrine of perishing seem to rule out naturalistic accounts of causality. But theistic accounts either beg the question or require God to interact with the world in a way which makes Him an exception to the metaphysical system.

Second, we saw that the ontological principle and the principle of relativity establish the need for God's existence as ground for the world (i.e., "creator") but that the same ontological principle has to be violated to find a ground for God's own existence.

These two incoherencies in Whitehead's system raise a final but very serious question. "Is there an alternative metaphysical theory that is *more* coherent than Whitehead's?"

Is Whitehead's "proof" for God any less circular than the more traditional cosmological arguments? Those arguments affirm that one causal principle applies to everything in the world, but because appeal to that principle cannot regress without end, they must affirm a Being which grounds the whole process. But to do so the Being must be an exception to the original causal principle. Such arguments are also circular.

Is God an Exception to Whitehead's Metaphysics?

Is Whitehead really so far from traditional Christian theology when he says that "No reason can be given for the nature of God, because that nature is the ground of rationality"?[41]

Is causality really in any better shape in traditional substantival metaphysics? Perhaps in traditional metaphysics there are no gaps of *actuality* to leap from occasion to occasion as is the case in Whitehead's system, because the continuing endurance of things through time that characterizes substances takes care of this. But are the problems of causality in traditional theories any less serious? Has Hume's criticism that we are not entitled to believe in the necessary connection of causes and effects without experience of that connnection really been answered? One might say that Hume's critique merely points to a temporary inadequacy of substantial metaphysics that may yet be resolved and that is much less serious than a demonstrable incoherence. But that is an argument from ignorance and ignorance is bliss! Who can say if causality can be accounted for coherently by traditional metaphysics until a successful proposal is seen?

To put this another way, there is an additional warning to be added to the one I made at the beginning of this essay where I pointed out that the internal issues of coherence need to be distinguished from external questions of theological adequacy. By that I meant that a gain in coherence may be a loss of theological adequacy and *vice versa*, so that a simultaneous use of both external and internal criticisms might turn out to be self-defeating for the Christian who is interested in attacking process theology. My added warning is against concluding too much. Even demonstrable incoherence in the process metaphysics (whether shown in this essay or not), would do no more than rule out the current form of such a metaphysics as a viable framework in terms of which to express Christian theology. It would not provide any evidence for the preferability of a metaphysics of substance which remains philosophically troublesome (to say the least) even after 2000 years of use. The search of a metaphysics that is both adequate and coherent must go on.

NOTES

* To reduce the number of footnotes and simplify things somewhat, all references to Whitehead's *Process and Reality* will be noted in parentheses. The letters PR

followed by page numbers will refer to Alfred North Whitehead, *Process and Reality*, Corrected Edition, ed. D. Griffin and D. Sherburne (New York: Free Press, 1978).

1. In such questions of adequacy, the critic and process theologian alike seek to discover how many, if any, of the traditional doctrines of the church can be retained, with perhaps some modification, on a metaphysical view which was obviously unknown to the writers of Scripture and to the early church fathers who first articulated these doctrines. A major part of this task reduces to asking which doctrines merely reflect an outdated, nonessential metaphysics, and may be re-expressed in terms of a novel set of categories and which doctrines on the other hand cannot be modified or sacrificed short of heresy.

2. For example, making God an instance of general principles rather than an exception to them may be theologically repugnant, but philosophically more coherent.

3. Christians need not be substantival dualists. But monisms are much less common (Berkeley's was a mentalistic monism).

4. See G. E. Moore's "naturalistic fallacy" as discussed in his book, *Principia Ethica* (Cambridge: Cambridge University Press, 1903).

5. See L. Eslick, "God in the Metaphysics of Whitehead", in *New Themes in Christian Philosophy*, ed. R. M. McInerny (Notre Dame: Notre Dame University Press, 1968), pp. 65f.

6. Whitehead also says, "Descartes, indeed, would ascribe to God 'existence' in a generically different sense. In the philosophy of organism, God's existence is not generically different from that of other actual entities, except that he is 'primordial' in a sense to be gradually explained" (PR 75). Even this primordiality, which Whitehead apparently did not see as troublesome, seems to me an illegitimate exception to his general principles as I point out later in the chapter.

7. Alfred North Whitehead, *Science and the Modern World* (New York: Free Press, 1967), p. 257.

8. For Whitehead, virtually all the collections ('societies') of actual entities which are the object of everyday life are repeated over and over again. This repetition is what explains the endurance of our familiar objects even though they consist of entities which individually become and perish. Some of these societies have a peculiar repetition of pattern which Whitehead says makes them persons.

9. J. L. Nobo, "Whitehead's Principle of Relativity,"*Process Studies* 8 (1978), pp. 276f.

10. V. J. Mannoia, "The Ground of Givenness of the Past in Whitehead's Theory of Causal Objectification", *Modern Schoolman* 61 (1984).

11. Without such an interpretation, it seems to me that Whitehead's fundamental intuition is lost. His metaphysics would be incoherent from the *start*, in a way not unlike a "dualistic substance" view. It would begin with *two* fundamental kinds of reality, becoming *and being*, instead of becoming alone. I believe that to maintain coherence at this fundamental level at least (i.e., to satisfy the ontological principle and the principle of process) reasons must at bottom appeal to some actual entity *in concrescence*.

12. I have addressed the questions of whether either the *present* occasion itself, or what Whitehead calls 'eternal object' might be available for this purpose in my Ph.D. dissertation, "Whitehead's Ontological Principle: A Defense and Interpretation", Washington University-St. Louis, 1975.

13. See D. Sherburne, "Whitehead Without God", in *Process Philosophy and Christian Thought*, ed. D. Brown, R. James, and G. Reeves (New York: Bobbs-Merrill, 1971) pp. 305-328; W. A. Christian, *Interpreting Whitehead's Metaphysics* (New Haven: Yale University Press, 1967); C. Johnson, "On Prehending the Past," *Process Studies* 6 (1976), pp. 255-269; and L. Ford, "An Appraisal of Whiteheadian Non-Theism," *Southern Journal of Philosophy* 15 (1977-78), pp. 27-35.

14. Christian, *Interpreting Whitehead's Metaphysics*, p. 29.

15. Johnson, "On Prehending the Past", p. 264.

16. Ford, "An Appraisal of Whiteheadian Non-Theism," p. 29. In a more recent work, Ford makes "being dependent on ("ingredient in") "becoming" and concludes that God must be invoked for the prehension of the *distant* past, but is still unnecessary for the prehensions of immediate past occasions. This dependence of being on becoming is something he does not believe Whitehead ever expressed (See L. Ford, "Divine Activity of the Future", *Process Studies* 11 (1982) p. 177), and calls it a kind of "perfected ontological principle". I believe this is the only way the principle can be interpreted (See my "Ground of Givenness" in *Modern Schoolman*). So we agree on the interpretation but disagree on whether it is Whitehead's or a new modification. Furthermore, we agree that the principle makes God necessary for prehension of the distant past but disagree on whether God is necessary for the prehension of the immediate past. See footnote 22 below.

17. Christian, *Interpreting Whitehead's Metaphysics*, p. 29.

18. Ibid. D. Sherburne (in "Whitehead Without God") says that this problem of givenness exists only for the givenness of the *distant past* (long gone) for the present, and if we deny such long past causal effect then the givenness of the immediate past is no problem. But Whitehead does *not* want to deny the givenness of the distant past (PR 227-227). Furthermore, Sherburne never explains how even the immediate past manages to linger to be its own ground of givenness for the present or why if the immediate past can do this, then the distant past cannot.

19. C. Johnson, "On Prehending the Past," p. 262.

20. Ibid., p. 264.

21. Ibid., p. 261.

22. It seems to me that this same basic criticism also applies to the naturalistic component of L. Ford's account of objectification. I say naturalistic *component* because, like Sherburne, Ford distinguished between the distant past and the immediate past. Notwithstanding his own criticism of Sherburne's means for drawing such a distinction, Ford provides a naturalistic account of the givenness of the latter (see Ford's "An Appraisal of Whiteheadian Non-Theism"). The criticisms above do not apply entirely, however, because Ford makes the being of the satisfied entity dependent upon becoming (i.e., a subjectively immediate entity). (See Ford's "Divine Activity of the Future", p. 177). Ford also says this is a modification of Whitehead, a kind of "perfected ontological principle". I say this is Whitehead himself (see my "Ground

Process Theology

of Givenness," *Modern Schoolman*). But if its usefulness in satisfying the ontological principle by providing a reason for the givenness of the immediate past for the present requires reference to becoming then we seem to be back to where we started. We must ask of Ford which subjectively immediate entity provides the reason for the givenness of this past being for the present. The question goes begging.

Where Ford parts company with Sherburne, and consequently with the naturalistic approach is in affirming with Whitehead (PR 226, 284), the givenness of the distant past for the present is as important as the givenness of the immediate past. And furthermore, even if naturalistic explanations for the latter do work, they would be inadequate as explanations for the former.

23. Ironically, it was in reaction to just such a divine solution that the naturalistic approaches were first suggested. In Sherburne's article "Whitehead Without God" and Ford's "An Appraisal of Whiteheadian Non-Theism," both men allude to the incoherence of any view which appeals to God as a sort of *deus ex machina* who holds the world together by providing the reason for the givenness of the past (immediate or distant or both) to the present.

24. D. Sherburne, "Whitehead Without God", L. Eslick, "God in the Metaphysics of Whitehead," and L. Ford, "Divine Activity of the Future."

25. D. Sherburne, "Whitehead Without God", pp. 308-309.

26. Ibid., p. 309.

27. For more discussion of God's atemporality, see W. Norris Clarke's "Christian Theism and Whiteheadian Process Philosophy: Are They Compatible?" *Logos* 1 (1980) pp. 34f.

28. L. Eslick, "God in the Metaphysics of Whitehead", p. 80.

29. Ibid.

30. Ibid., p. 81.

31. The attempt to resolve the problem of how God might mediate causal objectification not only seems to come at the cost of incoherence, but it creates problems in other areas of Whitehead's system as well. God's role as giver of the subjective aim to each occasion is affected because if God is everlastingly immediate, how is *he* ever objectified to provide intitial aims (see L. Ford, "Divine Activity of the Future", p. 169)? And again, if everlastingly immediate, in a unison of becoming with every occasion, does this not imperil Whitehead's case for freedom in the individual (See L. Eslick, "God in the Metaphysics of Whitehead", p. 80).

32. This modification has been adopted by many process theologians but it takes us beyond a critique of the incoherence in Whitehead's own views. It is important however in any analysis of process theology. I suggest L. Ford's excellent account.

Hartshorne proposed that God be reinterpreted as a "personally ordered" society (Pr 34-35). Making God such a society brings gains in coherence. God can be meaningfully described as a person, he is, like all other societies, alternately subjective then satisfied and objective, then again subjective. Since God is periodically complete (satisfied) and thus objective, he is capable of being made available to others (i.e., objectified) so as to influence the world and in particular to provide the initial aims of occasions in the world. And God is now temporal, a part of nature and hence more clearly a part of Whitehead's system.

Unfortunately this modification comes at a cost. In the first place, it seems to leave the question we have been addressing completely unanswered. If God is a society how do we explain the givenness of God's past to God's present? If naturalistic accounts fail as we have seen above, then there can no longer be a theistic alternative because God is not just a *case* of nature. In the second place, one is forced to wonder *how* God's repeated completion ('satisfactions') could ever occur? How can an unlimited aim of unlimited potential (what Whitehead calls the 'Primordial Nature of God') ever be satisfied? And if it could be satisfied how could it do so instantaneously through all space? (This it would need to do in order to interact with all occasions and to mediate all causality if naturalistic accounts fail as we have argued above.) This would seem a serious violation of relativity physics and perhaps even of Goedel's Incompleteness Theorem (See Ford's "Divine Activity of the Future", p. 170). Because of such problems, some scholars have abandoned Hartshorne's account here and returned to Whitehead.

33. L. Ford, "Divine Activity of the Future," p. 171.
34. Ibid., p. 173.
35. L. Ford, "An Appraisal of Whiteheadian Non-Theism," p. 29.
36. L. Ford, "Divine Activity of the Future," p. 176.
37. Ibid., p. 172.
38. Whitehead's use of the phrase 'formal constitution' here is one of the clearest bases for interpreting his ontological principle the way I have; i.e., that reasons can only be actual entities in concrescence.

As L. Eslick points out, there are at least two corollary functions served by this Primordial Nature of God (PNG). (See Eslick's "God in the Metaphysics of Whitehead," p. 72). The first is to account for the emergence of novelty in the world. Without an actual entity in which to ground possibilities hitherto never realized in the temporal world, no true novelty could ever appear. Even David Hume thought it obvious that people can form a very good idea of the color shade missing in a spectrum with a small gap in it even if they have never before experienced that color. But his empiricism could not account for this idea unless it was traceable to a previous sense impression. Whitehead sought to supply the answer, and empiricist that he was, he traced it back to the "experience" which is the formal constitution of God. So the scandal of Hume's missing color shade is here resolved by positing the existence of this non-temporal actual entity who completely realized ('envisages' is Whitehead's term) all possibilities and thereby makes them relevant to the temporal world.

The second function of the primordial nature has to do with the origin of the subjective aim. The creation of a new actual entity requires that it be given an initial aim. This aim guides the concrescence, and shapes how the entity will respond to what is possible. Within the limits of the entity's freedom, the aim determines how the many which are its past are uniquely synthesized into a new unity which is the entity's satisfaction. But again the ontological principle requires that the initial aim must be traced to an actual entity other than the one it begins. This entity is God in his primordial nature, functioning as Creator.

39. It will not do to appeal to a world without beginning for the demand of the ontological principle is not for *temporal* priority, but precisely for *ontological* priority.
40. Whitehead, *Science and the Modern World*, p. 178. Compare L. Eslick, "God in the Metaphysics of Whitehead," p. 74.
41. Whitehead, *Science and the Modern World*, p. 178.

God and the World

Thomas V. Morris

Thomas V. Morris

Thomas V. Morris received his A. B. degree in religion from the University of North Carolina (Chapel Hill) where he was a Morehead Scholar. He earned his M. A. degree from the Department of Religious Studies at Yale University and his M. Phil. and Ph.D. degrees jointly from the departments of Religious Studies and Philosophy at Yale. He is currently Assistant Professor of Philosophy at the University of Notre Dame. Dr. Morris has published two books: *Francis Schaeffer's Apologetics: A Critique* and *Understanding Identity Statements*. His articles have appeared in such journals as *American Philosophical Quarterly, Christian Scholars' Review, Faith and Philosophy, Mind, Philosophical Review, Religious Studies*, and *Theology*.

In this chapter, I want to look at a few of the more interesting claims of process theology having to do with the relations that exist between God and the world. The process theologians have done us a favor by insisting that our concept of God be such as to square with the central religious conviction that God can interact with us, his creatures. Some strands of medieval theology stand in tension with the biblical portrait of God as a responsive agent in history. Process theologians have sought to point this out and develop a concept of God more adequate to the biblical picture. By looking at this criticism of one feature of some medieval theology, even briefly, we can come to see something very important about our idea of God.

Unfortunately, not all that process theologians say about God and the world is equally valuable, or even acceptable to traditional Christians. I want to take a look at two points at which numerous process theologians have gone wrong concerning God's relation to the world. First, it is a standard tenet of process thought that God needs the world in order to be who he is. As we shall see, this involves a denial that God freely created the world *ex nihilo*, the denial of a central belief of orthodox Christian thought. I hope to show how the process theologians, starting from a genuine insight, go wrong at this point for no good theological reason. It will be fairly easy to see that we can preserve their insight while avoiding their error on this point.

Lastly, we will look at what a number of process theologians have said about God's eternal preservation of his world, and specifically at the idea of immortality they ordinarily endorse. The sort of immortality they promise is very different from the personal afterlife in which Christians have believed over the centuries. We will see that the one and only argument presented against the traditional view by one of the most prominent process theologians not only is itself unconvincing, but also may be inconsistent with one of the central claims distinctive of process thought.

I aim here neither at completeness nor at any measure of comprehensive scholarship concerning what exactly this or that process theologian has said in one or the other edition of this or that book. Nor shall I concern myself much with the relation between the ideas of process theology I have chosen to discuss and the details of Whitehead's original metaphysical system, to which they are related in one way or another. This self-imposed limitation is possible due to the fact that the specific ideas of process theology we shall examine can be understood well enough for our purposes without the need of any Whitehead exegesis. This limitation is desirable for the sake of clarity, so that we can focus our attention more firmly on the substantive theological issues at stake and lay aside the complexities of interpreting Whitehead.

God's Perfection and Action in the World

In the twelfth century, St. Anselm, Archbishop of Canterbury, one of the greatest theologians of all time, wrote that he understood God to be "that than which no greater can be conceived"—a greatest conceivable, or maximally perfect being. This was meant by Anselm to be something like a definitional truth. In much the same way that it is true by definition that a triangle has three angles, it is true that God is a perfect being. Another way of expressing this point would be to say that just as no figure counts as a triangle unless it has three angles, no individual counts as literally divine unless he is altogether perfect.

St. Anselm's definition attempts to capture the core of the Christian concept, or idea, of God. To specify that God is a greatest possible, or maximally perfect being is not to display all of the Christian concept of God, it is just a way of summarizing a controlling feature of that concept. Anselm's definition can be thought of as a formula which can be used to help us arrive at a more complete conception of deity: God is to be thought of as having a maximally perfect set of great-making properties, where a great-making property is a property it is intrinsically better to have than to lack. For example, if it is intrinsically better to be powerful than not to be powerful, Anselm's formula will have us ascribe power to God. Likewise, if it is better to be omnipotent, or unlimited in power, than not to be omnipotent, we must ascribe omnipotence to

God. The same will hold true for such properties as omniscience and omnibenevolence. Applying Anselm's formula to intuitions we have about what properties are great-making properties, or perfections, we begin to philosophically develop our idea of God.

Most sophisticated philosophers and theologians over the centuries seem to have agreed that if there is a God, he must be a perfect individual. One thing they have not agreed on, however, is exactly what that perfection must involve. Intuitions can vary about what properties are perfections. A number of medieval theologians, including such great thinkers as St. Augustine and St. Thomas Aquinas, had a set of intuitions about divine perfection not shared by contemporary process theologians. Some of those intuitions gave rise to the view that a perfect being must be metaphysically simple or noncomposite in every respect whatsoever. The intuitions operative here seem to be that anything which is composed of parts or which can be analyzed into parts depends for what it is on what those parts are. But it is greater not to be dependent on anything else for what one is than to be so dependent. Thus God, the greatest possible being, must lack any sort or part whatsoever, and must be such that his nature cannot be analyzed into parts. This conclusion which has come to be known as the doctrine of divine simplicity, has had important implications for the conception of God developed by many philosophers and theologians since the early Middle Ages.

If God has no parts, he has no spatial appendages such as arms or legs. He thus cannot be a corporeal being located in physical space. This is an implication of divine simplicity accepted by many orthodox theologians. Likewise, simplicity theologians reason, God can have no temporal parts either—there can be no before and after in the divine life. God is outside time altogether. His eternity is thus not to be understood as unending, everlasting existence through infinitely many moments of time, but rather is to be understood as a-temporality, or timelessness, existence outside the bounds of any temporal framework.

If God is outside time, it follows that he is absolutely immutable, that he cannot undergo any sort of real change, for any real change must occur over time. In any case of real change, an object comes to lack at some time a property it had at a previous time, or it gains a property it lacked at an earlier time. In either case, the object must exist through different times in order to change.

God is described in the Bible as having done different things at different times. At one time he called Abraham out of Ur, at a later time he spoke to Moses, later still he revealed his will to the prophets, and, at the culmination of the biblical account of his dealings with his people, he himself became a man and dwelt among us. This seems to implicate God in change—he changes from doing one thing at one time to doing something different at a later time. In the biblical account, God seems to be ever-changing not only in the actions he initiates but also in his responses to ever changing circumstances and needs on the part of his people. In short, the biblical portrayal of God does not appear to be the portrayal of an absolutely immutable being. Granted, the biblical God does not change in his character, or, with respect to the basic attributes distinctive of deity, such as omniscience and omnibenevolence, but along with these continuities in who he is, he appears to be characterized by a ceaseless and appropriately changing activity in what he does.

This is a point not ignored by medieval theologians who held to divine simplicity, a-temporality, and immutability. They and their contemporary followers have attempted to explain away the appearance of change on the side of God by drawing some fairly simple distinctions. First, we need to distinguish real change from merely relational change. Suppose that, unknown to me, there is now a man standing exactly two miles to my right, and that suddenly he walks farther away. Due to his move, I come to lack a property I earlier had—the property of having someone exactly two miles to my right. Yet have I undergone any sort of real change; has there been a change *in me*? Most of us would agree that it was not I who underwent a real change here but rather my right hand man, who changed by moving away. In this story, I lose a property I had, but I can be said to change only in the loosest sort of relational sense: I underwent a merely relational change.

Likewise, suppose some man named Smith dreams of vanilla ice cream daily. But then at some point in time he ceases ever to think of vanilla and begins to dream of chocolate. Vanilla seems to lose a property it formerly had—the property of being dreamed of daily by Smith—and chocolate gains that property. Yet have these flavors themselves undergone any sort of real change? Surely not, the real change is in Smith and his imagination, not in the ice creams of his dreams. They can be said to have changed only in the loosest of senses, having undergone merely relational change.

Defenders of divine immutability attempt to use this distinction to help explain away the appearance of change in God. There are two ways the distinction between real change and merely relational change can be used for this purpose. The simplest is just to apply the category of merely relational change to God and claim that all divine change is merely relational change—God never undergoes real change, change *in himself*, but rather always is characterized by merely relational change. Suppose that at some point in time God created our physical universe. Defenders of immutability will insist that upon the creation of this world, nothing really changed on the side of God; it merely began to be true at some time that this world existed. Any change here was extrinsic to God, not intrinsic to him. Likewise, they argue, as various biblical characters are spoken to by God throughout the centuries, there is no real change on the side of God, only on the side of those receiving his Word. On this view, God changelessly and eternally wills to speak to Abraham at time *t*, to Moses at *t + n*, and so forth. The claim is that from God's willingness to do different things at different times, it does not follow that God's act of willing changes from one of those times to another. Although his will has to do with the changing times, he does not himself really change with those times. His eternal will is changeless in any but a merely relational way.

Notice however that in the two stories used to illustrate the distinction between real and merely relational change, the object or objects said to change in the merely relational sense did undergo the gaining or losing of some property. In each case it was a relational property, a property of standing in relation to some other object, but a property nonetheless. It is possible for an object to gain or lose a property only if that object is a temporal individual. But God, according to the simplicity/a-temporality/immutability theologians, is not in time. So if gaining or losing a property, and thus existing throughout successive moments of time, is a necessary condition of undergoing merely relational change, God cannot undergo even this minute sort of change. At this point, the defender of extreme immutability who, remember, needs to explain away the appearances of real change on the side of God, can make one of two moves. He can deny that gaining or losing properties is necessary for undergoing merely relational change, and so characterize that form of change that God can undergo it. Or he can say that in much the same way that we distinguish merely relational change from real change, we must distinguish the appearance of relational change from the actual occurrence of relational change. In this case, he will deny that God ever undergoes even merely relational change.

A realist account of truth typically specifies that a statement about an object is true just in case the object has the property predicated of it in that statement. My statement that the grass outside my office is green is true just in case the object my statement is about—the grass in question—has the property predicated of it—the property of being green. Suppose however that at t a statement made by Aaron that God is speaking to Moses is true. Later at $t + 1$ a second statement by Aaron that God is speaking to Moses is false, God's having ceased the communication. On the view that God is outside time, this situation cannot accurately be described by saying that God had a property at t which he had ceased to have by $t + 1$—the property of speaking to Moses. For to be so describable truly would implicate God in time as well as change. The classical theologian must deny that Aaron's true statement uttered at t was true in virtue of a property God had at t, because he must deny that God has any properties at any times. Some theologians have tried to claim that God has all his properties timelessly, but the classical theologian who endorses divine simplicity as well as a-temporality and immutability cannot say even this. For on the standard explication of simplicity, God cannot be said literally to have properties at all, distinct from each other and from him, since that would involve a sort of composition simplicity theologians have found objectionable. Now this aspect of the doctrine of simplicity is itself far from simple, far from easy to understand, and it has been amply criticized by others.[1] The point to be made here is that the classical theologian who endorses divine simplicity either must interpret the category of merely relational change in such a way that undergoing such a change requires no gaining or losing of properties of any sort, or else must deny even this loosest sort of change to God, holding instead that in the case of God we have only the appearance of merely relational change.

Let us suppose the classical theologian takes the latter course and denies that God is capable of change in any sense. His strategy for dismissing the appearance of change on God's part as he interacts with his creatures can turn on the following claim: Just as real change in one object can be reflected in merely relational change in another, so real change with respect to God's creatures can be reflected in the appearance of merely relational change on the part of God. We are presented then with an analogy. How successfully the theology of simplicity, timelessness, and immutability can be squared with the biblical and religious picture of God as an active agent in history will turn at least in part on how well this analogy holds up.

Consider this standard story of merely relational change. A woman's husband on an ambassadorial trip to a foreign land dies at the hand of a terrorist, unknown to her for some hours. At the moment of his death, she becomes a widow. But at that time, the change she undergoes is a merely relational change. The circumstances involve no real change on her part. Contrast this with an alternate story in which the murder occurs in her presence, or an even worse story in which she herself pulls the trigger. In neither of these cases is her becoming a widow a set of circumstances involving only merely relational change on her part. In light of this difference, we can isolate at least three features of any situation in which one object has undergone nothing more than merely relational change, reflecting some real change in a different object. First, the ongoing existence of the really changing object and its having at least most of the nonrelational properties it has are matters in some sense causally and metaphysically independent of the object undergoing the merely relational change. Secondly, the real change in question involves no occurrent exercise of power on the part of the object undergoing merely relational change. And thirdly, the real change is not registered as a piece of knowledge or belief on the part of the individual going through merely relational change. Each of these three stories illustrate merely relational change (the man to my right, Smith and the ice cream, and the unknowing widow), all three features are present. And the same will hold true of any story noncontroversially portraying a case of merely relational change. But these are features which could never hold true of God and any of his creatures, such that the creature underwent real change and God was properly characterized as exemplifying all the features of merely relational change that the doctrines of timelessness and simplicity will allow. Each of God's creatures depends on God moment to moment for its existence. None can exist causally or metaphysically independent of God. Further, nothing can happen without at least the concurrent operation of God's conserving power. And nothing can come about without God's knowing it. Whenever we have a case of real change reflected in a case of merely relational change, we have an object undergoing the latter which exists in numerous sorts of isolation from the object going through the former. It is impossible for God to exist in such isolation from his creatures that exist. In light of this, it is hard to see how the classical claim could be made plausible that God stands to all creaturely change in much the way in which an object undergoing merely relational change stands to a really changing object. And without plausibility here, the immutability theory cannot be reconciled to the biblical portrayal of God, in which it seems so clear that God changes what he does as his creatures' circumstances require.

Other objections can be raised to the traditional defense of extreme divine immutability. However, I shall mention no more here aside from pointing to the central Christian doctrine it seems most difficult to square this conception of divine immutability with—the doctrine of the Incarnation, the core belief of the Christian faith that God once became a man and entered into our human history as one of us. I have seen no attempt to reconcile extreme divine immutability with the Incarnation which did not fall into some ancient heresy, or invent a new one.[2] I shall not declare categorically that this cannot be done, or that extreme immutability cannot be made consistent with other elements of the biblical picture of God. But the prospects for such a reconciliation seem dim. And I think it a sound method of theological reflection for a Christian, when in serious doubt about the coherence of a particular philosophical claim with central biblical claims about God and divine-human interaction, to avoid endorsing that philosophical claim and to explore alternate philosophical ways of articulating the aspect of deity in question.

If God is not immutable in the extreme sense, then he is not an altogether a-temporal individual. Nor is he metaphysically simple.

Such are the logical relations among these properties. It is important for us to realize that we can give up extreme immutability, a-temporality, and simplicity without detracting from the grandeur of our idea of God. For instance, for God to be such that his nature can be analyzed in distinct properties and temporal parts is not for God to be dependent in any substantive and objectionable sense on those parts for what he is. On the contrary, those parts can be held to be dependent on him.[3] So deciding that the notion of metaphysical simplicity has no application to God need not involve detracting from the divine perfection. Process theologians have repeatedly called our attention to those features of the classical conception of God, such as simplicity, a-temporality, and extreme immutability, which seem to comport ill with the biblical picture of God and the religious conception of God as in interaction with us his creatures, and have rejected vociferously those classical attributions. Their insistence at this point is that our idea of God be controlled by the data of revelation and religious experience seen as normative by the church. Thus, intuitions about what properties are great-making properties—for example, intuitions that it is better to be outside time than to be temporal—are only defeasible indicators of truth: they can sometimes be wrong. The idea of perfection is not itself rich enough to tell us alone what God is like in every way. And we should not expect to develop our idea of God just from the Anselmian formula together with supporting value intuitions. The revelation God has granted us in his Word and in his Incarnation must be attended to as the central source of any detailed conception of what God is like.

By challenging the classical conception of God, process theologians have helped open the eyes of many Christian thinkers to the role of revelation as an important control on purely philosophical theorizing concerning the nature of God. And the impact of their challenge is enhanced by their attempt to provide an alternative conception of God which can satisfy the requirements of perfection without creating the problems we find in classical theism.

Consider the claim that God is immutable. This is a claim that nearly all Christians want to endorse in some sense. But there are many ways of understanding it distinct from the classical conception we have been reviewing. Some theologians seem to understand it in the very minimal sense that God is reliable in the conduct of his affairs. They take divine immutability to be no more than God's moral dependability. On the other hand, there is a stronger, more comprehensive construal of divine immutability which stops far short of the extreme classical view. This would be the claim that it is impossible that God change either with respect to his defining attributes, those properties distinctive to and constitutive of deity—such properties as omniscience, perfect goodness, and almightiness—or with respect to his character and basic intentions.[4] For example, God could not ever have begun to be omniscient, nor can he ever cease to exemplify this attribute. This conception of divine immutability excludes certain very important sorts of change from the life of God, but also allows God to undergo the sorts of change involved in his being unceasingly active and in his interaction with his creation.

This dual aspect characterization of deity is somewhat like the conception articulated by many process theologians, including Charles Hartshorne, which often is referred to by them as dipolar theism. There is one pole of deity, one aspect of God which is necessarily as it is, and thus is immutable. There is, however, contrary to classical theism, a second aspect of deity characterized by receptivity, responsiveness, and change. On this conception of God, the immutability required by divine perfection is perfectly compatible with the sort of change required by God's interaction with his created world. In supplementing their critique of the classical conception with such an attractive alternative way of thinking about what God is like, process theologians have provided an important service to modern theology.

God's Relation to the World

In many ways, what process theology has said about God and his relation to the world has been of value, and has served as a needed corrective to some elements of traditional thought, as we have seen. Yet there are also process claims about God and the world which are unacceptable to Christian faith. Let us consider briefly one way in which a genuine insight had by many process thinkers has been translated into a theological commitment which is unacceptable to orthodox Christians. In process thought, every existent object is viewed as essentially related to other existent objects. Essential relatedness is a pervasive characteristic of reality. Prominent process thinkers such as Charles Hartshorne, along with many more traditional theologians influenced by St. Anselm, hold that God necessarily exists. Not only is it a matter of fact true that God exists, but things could not possibly have been otherwise. God's nonexistence is impossible. Now a property is essential to an individual just in case that individual could not fail to have that property without failing to exist. Since God cannot fail to exist, his essential properties are all necessarily exemplified. And so, if every existent individual is essentially related to other existent objects, and God is a necessarily existent individual, there must of necessity exist objects distinct from God to which he is related. And further, since every object distinct from God must be dependent on him as creature to creator, it follows that a created world necessarily exists. God is necessarily a creator. But any property an individual has necessarily, he does not have freely. So it follows that God never was free with respect to whether he would create a world distinct from himself. He may have been free to create this world rather than another one, but he was not free not to create.

On this view, God needs a world to which to relate himself. A number of process thinkers have given a parallel argument for this view, beginning not from the premise that all existent objects are essentially related to others, but from a specifically theistic premise that God essentially exemplifies a certain sort of relation—that of being loving. The sort of love intended here is not self-love, but what we can call 'other love'. It is thus impossible that God exist without loving another, some individual distinct from himself. But every individual distinct from God is a created being. It is thus impossible for God to exist without a creation. So, again, God has never been free to refrain from creating at all. To be who he is, he needs a world.

The conclusion common to both these lines of reasoning is at odds with a firm commitment of the Christian tradition, the belief that with respect to creation God was utterly free not only concerning what he would create but, also concerning whether he would bring into existence any universe at all. I think that process theologians who mount these sorts of arguments are starting from genuine insights about relatedness and divine love: Everything that exists is essentially related to other existent individuals, and it is an essential property of deity to be other-loving. But the process theologians' conclusions do not follow from these premises as they seem to think. A traditional Christian, upholding the orthodox belief in God's absolute freedom with respect to creation can capture both these insights by a properly articulated doctrine of the Trinity.

The minimal content of any acceptable formulation of Trinitarianism will specify that within deity there is an internal relatedness. On a traditional understanding of the Trinity, each of the three persons is distinct from the other two. Theologians throughout the centuries have differed over whether to stress the distinctions of these three persons, one from the others, or their unity, which is such that Christians can say there is one God who exists as three persons. There are thus two strands of orthodox thinking on the matter. What is called the social view of the Trinity, or Social Trinitarianism, is an approach which stretches back to the Cappadocian fathers, and which has had able development and defense in recent years. The other emphasis, on the unity of deity, which tends to see the three-ness of the Trinity as three modes of the existence of one being, was represented by, for example, St. Augustine, and has actually been the dominant view among theologians. The Augustinian emphasis, I think, has resources for countering the process view we are explaining, but it will be simpler, and possibly more interesting as well, to consider how a social view of the Trinity can capture the process insights at this point while avoiding their conclusion.

While discussing favorably the argument that the essentiality of divine love requires a creation, Barry L. Whitney has written that:

> If one were to reply that love could exist only in God himself among the persons of the Trinity, this would seem to imply an unacceptable "tri-theism" wherein the persons of the Trinity are considered as distinct centers of consciousness.[4]

Is a social view of the Trinity, as Whitney claims, an unacceptable tri-theism? Or can three distinct centers of consciousness, three individuals, three persons be acknowledged as God without any unacceptable theological results? These are difficult questions, which would require a great deal more treatment than can be given them here. But I shall address what many philosophers and theologians appear to have taken to be a decisive argument against any plurality of divine persons, and show how, in seeing what is wrong with it, we may be seeing how a Social Trinitarianism can be a completely orthodox view to hold.

No being is divine unless it has all the defining attributes of deity. Any divine persons must be essentially omniscient, omnibenevolent, and omnipotent, as well as necessarily existent, and so forth. With this in mind let us ask whether there could be two divine individuals or persons.

Let us begin with a thought experiment. Imagine two arm wrestlers of exactly equal power, skill, and determination. Their match presumably will end in a stand-off, clasped hands straight up, equidistant from each side of the table. Now imagine two essentially omnipotent beings 01 and 02. Suppose 01 wants some contingent object A to exist at some time t. And suppose 02 wants A not to exist at t. At t, what happens? There is here no equivalent to a stand-off. By reflection on this sort of imaginable scenario, numerous philosophers and theologians have been led to conclude that there cannot possibly be more than one essentially omnipotent being. Yet, our thought experiment does not support this strong a conclusion, only the interestingly weaker conclusion that there cannot be multiple, essentially omnipotent beings *with opposable wills*. However one philosopher, William Wainwright, has proposed a conceptual claim about persons which, when joined to this weaker conclusion, will entail the stronger one that there cannot be more than one essentially omnipotent person. The claim is that:

(C) Necessarily, given that two persons are genuinely distinct, it is possible for their wills to conflict.[5]

This is just a claim, in other words, that any two or more persons have opposable wills. If Wainwright is correct here, Social Trinitarianism of any clearly orthodox sort is ruled out.

But why think Wainwright is correct? It surely does seem to be a necessary truth of a conceptual sort that it is possible for the wills of any distinct persons to differ—01 for example willing A, 02 either just having no intention with respect to A, or else willing only that whatever 01 wills concerning A be done. But differing in this way is compatible with their wills being necessarily harmonious, such that it is impossible for them to conflict. Unless we have any good reason to endorse Wainwright's stronger claim (C), and I for one do not see any good reason to, we seem to be left with the real possiblilty that there be multiple, essentially ommnipotent persons necessarily harmonious in will. This is a far cry from any sort of pagan polytheism, whose gods were in continual conflict. As long as we recognize the conceptual requirement of necessary harmony in will, a belief in multiple divine persons, in particular three, will be far from any obviously unacceptable sort of tri-theism. And it may well be that the unity of deity among the three persons of the Trinity consists, at least in part, in that very harmony of will.

If we can endorse a social conception of the Trinity, a very simple way of blocking the process arguments for the necessity of creation we are examining will follow. But there is one further argument which can be given against a multiplicity of divine persons which draws on a distinctive claim of process theology. According to leading process thinkers, such as Whitehead and Hartshorne, God develops through time, progressively enriching his experience and thereby surpassing his own previous levels of greatness. According to them, it is a conceptual truth that any divine being is a greatest possible being not in the sense that he is so great he could not possibly be greater, but in the sense that he is so great no other being could possibly be greater. In short, God's greatness is unsurpassable by any other being. We shall return to the conception of divine perfection in the last section of this paper, but for now I want to look at another argument Wainwright has attempted to construct, this time from the process conception of unsurpassability to the conclusion that there cannot be more than one divine person. Wainwright very carefully lays out his argument in the following ten numbered propositions:

(1) Necessarily, any perfect being is more perfect at later times than at earlier times. (This follows from the dynamic process conception of perfection.)

(2) Necessarily, if there were two unsurpassable beings A and B, then A at time $t + 1$ would be more perfect than A at time t, and B at $t + 1$ would be more perfect than B at t. [from (1)]

(3) Necessarily, B at $t + 1$ is either more perfect than, just as perfect as, or less perfect than, A at t.

(4) Necessarily, if it is more perfect, then B at $t + 1$ surpasses A at t, from which it follows that A is surpassable by another being and is therefore not perfect.

(5) Necessarily, if it is less perfect, then A at t surpasses B at $t + 1$, from which it follows what B is surpassable by another being and is therefore not perfect.

(6) Necessarily, if it is equally perfect, then since A at $t + 1$ is more perfect than A at t, A at $t + 1$ is more perfect than B at $t + 1$, from which it follows that B is surpassable and therefore not perfect. Therefore,

(7) Necessarily, if there were two perfect or unsurpassable beings A and B, then either A would not be perfect or B would not be perfect. [from (2) through (6)]

(8) Necessarily, if there were two perfect or unsurpassable beings, then there would be two perfect beings at least one of which was not perfect.

(9) It is impossible for there to be two perfect beings at least one of which is not perfect. Therefore,

(10) It is impossible for there to be two perfect or unsurpassable beings. [from (8) and (9)][6]

This is an impressive argument whose only major flaw is that it depends on an artificial conception of unsurpassability which not even process theologians need to hold. The intuition, or claim that God is unsurpassable by any being distinct from himself is captured most naturally by an understanding of unsurpassability according to which a being A is unsurpassable just in case it is impossible that there exist a being B and a time t such that B-at-t is greater than A-at-t. And on this most natural understanding of surpassability the argument given by Wainwright will not work. For the unsurpassability of A will not be judged by how A at t compares to B at $t + n$ (for any positive value of n). To the extent that we have no good reason to accept the construal of unsurpassability on which Wainwright's argument turns, and reason to prefer a more natural construal, we have no reason to judge this to be a good argument against any multiplicity of perfect divine persons. So the possibility of Social Trinity still stands.

Suppose we endorse a social view of the Trinity, as many orthodox Christians of the past have. Can we account for the essential relatedness of all existent beings and the essentiality of the other-love of God without accepting the process claim about the necessity of creation? Yes, we obviously can, for the three persons of the Trinity exist in eternal and necessary relatedness to one another, a relatedness which includes an intra-Trinitarian relation of love. The necessity for any divine person that there exist an object distinct from himself as an object of relatedness and love does not entail the necessity of a physical universe or the necessity that there exist some contingent being or other distinct from God. So in the light of this understanding of the doctrine of the Trinity, we can capture the insights of process theology at this point without following the process theologians into their quite unorthodox conclusions concerning God's freedom in creation, or, rather, his lack of it.

God's Preservation of the World

It is a tenet of process philosophy that the changing aspect of deity reflects and registers eternally every thing, state of affairs, and change in the world. Every contingent being which comes into existence and then passes away only from the original physical stage of its existence, retaining a sort of foothold in reality in the mind of God. According to many process thinkers, it is impossible that God will ever cease to remember and preserve the objective reality of even the slightest and most ephemeral of entities in this world. God is ever changing with respect to the continually active registration in his omniscient knowledge of every new thing that happens in our world. He is never changing with respect to the strength with which he holds all these things in memory, eternally preserving their objective reality. At one time in the past, it was true that Socrates was drinking hemlock. It is now true that Socrates once drank hemlock, and it always will be true. It can never now become false. According to some process thinkers, this very fact about truth, the fact that truths about the past are forever true, along with the fact that we now can refer to Socrates at all, a being who no longer exists on the earthly stage of reality, reflects the objective preservation of the past in the mind of God.

What happens in this world is thus, to process thought, not merely ephemeral. The ongoing developments of history are not transient, evanescent, and ultimately meaningless. They are eternally preserved and they make a difference in the actuality of the ultimate being, God. Viewed in this way, process thinkers declare, the events of history are full of eternal significance concerning even the smallest details of life.

300

There is a grandeur about this view which cannot be denied. And it is true that many, if not most, people find a great deal of personal satisfaction and comfort in the thought that, in an ultimate sense, "Here today, gone tomorrow" is not the final truth about things in our world. It is interesting and important to note, though, that in so far as it commands widespread assent and provides widespread comfort, this view about God and the world, at least on the points mentioned here, is not unique to process thought. It is a fully orthodox and traditional religious view. What is unique to, and distinctive of, much process thought on these matters is the way in which the preservation picture is used to provide a conception of human immortality—the final end of man.

Immortality has been a central and driving concern in human thought throughout the centuries. Blaise Pascal, the great seventeenth century scientist and religious thinker once wrote:

> The immortality of the soul is something of such vital importance to us, affecting us so deeply, that one must have lost all feeling not to care about knowing the facts of the matter. All our actions and thoughts must follow such different paths, according to whether there is hope of eternal blessings or not . . . .[7]

And this sentiment has been echoed by many others. Tennyson, for example, once said:

> If there is no immortality I shall throw myself into the sea,

a pronouncement which many people on first reading find puzzling, since many of us would incline to say rather that if there is no immortality, we should be as careful as possible, avoiding the sea, great heights, and any other dangers. However the point, and profundity, of Tennyson's remark comes to light clearly when we meditate on the words of the nineteenth-century English historian Henry Thomas Buckle:

> If immortality be untrue, it matters little whether anything else be true or not.

Add those of Bismark, who said bluntly:

> Without the hope of an afterlife, this life is not even worth the effort of getting dressed in the morning.

301

The importance of the promise of immortality has been paramount to many of the most eminent thinkers of history. It is a central tenet of the Christian faith that those who love God and appropriate the saving work of Christ on their behalf will exist in communion with him forever. Personal immortality through resurrection into new life with Christ is a fundamental belief of orthodoxy. It is a concern with which any comprehensive theology must deal.

A number of process theologians, including Charles Hartshorne, whose work ordinarily sets a standard for process thought, have reinterpreted the idea of personal immortality and have argued that their version of this idea captures the only real hope we have for eternity. As John Cobb and others have pointed out, Whitehead's metaphysical system itself neither entails nor precludes the continuation of conscious human experience beyond bodily death. Whitehead himself seems also to have been agnostic on this issue. It has been left to other process thinkers to decide what should be said about personal immortality.

The view endorsed by Hartshorne and others is that there is no hope to be had in an eternal, and blissful continuation of personal conscious experience beyond bodily death for religious believers, or for anyone. Our lives are rather immortalized, or preserved forever, in the mind, or more specifically, the memory, of God. It is thus in the sense, and only in the sense, that everything else is preserved by God forever, that human beings will have an objective immortality. This is the promise of immortality allowed by Hartshorne.

Of course, this is obviously not the sort of immortality for which most people hope. What difference does it make to me if there are, in effect, divine snapshots of my life preserved forever in the gallery of omniscience? On the Hartshornian picture, my future reality one thousand years from now will be no different in fundamental nature from the present reality of dinosaurs: there will be truths about me, as I was, and I shall be remembered, as I was. What we must ask is why Hartshorne and other process thinkers have abandoned the traditional, full-bodied view of immortality in favor of this thin, mnemonic alternative.

In one of his most recent books, Hartshorne gives, or rather, hints at, only one argument against the traditional belief in a personal afterlife. The argument is basically quite simple, and is akin to arguments offered by other critics of traditional religious belief who are not process thinkers. It is an argument which arises out of no fundamental tenet of process metaphysics, but rather, as I shall point out, turns on a crucial premise which is actually either inconsistent with some central claim of process thought, or else is such that we have no good reason to think it true. Either way, it cannot be used by a process theologian to get us to abandon orthodoxy on this point and join his ranks.

In *Omnipotence and Other Theological Mistakes*, Hartshorne says:

> Those who want to go on being themselves forever and yet pass on to additional experiences after death are either asking for unbearable monotony, endless reiterations of the same personality traits, or they are asking for a unique prerogative of God, ability to achieve self-identity through no matter how great and diverse change and novelties. Unconsciously they either want to be bored to death, so to speak, or to be God.[8]

The traditional Christian promise to believers is that of a blissful eternity. It could be argued that the notion of a blissful eternity is incoherent: There are many sorts of pleasures, or aesthetically positive experiences to a person. Throughout an infinite span of time, each type of experience would have to be repeated over and over and over again. But at a certain point, what was once of positive value would eventually become cloying, or at best unbearably boring. Such an existence would not be blissful. So a life can be blissful or it can be eternal; it cannot be both. The concept of blissful eternity is then something like a concept of square circularity—a conception of an impossibility, a logically incoherent notion.

If this were a good argument, if there could be no blissful eternity, then the traditional Christian promise of everlasting life would have to be rejected, but so would a central tenet of process theology—the claim that God's perfection is eternally progressive, that he eternally surpasses his previous states of value by virtue of the ongoing and ever positive aesthetic experiences he has of the world. For the process God exists in a state which cannot be denied to be one of blissful eternity. If positive value through infinite time is possible in the case of God, the very notion of a blissful eternity is not itself logically incoherent. If it were incoherent, this major claim concerning the progressive perfection of the process God would be ruled out as false, and, moreover, as impossible.

The argument just presented for the incoherence of the notion of a blissful eternity is not a good one. Supposing that there were only finitely many positive sorts of experience to be had, it is only a contingent fact of our psychology that repetition bores and cloys. It is part of the Christian hope that in the resurrected life our psychology, as well as the bodily form of our existence, will be transformed. But this need not alone circumvent the threat of tedium. For what reason do we have to suppose that, for any sense of 'kind' relevant to the ongoing experience of an immortal, transformed soul, there are only finitely many kinds of experience possible? There is no reason that I can see for thinking this, and there is no reason that Hartshorne or anyone else offers. In fairness to Hartshorne, he seems to assume neither that a blissful eternity is impossible, nor that the types of positive experience available in principle are of finite number. He does not imply that to enjoy eternal bliss, one would have to be God. But why think this? Why not allow that in order to enjoy such a state of existence one would have to be either God himself, or a being created in and conformed to the image of God? This is what Christians traditionally claim, and Hartshorne has given us no reason to conclude otherwise.

Many theologians have said that part of what it means, in traditional terms, to be in the image of God is to be creative. Creativity, or the capacity for creativity, is a key feature of our nature reflecting what it is to be God. It is one aspect of human nature which images deity. And it is the essence of creativity to be openended and inexhaustible. Our union and communion with God in the afterlife will not extinguish this feature of ours which reflects his nature. Rather, there is every reason for the Christian to suppose it will be magnified in the hereafter. And it is impossible for an individual to be both eternally creative and at the same time infinitely bored. Human creativity, and what it manifests, is a key to the real possibility of eternal bliss for human beings. One need not wish to be God in order to wish to be in a state of eternal bliss. For an infinite span of life, monotony and deity are not the only two options as Hartshorne claims. His argument contradicts this perspective, implies it is false, but his remarks do absolutely nothing to show it to be false.

And in the last analysis, it is hard to see how a process theologian could resist an argument in favor of traditional belief based on the importance of creativity. For the pervasive presence of endless creativity in the world is a central idea of process thought. Some critics even contend that in process theology, creativity is more fundamental and ultimate than God. It cannot be denied that it is a most important feature of reality from the process perspective. And once we have a fuller appreciation of what creativity is, we can appreciate a bit more how a creative personal existence can continue on in blissful eternity as traditional Christian theology claims. There is no good reason to abandon the traditional promise in favor of the extraordinarily weak Hartshornian alternative of eternal preservation as a memory in the mind of God.

Process theologians most often present all their views to us as a package deal. And certainly, this is an inveterate human tendency: "Love me, love my dog." But it seems to me very clear that toward process theology we must have an attitude of critical appreciation at best. Process theology has issued some important correctives concerning the medieval conception of God. But process theologians, in a spirit of innovation, often have departed unnecessarily, and dangerously, from the traditional claims of the faith they most often purport to be preserving. I think it is entirely possible to profit from what is laudable in process theology, while eschewing what is lamentable. By exercising critical discernment, we can in the end come from an examination of process thought with an enhanced conception of God and the world.

NOTES

1. For recent criticisms, see Alvin Plantinga, *Does God Have a Nature?* (Milwaukee: Marquette University Press, 1980), pp. 22ff; Ronald Nash, *The Concept of God* (Grand Rapids: Zondervan, 1983), pp. 85-98; and Thomas V. Morris, "On God and Man: A View of Divine Simplicity," forthcoming in *Religious Studies*.

2. For some of the best attempts to develop and defend the classical conception in recent years, see Norman Kretzmann and Eleanore Stump, "Eternity," *Journal of Philosophy* 78 (1981), pp. 429-458; and William E. Mann, "Simplicity and Immutability in God," *International Philosophical Quarterly*, Vol. 23, no. 3, pp. 267-276.

3. For an adumbration of this view, see my article "Necessary Beings," forthcoming in *Mind*. A further articulation of the view is attempted by Christopher Menzel and Thomas V. Morris in "Absolute Creation."

4. Barry L. Whitney, "Divine Immutability in Process Philosophy and Contemporary Thomism," *Horizons* 7 (1980), p. 67.

5. Wainwright discusses this in a paper entitled "Monotheism," presented at the Research Conference in the Philosophy of Religion held at the University of Nebraska-Lincoln in April 1984, sponsored by the National Endowment for the Humanities.

6. In the draft of "Monotheism" read at Nebraska.

7. *Pensees* (Penguin Classics Edition), p. 156.

8. Charles Hartshorne, *Omnipotence and Other Theological Mistakes* (Albany: State University of New York Press, 1984), p. 35.

PART FOUR

Personal Reactions

Between Classical
and Process Theism

Clark H. Pinnock

Clark H. Pinnock

Clark H. Pinnock is professor of theology at McMaster Divinity College in Hamilton, Ontario. Prior to this he taught at Regent College, Trinity Evangelical Divinity School, New Orleans Baptist Theological Seminary, and the University of Manchester (England) where he also took his doctorate in New Testament. He is the author of *Reason Enough, Biblical Revelation* and *Set Forth Your Case*.

The writers in this volume have been asked to explain what process theology is and to offer a fair evangelical criticism of it. In my essay I would like to go beyond that, and have us start to think about why process theology got started in the first place, and what it tells us about what we as evangelicals ought to be saying. Because its doctrine of God is the most important topic in the process way of thinking, I will concentrate entirely upon it.

When I first thought about what my criticisms of process theism might be, it was not hard to think of several objections to it. But as I continued to ponder the assignment, I came to realize that I could hardly criticize process theism without at the same time objecting to certain features of classical belief in God. Imagine, if you will, a marriage dispute in which both partners are in the wrong, and you are asked to criticize only the wife. It would be an awkward request to fulfill because fairness would require that you say something like that in this case. It is impossible for me to set forth a case against process theism without at the same time calling attention to certain deep inadequacies in classical theism. There are, in my opinion, strengths and weaknesses in both classical and process theism, and it is important for the evangelical not to be blind to the full picture. Getting our thinking straight on this can help us see the way to an improved understanding of evangelical theism.

I am by no means the only evangelical scholar who has seen the need to move beyond both classical and process theism.[1] A serious one-sidedness in the direction of transcendence crept into classical theism owing to the Hellenistic influence, and process theism is an equally one-sided reaction to it tending toward radical immanence. This pattern of one-sidedness on both sides means that we have to move in the direction of a model which keeps a proper balance between transcendence and immanence, and makes such adjustments in our thinking about God as will serve the dynamic biblical presentation in a faithful way.

Therefore, rather than limit myself in my essay to negative comments about process theism, I would prefer to set forth what is wrong in classical theism, then process theism, and in the final section to sketch a constructive alternative to them both. I am quite convinced that we evangelicals need a model of the divine which is open to the world and dynamically involved in what transpires in it.[2]

What is wrong with classical theism?

Evangelicals are caught in a bind in the matter of their doctrine of God. On the one hand, their loyalty to the Bible makes them want to affirm the living God of the scriptural narrative. God is not aloof and remote from the world, but is dynamic and active on behalf of his people. On the other hand, their theological tradition stemming from Augustine gets them implicated in a systematic way of thinking which brings the dynamic openness of God into doubt. They find themselves thinking of God's relation to time and space in such a way as to give the distinct impression that events in the world from beginning to end are all sewed up and that God is utterly unaffected by what goes on here below. Process theism is correct, in my view, to call attention to the tension and even contradiction which exists between evangelical biblical theology and evangelical systematic theology.[3]

The basic problem with classical theism as we find it in Augustine, Anselm, and Aquinas is that it does not present God as a dynamic personal agent involved with us in our joys and sorrows, but rather as a closed and immobile structure. It tends to threaten the biblical picture of God as a person who engages other persons in dynamic interaction. Although Aquinas, for example, certainly attributed personal qualities like love and mercy to God, he construed them in so transcendent a way as to cast doubt upon their reality and intelligibility. We hardly know what it means to say that God is love and wisdom. They are brought to perfection in such a way as almost to disappear from sight. But while the God of the Bible plans and decides, acts and responds, remembers and predicts, it is not clear how the God of classical theism does any of these things. How can a God who is timeless act in time? How could God create the world at a specific time? Without meaning to, classical theism presents God in such a way as to make God appear to be inert.[4]

The classical view presents God as a being which is immutable and impassible. This means that God does not change in any way at all. He has no potentialities that are not already actualized. There is no form of being which God can acquire or lose. Being impassible means that God is not able to be affected by any external event or cause. If God could be affected in any way by the world, it was thought that he would not be wholly self-sufficient and self-determining. God would have to endure experiences which he did not choose and be caught up in the temporal world of becoming and change. Though to us these qualities bespeak a static condition, to the ancient mind they suggested stability and solidity. They felt it was reassuring to know that God could not be affected by the world or have his blessedness in any way disturbed.

For most of us today, however, this immobility in God is by no means attractive. We are not thrilled to learn that God is self-enclosed reality and utterly changeless. When we read the Bible and see how full of passion God is, how far God is from being apathetic, we rejoice. We are not impressed when classical theism tells us that God takes in the whole of history in a single glance, because what that means to us is that history is meaningless. If the day after tomorrow is as fixed in God's timeless present as the day before yesterday, then there is no meaning to our freedom and power to shape what will be in the future. In the classical view, God knows everything that ever will be and knows it infallibly and changelessly. Nothing new can ever penetrate God's experience which was not always there. That can only mean that everything about the future is closed and settled in advance down to the last detail.[5]

The way in which classical theism thinks about God has a definite tendency to diminish the dynamic dimension of God's nature and to threaten the reality of creaturely freedom. Aristotle's God, though unchangeable and timeless, at least was held not to know the world or its history, and thus did not endanger it. By keeping God separate from the world, the Greek philosopher was able to affirm both God's immutability and the world's contingent reality. But when the Greek ideal of immutability got mixed up with the biblical category of history it had a deleterious effect. As Griffin, a process theologian, correctly puts it, "When the Aristotelean unchanging God was combined with the biblical God who knows the world, it became necessary in order to achieve a self-consistent position, to deny all genuine contingency. . . .For if God knows everything that occurs in the world, and knows this infallibly and unchangeably, without any additions to the content of the divine knowledge, then the total truth about reality, including what is future for us temporal beings must be completely determinate."[6] The classical model of God conflicts with the need to affirm the reality of freedom and genuine contingency.

But let the reader notice that I do not wish to exaggerate the difficulties of classical theism. There is a strong tendency on the part of process theists like Ogden and Hartshorne to caricature the position. Just as a political cartoon about President Reagan, for example, can affect the mind more than a serious piece of analysis, so the critique of classical theism can overstep the bounds of good judgment, and fail in the minds of fair people. Indeed, if the choice were exclusively between classical and process theism (which it is not), I would certainly opt for classical theism. Nevertheless, the defects are there and must be pointed out.

In the Gifford Lectures for 1983-84, the Anglican theologian John Macquarrie speaks of a one-sidedness in classical theism. It does a fine job of presenting God as sovereign over the world, but not a good job in conveying God's immanence. God can act upon the world, but the world cannot act upon God. God can affect the world, but the world cannot affect him. God is in no way enriched by the world, and could be perfectly happy if it ceased to be. Mutuality and reciprocity are in short supply. God is said to be loving, and yet is in no way vulnerable and supremely untouched by the pain of his creatures.[7]

Now if we are honest, we would have to admit that it has been process thinkers who have called our attention to some of these problems. I have to acknowledge the stimulus I have personally received from them, and how they have made me aware of the need to introduce changes into the received doctrine of God. Hartshorne, for example, has put a lot of effort into exposing the difficulties and suggesting alternatives. I have been helped by his ideas on various things. He has taught me that thinking of God as literally *all*-powerful divests the finite universe of a degree of power. He has pressed the point that God, though unchanging in his character, is certainly able to change in response to a changing creation.[8] In my theology, at least, God has used process thinkers to compel me to change certain ideas which I had and bring them up to scriptural standards. Without being a process theologian myself, I am certainly indebted to such thinkers for many good insights. And, I suppose, what worries me a little is the fear that evangelical theologians in general may not be willing to learn what they need to learn or change in ways they really ought to change. My fear is that if evangelical theologians refuse to recognize the moments of truth in process thought, they will force many to accept process theology. Unless we construct a model of the divine somewhere between classical and process theism, I fear that we will lose some of our keenest minds to process liberalism.

I admit that modern culture has influenced me in this matter. The new emphasis upon human freedom requires that I think of God as self-limited in relation to the world. For the Greeks it may have been natural to place God completely beyond the temporal flow, in a serene magisterial aloofness. But for us it certainly is not. We read it in the Bible, and we know it in our hearts, that God is the creator and sustainer of a world with genuine freedom in it, and that he does not crush it with overwhelming and coercive power. On the contrary God shares his power with us, and invites us to work along with him in the re-creation of the world. Although to the ear of a classical theist, this may sound too radical, nevertheless, to the biblically attuned ear this wonderfully dynamic concept of God is precisely what the Bible attests. Early in our theological development, we allowed Hellenistic ways of thinking to give the Christian doctrine of God an overly negative view of time and space in relation to God. The modern world invites us to restore the positive assessment of history and change and in so doing draw closer to biblical teaching. Let no one say that modernity always lures us away and never beckons us toward the truth.[9]

What is wrong with process theology?

Obviously the process theologian hopes that evangelicals who wake up to the severe difficulties in classical theism will come over to his side. After all, he has a dynamic doctrine of God. But we cannot do so for reasons which I shall now try to explain.

The basic problem with process theology for a biblically and rationally oriented evangelical is that it is clearly an extreme correction and a great overreaction to the classical theism it proposes to improve. As a result it fails to improve the situation, but instead creates new problems of its own. Although process theology is certainly in tune with the modern emphasis of freedom, it presents us with a God who is not even the creator of the world, but rather one of several factors interacting with each other in the process of evolution. God introduces order and value into the process and empathizes with us in the experiences of life. But God is not the ground of the world's existence and has no final control over what is going on. It is not just that God allows the world some liberty while reserving the right to intervene. God is finite and metaphysically incapable of determining events. Although one might say God preserves items of value in the world by storing them in his everlasting memory bank, it would not be true to say that God redeems the world. One could not really speak of God's judgment against sin, or his reconciling actions to justify sinners. When presented with this doctrine of God, I think most evangelicals would shudder and feel that such a God is hardly worthy of our praise. Although Ogden mounts an impressive argument for the way a process deity can supply a firm basis for our confidence in the worthwhileness of our existence, I think many people will feel that a godling of this small proportion is not big enough to satisfy their religious needs. They would naturally feel that a God who is neither the creator or redeemer of the world in any strong sense does not deserve to be called God, and is vastly inferior to the God of the Bible and evangelical experience.[10]

Let me state the basic biblical case against process theology. It begins with the doctrine of creation. Process theism suggests that the Bible is ambiguous about God being the creator of the world. But surely it is not. The verb 'create' in Hebrew is used only of God's activity and never mentions the material out of which God makes things. There is a strong implication in it that God called the world into being in an effortless way and sustains it in existence. As the psalmist says, "He spoke, and it came to be" (33:9). The world exists because of the good pleasure of God. If it did not, then we would have to be dualists. That is, we would have to believe that the world always existed as a second ultimate alongside God. Although there is a relative dualism even in the Bible, as when there is a struggle between good and evil, God and the Devil, there is no ultimate dualism of this kind. It would mean that God is a finite being and unable to make plans and realize them. It would mean that the world is a kind of evil power against which God has to struggle eternally. No one with a high view of the Bible is going to be able to accept such a model.

When all is said and done, process thought robs God of his sovereign freedom. It makes him metaphysically dependent on the world and unable to do what he chooses. It would mean that his actions are always determined by something outside himself and his being controlled by the structure of reality of which God is only one element. God would be like a Greek god who was in the grip of a more ultimate metaphysical ground. Our belief and reliance on the freedom of God would have to be abandoned. That feeling requires that God be independent of the world and able to act unhindered. God must be free in this sense in order to be the kind of personal agent the Bible describes. I agree with the process thinkers that the traditional notion of omnipotence must be revised, but I cannot possibly revise it to such a radical extent as they do. The ontological transcendence of God is essential if we are to maintain the biblical picture of God's freedom and redemptive activity.[11]

But it is not just a biblical objection. I do not think the process model of God is superior to classical theism even in terms of rationality, and especially not if certain adjustments are made to the received doctrine. Process theology is not only attenuated from a biblical point of view, it is also deficient intellectually. It is a simple fact that philosophers and theologians have not generally found process metaphysics to be very convincing or helpful, and for good reasons.

If one is looking for a God who can explain the world and supply assistance to us in the living of life, process theology is pretty thin soup. Process thinkers have reacted so sharply to the monarchial model of God that they have reduced him to a puny godling who behaves like a cosmic sponge soaking up the positive things that happen in the world or a hapless victim of a world completely out of his control. This God is hardly more appealing than one who sits enthroned, entirely out of touch with the world. An atheist might be inclined to think that the God of process theology is little more than nature itself in which he already trusts.

Certainly it is doubtful whether the process God can be considered a person. It is much more like a principle in the overall organism of the process. When God is said to wipe away every tear, it is not so much that the divine Agent actually deals with us personally, as it is that the metaphysical system implies that the tears which fall get soaked up by the cosmic sponge. And as Robert Neville says, "My own religious intuitions tell me that, if God wipes away the tears, it is out of divine freedom, not because God is metaphysically obliged."[12] Indeed, process theology sounds more like religious naturalness than theism.

The evangelical theist is not attracted to a view which binds God to the world in a necessary and nonvoluntary way. This move cannot serve him even if he sees the need to make some adjustments in classical theism. The correction is far too extreme biblically and rationally. The world is not necessary to God in the same way God is necessary to the world. God would exist whether there was a world or not. And, although God respects the freedom he gave to the creatures, the world does not bind his hands. God remains gloriously free to act upon the world and be an agent in history.

Let me offer a suggestion. It is acknowledged that Hartshorne modified Whitehead's ontology to bring out a clearer picture of God. What is now needed is for evangelical theists to go much further. Let them work on the classical concept of God to bring into it such good insights as process theology has identified, but without going to those extremes we have mentioned. Let them develop a dynamic model which would really deserve the name neo-classical.[13]

Classical Free Will Theism, the Alternative

I believe there is a way to avoid the Scylla of classical theism and the Charybdis of process theology, the one a rock, the other a whirlpool, appropriately enough. There is a way to think of God which is both biblically and rationally superior to the immobility of the first and the sheer flux of the second. David Basinger has made the same point, and called the alternative classical free will theism.[14]

Or we could call it open theism, as Richard Rice does.[15] The tactic involves taking what is positive from classical and process theology, and abandoning what is not helpful. It means that we affirm God as creator of the world as classical theism does and process thought does not, and also affirm the openness of God as process theology does and classical theism does not sufficiently. This leaves us with a model of the divine which sees God as transcendent over the world and yet existing in an open and mutually affecting relationship with the world. It is a doctrine of God which maintains mutuality and reciprocity within the framework of divine transcendence. Against classical theism it affirms that God is dynamic not static, and against process theology it says that God is the Lord of the universe and not a finite deity. I think it would be fair to say that my proposal constitutes a *via media*.

This model of God involves seeing God as the ontological creator of all finite beings and an agent unlimited by metaphysical necessities beyond his control. In this respect it is like classical theism. And it places emphasis upon God as a dynamic personal agent in a mutually affecting relationship with the world. In this respect it is like process theology. When you add it all up, you find a doctrine of God which is superior to either of them and maps a path between them. With Aquinas we maintain God's aseity (self-contained existence), while with Whitehead we grant true reciprocity with the world. As Thomas Tracy puts it, "This proposal maps out a path between two of the most sharply opposed options in contemporary discussion of the doctrine of God."[16]

To view it from another angle, my proposal involves an open view of God. It was wrong of classical theism to think of God, in line with Plato and Aristotle, as absolutely changeless. If God is closed to novelty as He must be according to this ideal of perfection, it means that the world God relates to is absolutely changeless too. It means that everything is fixed and definite, and there is no new thing the creature can inject into reality. We cannot think of God's experience as already determined by a timeless intuition. The Bible forces us to think of God as open to what happens in the world. Only in this way can we do proper justice to the value of creaturely events and decisions.

Notice that I am not motivated here by a desperate desire to defend man's autonomy even if it requires us to revise the doctrine of God. Rather I can see no other way of showing respect for the biblical presentation of God as a dynamic personal agency. It is not modernity we are trying to catch up to but the Bible itself. Ours is a God who rejoices when the news comes of a sinner repenting, and who tests Abraham to see if he will obey God. He is a God who changes his mind if people respond to his warnings, and who feels the sufferings of his people along with them. God is open, not closed. This is both the testimony of the Bible, and the only message people today are going to be able to hear. So let us seize the opportunity to tell them the truth so long obscured.

God is both changeless and changing. He is changeless in his nature and character—He is changing in his experience of a changing creation. There is nothing contradictory in this, as long as we differentiate what in God is changing and what is not. In John Macquarrie's Gifford Lectures for 1983-84, the term 'dialectical' is used for a proposal similar to my own. The term is a dangerous one because it tends to connote an opposition between concepts. It can sound as if Macquarrie might mean that God is both changeless and changing, or timeless and temporal, or even good and evil at the same time. But this is surely nonsense and self-contradictory. I am not suggesting anything of that kind. I simply want to affirm that God is an unchangeable God in respect of his deity and personality, and a changing God in respect of his experiences and actions. It makes perfectly coherent sense, and is of course biblical.

In reading Macquarrie, however, I cannot believe that he himself wants 'dialectical' to mean a coincidence of oppositions even though he strays into such language at times.[17] Trying to introduce needed changes into classical theism, Macquarrie wants to achieve a better balance of transcendence and immanence. In a key illustration he speaks of God as an artist who, though He wholly transcends the art-work, nevertheless puts Himself into it so that it reflects His personality and gives Him a vehicle of communication. Though transcendent, God goes out from himself in creation and fills the world. As the poet said, "In Him we live and move and have our being" (Acts 17:28). God is not then wholly external to the world, but is a participant in history and a fellow traveller with us.[18]

It is simply a dynamic model of deity which we need, a doctrine of God who can relate to us is our creatureliness. God has created a significant universe and limited the exercise of his sovereignty in order to relate to the world without crushing it. We cannot think of history as the shadow of a timeless eternity or as the temporal unfolding of an eternal blueprint of the divine decisions. Rather, history is the theatre where new situations are encountered and fresh decisions are made, the scene of divine and human creativity. Classical theism was wrong to suggest that God was unconditioned by the world and unaffected by what goes on in it. No, there is a passivity in God which enables him to exist in a reciprocal way and be affected by the novelty which arises out of history. In some mysterious way we cannot understand how God shares in the temporality and changeability of his creatures. The past is decided, but the future is open and undecided even for God. God's experience of the world moves forward with time as possibilities become actualities. If this seems too radical for evangelicals, let them remember that it is no more radical than the dynamic picture the Bible gives itself.[19]

Now it is obvious that the model of deity which I am proposing will require us to redefine certain of the attributes of God as these have been traditionally conceived. I have already said how it is necessary to limit God's unchangeability to his eternal person and not apply it to God absolutely. To do so would be to destroy the world as a relatively autonomous creation of God. I have also hinted that we cannot possibly agree with Aquinas that God is impassible in the strong sense of being incapable of being affected by anything outside himself. The idea of course was to deny that God could be swayed by passion as we are, but the result was to deny God the feeling of love and wrath and so forth. As even H. P. Owen admits, "This is the most questionable aspect of classical theism."[20] Indeed it is! In fact, it is completely unacceptable. The central insight into the character of God in the Christian gospel is God's love revealed in the Cross. Here the gospel truth about God's suffering collides head-on with the Greek opinion that God cannot share in any kind of weakness at all. There is no clearer proof of the necessity of revising classical theism than the doctrine of the divine impassibility.[21]

Omnipotence is another attribute that cannot be taken the way theologians like Augustine and Calvin did. They thought that God decrees everything that happens, and that nothing ever happens contrary to the will of God in some sense. This is clearly unacceptable. People do monstrous deeds every day which shock and offend God, actions which God certainly did not predestine. Although we must say against process theology that God suffers no metaphysical or necessary limitations on his power, we must also say that God created human beings with a degree of real freedom, making them morally accountable for their actions, and thus measures his own actions with that in view. God, we must suppose, exercises his power appropriately, given the kind of universe he made, and therefore allows us to act freely even if we choose to go contrary to his express will for us. There is no other way, in my judgment, to make sense of the biblical story of fall and redemption. Omnipotence cannot mean that God has determined history down to the last detail. It must mean the complete freedom to act even though God uses this freedom in self-limiting ways.

I would go further and say that it makes little sense to think of God's eternity as timeless, and a good deal of sense to think of him as everlasting as the Bible does (Ps. 90:2). Although Plato and his Christian followers thought that timelessness was the only way to affirm God's true infinity and transcendence, to me timelessness simply threatens God's dynamic agency. How can God act at any particular time, or know things that happen in sequence, or experience any feedback from the world, if God is timeless? The Bible says that God plans, decides, acts, remembers, predicts, and responds to events. But if God is timeless, he cannot do any of those things. There is a better way to look at God's eternity. God is not limited by time the way we are limited. He is certainly in some way supertemporal. God transcends our experience of time. But that does not make God atemporal or supra-temporal or timeless. Rather it makes God temporal to the nth degree so to speak. He does not experience time in a creaturely way, but he does enter into time and act in time. If he did not, we would still be in our sins. In ways we cannot understand, God transcends time. God *is* even when the world is not. But given a temporal world, we must say that God has a temporal dimension to his being that enables him to fill time. I do not know exactly what God's relation to time is. But I am sure it is wrong to say God is timeless.[22]

Let me go one step further even though I suspect I may have to walk alone down this path. I believe that we must adjust our understanding of the knowledge of God.[23] According to the traditional doctrine of God's omniscience, God knows everything that has ever happened and everything that ever will happen from the beginning to the end. It is based upon the notion that it would be impious to think of God learning things he did not know before. It also helps to explain how predictive prophecy might work. It is easy to see why people take it more or less for granted. However, I do not see how we can possibly take it for granted. If God knows ahead of time exactly what we will decide to do tomorrow, we are not free to do otherwise. Now I grant that God might have a pretty shrewd idea what we will decide to do because he knows us so well. But he cannot know precisely what we will decide if we really are the decisions makers. Nobody, not even God, could know that, for the simple reason that the decision is not available to be known. It has not been made yet. My view then of God's omniscience is that God knows everything it is possible to know, but that this cannot include future free decisions because they cannot in principle be known by simple definition. If they could be known, they would not be free.[24]

Conclusion

There is a need for evenhandedness when we hand out criticisms concerning theism. Process theology richly deserves to be criticized, but then so does classical theism against which it rails. In so many areas of theology we have to seek balance and try to avoid falling into a pit on one side or the other. When I read process theologians I realize two things: first that we need a theism which is more dynamic than the traditional view, and second that we need a God who is more deserving of that title than Whitehead's godling is. I hope the reader will agree that the model of the divine which I have sketched is both dynamic and deserving to be called God, to whom be glory forever.

In closing I ought to add a comment on the anticipated objection to my line of thought that this is nothing more than 'the halfway house of conservative process theism.'[25] This may be the way it looks from the vantage point of unrepentant classical theism, or even from the citadel of process theology. But the fact of the matter is that what I am proposing constitutes a viable approach lying between the two feuding protagonists and which hopefully will outrun them both.

NOTES

1. Let me mention three scholars who declare themselves on this point. John C. Moscop, *Divine Omniscience and Human Freedom* (Macon, Georgia: Mercer University Press, 1984); Ronald H. Nash, *The Concept of God* (Grand Rapids: Zondervan, 1983), pp. 22, 30, 36, 115; and Thomas F. Tracy, *God, Action, and Embodiment* (Grand Rapids: Eerdmans, 1984), pp. xix, 147-54.

2. The reader may wish to compare other efforts of mine to do this: Pinnock, "The Need for a Scriptural and Therefore a Neo-Classical Theism," in *Perspectives on Evangelical Theology*, edited by Kenneth S. Kantzer and Stanley N. Gundry (Grand Rapids: Baker Book House, 1979), pp. 37-42; and an essay to be published in 1985 by Inter-Varsity Press in a debate volume on divine sovereignty and human freedom.

3. I see the tension in Jack Cottrell, *What the Bible says about God the Creator* (Joplin, Missouri: College Publishing Co., 1983), chapters 6-8.

4. Thomas Tracy pursues this point in his book *God, Action, and Embodiment*.

5. Richard Rice develops this point most capably in *The Openness of God. The Relationship of Divine Foreknowledge and Human Free Will* (Washington, DC: Review and Herald, 1980). Though withdrawn from print, this book will be reissued soon by Bethany Fellowship, Minneapolis.

6. David R. Griffin, *God, Power, and Evil: A Process Theodicy* (Philadelphia: The Westminster Press, 1976), p. 44.

7. John Macquarrie, *In Search of Deity, An Essay in Dialectical Theism* (London: SCM Press, 1984), ch. 3.

8. Here are a few of Hartshorne's books on theism: *The Divine Relativity. A Social Conception of God* (New Haven: Yale University Press, 1948); *Man's Vision of God and the Logic of Theism* (Hamden, Conn.: Archon Books, 1964); *Omnipotence and Other Theological Mistakes* (Albany, NY: State University of New York, 1984).

9. I have appreciated Langdon Gilkey on these matters: *Message and Existence, An Introduction to Christian Theology* (New York: The Seabury Press, 1979) and "God" in *Christian Theology. An Introduction to its Traditions and Tasks* edited by Peter C. Hodgson and Robert H. King (Philadelphia: Fortress Press, 1982).

10. Schubert M. Ogden, *The Reality of God and Other Essays* (New York: Harper and Row, 1966), ch. 1.

11. Langdon Gilkey, *Maker of Heaven and Earth* (New York: Doubleday & Co., 1959), pp. 109-116.

12. Robert C. Neville, *Creativity and God, A Challenge to Process Theology* (New York: The Seabury Press, 1980), p. 68.

13. For further help with process theology, see Alan Gragg, *Charles Hartshorne* (Waco, Texas: Word Inc., 1973) and Eric C. Rust, *Evolutionary Philosophies and Contemporary Theology* (Philadelphia: The Westminster Press, 1969).

14. See chapter 11 by David Basinger entitled "Divine Power: Do Process Theists Have a Better Idea?"

15. Richard Rice, *The Openness of God* (see footnote 5).

16. Thomas F. Tracy, *God, Action, And Embodiment*, p. xix.

17. John Macquarrie, *In Search of Deity*, p. 128.

18. For Macquarrie's dialectical model of God, see *In Search of Deity*, ch. 13 and 17 especially.

19. While Ronald Nash can be numbered among those evangelicals seeking a middle ground between Thomistic theism and process theology, he strongly rejects attempts to limit God's knowledge of the future. See Ronald Nash, *The Concept of God* (Grand Rapids: Zondervan, 1983), pp. 51-66.

20. H. P. Owen, *Concepts of Deity* (New York: Harper and Herder, 1971), p. 24.

21. Richard Bauckham, " 'Only the suffering God can help': divine passibility in modern theology" *Themelios* 9 (1984), pp. 6-12.

22. Stephen Davis agrees in *Logic and the Nature of God* (Grand Rapids: Eerdmans, 1983), ch. 1.

23. On this point, for example, even Stephen Davis declines to follow, ch. 2 and 4.

24. Let me refer to a few theologians who agree with me and I with them on God's knowledge. Richard Swinburne, *The Coherence of Theism* (Oxford: Clarendon Press, 1977), ch. 10; Keith Ward, *Rational Theology and the Creativity of God* (New York: The Pilgrim Press, 1982), ch. 6; and surprisingly H. P. Owen, *Concepts of Deity* (note 20), p. 32-33.

25. This is the epithet Royce Gruenler hurls at Richard Rice. *The Inexhaustible God: Biblical Faith and the Challenge of Process Theism* (Grand Rapids: Baker, 1983), p. 44.

Reflections on a
Journey in Process

Royce Gruenler

Royce Gruenler

Royce Gruenler is Professor of New Testament at Gordon-Conwell
Theological Seminary. Formerly, he was Professor of Religion and
Philosophy at Hiram College where he worked with scholars who
were members of the process school. Gruenler's own analysis and
critique of process theology can be found in his book, *The Inex-
haustible God: Biblical Faith and the Challenge of Process Theism*.
His other books include *New Approaches to Jesus and the Gospels*.
In addition to his Ph.D. from the University of Aberdeen where he
was a Fulbright scholar, Dr. Gruenler also holds degrees from
Williams College and the Reformed Episcopal Seminary. He has also
studied as a Fulbright post-graduate fellow at the University of
Heidelberg.

One of the compelling themes in J. R. R. Tolkein's *Lord of the Rings* trilogy is the journey of the smallish hobbit Frodo to the forbidding fortress of the evil Sauron in the land of Mordor to destroy a seductive ring with the power of making one invisible. This ring must be destroyed in the fires of its original forging or its bearer will be drawn little by little but inescapably into the wraithlike circle of darkness and become a minion of evil rebellion against true Light and Fellowship. Tolkein's wonderfully imaginative story (drawn from Plato and Wagner and the Bible) parallels the primary world where each of us is tempted to put on the ring of self-sufficiency that will give us power, so we think, to do the things we want to do, to fashion the world as we want to fashion it, and to be masters of our destiny, invisible to the moral constraints of God and Scripture. Frodo almost didn't make it, so seductive was the appeal of the ring, and had it not been for his simple but morally steadfast companion Sam, he probably would have kept the ring upon his finger and perished with the dark forces of Sauron in the final battle. But by grace he decided to reject the temptation, the ring was destroyed, and Frodo and his friends returned to happier times in more pleasant places. He had been there and back again.

Demanding My Rights And Shaping God To Size

In a sense my own journey has been a pale image of the perennial quest. Everyone faces a temptation designed for him or for her to slip the ring of power upon a finger. But perhaps the temptation of the scholar is subtlest of all, for we begin with considerable pride in our intellects and place ourselves in positions of superior vantage simply because we know so much, or so we think. The ring of seduction for the intellectual whose principal interest is in biblical studies, theology or philosophical theology is especially attractive because it affords the scholar a special dispensation to criticize and improve upon the Scriptures which the sovereign God has given as a special revelation of himself and of his will and purpose for the created world. Allow me to say forthrightly that process theology, attractive and promising as it is at first appearance, and as it was for me, is in reality a seductive ring that gives its wearer the illusion of power to design the universe and God according to human imagination, but in the doing discards the only means by which we can truly know God and be reconciled to him on his own terms. In the following pages I want to sketch as clearly and simply as possible some of the important lessons I have learned (at considerable cost) about the ring of process theism and give fair warning for those who are tempted to put it on.

First, we will spend some time together trying to get a simple overview of process theology so that the system of thought will not be confusing because of its heavy vocabulary. At its center the whole thing is really very simple. It comes down to the matter of a contest of wills, like an adolescent child arguing with its parents. Process (let's use that as an abbreviation for process thought, process theology and process theism)—process doesn't like the idea that God is all-powerful, all-knowing, and everywhere present. It wants to stake out some territory where we as free individuals can enjoy some independence from the all-searching eye of the Almighty, the sovereign God portrayed in the Old and New Testaments. A God like that doesn't seem to leave any breathing space, so in order to protect my freedom and my rights to my own life and creativity I need to slip on the ring of invisibility that will give me some shelter from that searching Eye that is always looking over my shoulder and making me feel uncomfortable. I don't want to be answerable to such a God, and my mind tells me that if He has all the power in the universe then I don't have any of my own. And I demand my right to claim some freedom from such an intimidating God.

How can I do it? Well, given the priority of my claim to my rights something has to give, and it can't be my right to be free. So God has to give, and what he has to give up is some of his power. Not all of it but certainly some of it, enough so that he is not always poking about in my affairs and leaving me no choice in shaping my own life. This means now that God, as I refashion him in my mind according to my agenda to be free, must relate to the world in a different way from what the Scriptures say. Instead of being the sovereign creator of the universe who brings everything into being (eventually even me) by simply saying, "Let there be" (Gen. 1) and upholds this vast and glorious universe right up to the present moment by the simple word of his power (Heb. 1:3), God needs to be seen as part of a larger family that contains him and the universe. Instead of the Genesis creation story (a misleading myth in the eyes of process people), God is contained in a larger circle. And the name of that circle? Creativity. What is creativity? Creativity is time and the process of time, hence the term "process" that describes the invisible core of this ring we are looking at.

Now if God is inside this ring of time along with the rest of us, though of course on a gigantic scale (otherwise he wouldn't be God), there are a lot of things that are invisible to him because he has to wait and see how they are going to turn out. This is a neat arrangement for getting rid of a meddling God who is always poking about in our affairs and doesn't allow us any breathing space. Not that we want to get rid of him entirely. Process thinkers are sharp enough (much sharper than atheists and agnostics) to know that if you don't have any God at all there will be sheer chaos inside that ring and no order or meaning to things at all. God needs to be there, all right, but mainly as one who gives us suggestions that we will decide to adopt or reject. In a sense you might say that God tries to "lure" us to do good and beautiful things, or if you prefer, to persuade us to respond to his desire for the shaping of a processing world and universe.

This means that the God of process is there inside the ring of time and creativity trying to set an agenda, but because we human beings, and all the trillions and trillions of free agents that make up the world and universe, have some measure of freedom independent of God to act on our own, he doesn't know exactly how things are going to turn out. Accordingly, we've gained some comfortable invisibility by putting on the ring of power. To be a little more specific, God doesn't control the beginning of things because he always has had and always will have some universe of free agents that he cannot completely control; and he doesn't control the end of things because he cannot know the future in detail. So both the first and last books of the Bible and just about everything in between is discarded when we slip the ring on our finger. We have now determined what God is going to be like because our right to be free demands it.

Let us look at this demand a bit more closely and see how it limits God and makes us invisible to his power. Remember that the outer circle of the ring that contains everything, including God, is Creativity, or the process of time. Catch this concept in your eye and you've got the secret of the process school. Now watch carefully. God is moving along in time the same as you and I, though he is supposed to be encompassing everything that is happening, and of course he does it forever, where we are limited to a short duration and a small segment of the world. But the idea of movement is the same whether it is God or ourselves. Now one of the consequences of this invisibility agenda we've set up for God is that he cannot participate in our experience as it is going on. We've already determined that we are going to be independent of God in our choices, and that God is always excluded from the present moment of our lives. He has his own present moment which we cannot enter, but we also have our present which is our staked-out and sacred territory and off limits for God. He cannot enter my present moment of decision because his power would overwhelm my freedom and I wouldn't be free. Hence God is excluded from the immediate present of everything in the vast universe.

What does God experience about us then? He cannot experience our present while we are making free decisions and he cannot experience the future that we haven't yet met. There is only one segment of time left where God is free to poke about in our affairs: the past. After we have made our decisions and chosen from several possibilities while wearing the ring of invisibility, then and only then are we willing to take off the ring and let our finished acts and words appear visibly before God. Our thoughts of course always remain our own in the present moment of invisibility.

An illustration may explain the situation a little more clearly. Imagine that everyone and everything, including God, is lined up along the front line of time as it marches continuously forward, single file, sideways, eyes straight ahead with never a glance to the left or to the right. The line has to be single file sideways because each individual is totally private and invisible to those on the left and right in the present moment of decision. That is the price of freedom on our own terms. My right to be free requires that I be invisible to everyone and everything else that is also making free decisions in the present moment of time. Rather lonely, isn't it, especially when you consider that God is forever locked out of my present experience?

If you are thinking ahead, you may have discovered a rather disconcerting effect of this invisibility business, and it is something that eventually disturbed me and sent me back to the biblical promises of the God who is with us in thick and thin and who knows the sparrow that falls and the hairs on our head. If God never knows us as we really are in our lively moments of experiencing and choosing because we have on the ring, then what he finally sees when we take it off is not our complete self. The past he sees is minus all that former vitality of the living self. All he sees is a dead shell, a chambered nautilus. Everything vital has been lost forever. God can't remember it because he can't see it. Our demand to be free on our own terms has brought upon us the bane of the ring wearers. It is indeed a tragic vision.

If that isn't enough to send us back to the Bible, let's pursue the logic of the process folk and see what further problems arise. There are so many that it is difficult to know where to begin. But let's continue with the argument that in order to be free I must limit the power of God. Then the question arises, "How far shall I limit him, because I need him around to ensure that there is some order in the world and not just sheer chaos, and I need him to dangle the lures to things that are creative and not destructive? I want God, but not too much of him. But how much?"

That is the first big question. I don't want a sovereign God, the kind found in the Bible, because that is a threat to my rights and lifestyle; on the other hand I don't want a God so weak and effete that he can't do anything. At this point the process person is faced with the dilemma of power distribution: "Where's the beef?" This translates into, "Who's got the beef?" As you can see, the motive behind the decision of many people to go for process and put on the ring is really a kind of power grab. It is a carbon copy of what went on in the Garden in Genesis 3 and raises the perennial question of rebellion first posed by the chief power grabber, "Hath God said?" Ever since the Fall, the human race has been trying to hide from the disturbing and demanding presence of God (notice the attempts of the first couple to hide and become invisible to God's presence, Gen. 3:7-13).

Suppose though that in spite of my preachments on Genesis you are tempted to put on the ring of invisibility to protect your rights. Let me ask you how you are going to divide up the power between yourself, the rest of the world, and God. How much to each? How much to yourself? What percentage will you reserve for God? Remember that you have to assign him enough to make it worth his while. There's no sense having a deity so weak that he is simply a drag on the system. I think you will agree after some reflection that this is a pretty tough question to answer. One prominent process thinker, Charles Hartshorne, suggested that the amount of power any one of us human beings has at any given time is pretty small: as a matter of fact, one over everything else in the universe that might in any way touch upon us at the moment. Of course if everything somehow affected our decisions, that would amount to one over infinity, and that as you know amounts to zero. Hartshorne surely didn't want to say that, but in suggesting the image he certainly held a tiger by the tail. So I will leave you with the question of how much power you want and how much you are going to assign to God, requesting only that you be fair about it. Unless of course you decide not to put on the ring after all, which would be by far the better decision, and let God suggest to you what the ratios are in his own way in the Scriptures. You probably won't find process much good either in answering the problem of evil, although this is another argument advanced by proponents of the school in favor of a limited God. If he has enough power to sustain this world, he could also destroy it and be done with its evil. If he is too weak to destroy it he is not worth considering.

Who Am I?

We have seen that the price of standing on our rights and defining freedom as freedom from God and others leads to total privacy and invisibility in the present moment. Each of us is marching shoulder to shoulder from the top of the page to the bottom of the page along the front line of time as it processes into the future, and we all have blinders on. No one can see or experience anything or anyone left or right. I want to introduce you now to a new problem that arises in the process system. It has to do with the make-up of your very self. Do you remember looking at those old pictures of yourself as a child and wondering how you could ever have been that person? Process folk use that illustration to prove that you really do change and that you are really a succession of persons, tied together from moment to moment by anticipation and memory. But there is no essential you in all those picture frames as they whiz by. You may have the illusion that there is, but actually one self succeeds the previous self as it fades away so that what you are is a continuous series of new selves. When you go to sleep your self actually turns off for a brief period.

This concept may boggle your mind, though it is really a very old idea that some of the ancient Greeks came up with when they were trying to figure out what life was ultimately made up of and decided it was process and change. Heraclitus and Protagoras were two who thought this way, and Plato deals nicely with the latter in a dialogue that bears his name. And of course, as Plato pointed out, there are problems when you make time ultimate and yourself the measure of all things. Everything becomes relative and there is no truth that doesn't change, including the statement that everything is in process. Aristophanes, the Greek comedian, has a hilarious play called *The Clouds* in which he pokes fun at the process types who try to excuse their responsibilities in court by claiming to be different persons from those who originally contracted their debts. What I eventually found disturbing about the process view of the self was its inability to account for the identity of the self from moment to moment and from one stage of life to another. I certainly look different as a boy of eight who stares out at me from the photograph on the wall, but I claim him nonetheless as myself, and we bear the same name. There are differences of course, but there is a basic identity, an essential sameness that accounts for my ability to use the personal pronoun "I" at every stage of my life.

Process people have trouble with this because they are really existentialists, not essentialists. Let me define the terms. An essentialist is a person who believes that God and creatures have certain characteristics that identify them wherever and whenever you meet them. In fact they have these essential identities whether you meet them or not. An existentialist is a person who makes a good deal of the fact that we are not finished yet but are always on the way to expressing more fully who we are. There is a fair amount of truth in this and it depends on what sort of existentialist you happen to meet on the street. Some Christian existentialists, like Gabriel Marcel (whom I happen to like a lot) can be very helpful in giving new insights to what it means to be a Christian. Others, like Jean-Paul Sartre, can be very disconcerting. He denied the existence of God, mainly because his view of freedom as "freedom from" demanded complete privacy and invisibility, and the best way to ensure invisibility was to make God invisible, that is, to rub him out, so to speak. Sartre was also very opposed to the notion that people could be pigeonholed. He detested the past and resolutely refused to allow anyone to define him by what he had said or done, since he was always on the move, redefining who he was in his immediate present. In his own terms, his ego transcended the past continuously in its ceaseless trek into the novelty of the future. Reality, he said, cannot be defined as being "in itself" (*en soi*) but only in terms of "for me" (*pour moi*). There are deep problems there, as you can see.

I have used Sartre as an extreme example of the existentialist posture because he illustrates something in process theology that is disturbing. The existentialist believes that I define myself as I step outside my just past moment into the open future of novelty and possibility (it helps if you know that the word existential comes from the Greek *ek histemi*, to stand outside, which gives us the Latin *existere* and the English exist and exit). This notion is deeply imbedded in process thought, so much so that process theologians include God in the process and define him as One who continually surpasses his past in an everlasting succession into the novelty of the future.

So that you may clearly perceive a difficulty here let me ask you to imagine that you are moving along your timeline from past, to present, to future. At this point you need to know something more about the process view of the self. One of the fundamental beliefs of the process school, going back to Alfred North Whitehead, this century's greatest interpreter of the view, is that the individual units of experience (he called them entities or occasions) are the starting point of everything. Basic atomicity, he said, is the foundation of all reality. What does this mean? It means that you and I as persons do not have essential natures when we are conceived and as we move through our life's journey, but come into existence as conscious human beings as the result of a long and complicated process. As a conscious person I am the end product of a collection of experiences by myriads of atomic occasions that make up my body. They form the pyramid and I pop out at the top like a flower. That's the first thing to bear in mind.

The second is that these atomic occasions that make up my body and my person are constantly emerging, peaking, and perishing and being replaced by new occasions. As they change so do I, and as I change and make new decisions so they change. The rub comes here. No one in the process school has ever given a satisfactory account of how one occasion that perishes passes on its identity to the new occasion that succeeds it. Remember that a cardinal rule of the school and its expensive insurance of freedom is the sacred privacy and invisibility of the present. All you can pass on to the next occasion that succeeds you is the hollow shell of the perished past, never the living vibrancy of the present. This is true of everything in the universe, so that when it comes time for God to have all the immediacies passed on to him, all he gets is the empty chambered nautilus. It's a colossal problem. Process thinkers say that memory is the key; but if memory can be only of what is perished and past, then what you have in the flickering film of a person's life is the serial succession of one private and invisible frame by another, with only the barest outline of the frame itself passed on, which is insufficient to account for the sense we have of being the same person from one experience to the next.

The rebellion that began in Eden has purchased freedom on its own terms at a terrible price. The demand for the right to be free has conjured up a system in which not only every nonpersonal entity in the universe suffers from want of identity, but persons themselves are different in every successive moment. One of my process friends remarked that the process doctrine of successive selves had helped him understand what Jesus meant by loving others as we love ourselves, for in loving my past selves, he said, I have a better sense of how to love other selves. Interesting, but hardly what Jesus had in mind, I should think. It is almost as though God had said at the Fall, "You desire freedom in terms of invisibility from me? Then

I will give you more invisibility than you bargained for. I will make you invisible to one another and to yourself. You will be so sick of your freedom in privacy that other people will become hell to you, and you will ever seek to escape the nausea of being with yourself." So Sartre, at least.

But with Whitehead and Hartshorne I detect more of a sense of well-being, at least on the surface. The process school has been accused (not least of all by myself) of being bourgeois. Though we have pretty much demolished the self by now and answered "I don't know" to the question "Who am I," it is of interest to ask what the motivating lures are that God is supposed to hold in front of us as he seeks to persuade us to follow his course in our procession of selves. We will discover that process theology aligns itself more with a sense of good feeling than with ethical responsibility. This does not imply that process theologians are disinterested in ethical matters, for many of them have written extensively in that area. But as far as our relationship to God is concerned there is little regard for the seriousness of sin, with the righteousness of God, with eternal judgment of sinners, and the absolute necessity of salvation by faith alone in the crucified and risen Christ. There is no need of satisfying a righteous and wrathful God since he is tenderly turned on to everyone and is doing all he possibly can to lead all entities in the universe to as full and beautiful an experience as they are capable during their brief tenure. The primary theme of process theology therefore is the quest for beauty and happiness in this life, not ethics and sin and the quest for righteousness. Let us look a little more closely at the role of beauty in the process system.

The Lure Of Beauty

God's principal role in process is to give creativity a positive direction so that it won't be chaotic and destructive. If you have detected something strange in that first sentence, I agree; for I have thought for a long time that it is not really correct to call the outer circle of the ring that contains everything, including God, by the name of "creativity" because the term creativity is already a positive word and shouldn't need God to give it a positive direction. If God is the one who offers positive and beautiful lures to the process of time, then the ring that contains God should not be called creativity; in fact it might as well be called destructivity, since God has to bring order out of it. Perhaps it would be better if process thinkers just stuck to the word "process" and let it go at that, assuming that process is a neutral word that allows for destructive as well as creative occasions to flow out of it. Then God would enter in at stage two to try to ensure that as much creativity as possible (given a universe with so many free and independent entities he cannot totally control) would flow forth.

The problem with the word "process" is that it is also loaded in the direction of the positive, and as we've seen, the positive element is not supposed to come into the picture until God lures it out of brute atomic possibility. Process means to proceed (same root) and to proceed means to go somewhere meaningful. Process equals evolution. Thus process people ought to scout around for a new term that isn't already loaded with positive value; otherwise God really isn't needed in the system. Nontheistic types (the Carl Sagans of the modern world) seem to get along very well without a second-stage God and appear content to view process and creativity as capable of producing its own order and evolution (although some, like Sagan, have flirted with the Hindu mythology of a pulsating universe).

There is a lot of humbug in this position too, for you never get something for nothing in this world (even justification by faith in Christ is very costly to God), though we are not dealing primarily with nontheistic evolution in this chapter but with process theology's view of God as lure to the process. I think, though, that before we go on with our subject you will agree that there is a lot to be cleaned up in this matter of evolution, order and process without God, as well as in process theism's not very logical use of "creativity" as bigger than God yet requiring God to guide it creatively.

How then is God the lure to creativity in process thought? To explain this process thinkers like to use the word "persuasive." God is persuasive, not coercive. That is the key to the system. Let's place the key in the lock and see what opens up. As the door swings wide we see inside a whole room filled with empty nautilus shells. This is all we can see and all God can see. That isn't all there is in the room but it is all God and we can see: a heap of dead shells that represent the past of entities that were once alive and well. What neither God nor we can see are all the invisible happenings ("occasions" they are called) that are now processing in some stage or other, emerging, peaking and perishing, but remaining invisible to his eye as to ours because to be free is to be free from outside meddling.

But God has a dream. He is limited by the outer circle of creativity which makes him subject to time and space, and he is limited by whatever degree of freedom you and I and all the occasions of the universe possess (remember the ratio problem we discussed earlier?), but he has a good deal of power nonetheless and a lot of ideas as to how evolution ought to flow. I say "evolution" because by now you have probably guessed that process thought is evolutionary to a fault and sees the creative advance going on until "the crack of doom,"as Whitehead described it (not a very good metaphor for him to have used, actually, as he thought of the process as going on forever, and the crack of doom image smacks a little too much of biblical prophecy).

' At any rate God has a dream about the future. Remember that he moves in time too and has to wait for things to happen before they become definite fact, so it is true to say that he dreams about possibilities he hopes we'll bring to pass by our free decisions. Here our discussion becomes a bit sticky because God's ability to set the framework within which we have to operate is determined by that ratio of power distribution we talked about earlier, and until that is more or less settled we can't say just how extensively God controls the outlines of our destiny. Process thinkers will vary here, but actually they haven't given enough attention to this very important question of ratios of power. It is, after all, important to know how powerful or weak God really is in order to know how invisible we really are to his control. Whatever the ratio is, God does have a dream about the future that comes from his own goodness and sense of beauty and his desire for the greatest degree of social relationship possible among entities in the universe. (An irony here is that social relationships have to be a little past or a little future, that is, with perished persons or possible persons, but never with present persons who are invisibly locked in to their immediacy and are therefore inaccessible because of their right to be free in the moment of decision.)

God seeks to realize his dream by working on us from two directions. From the direction of the past he tries to condition us by bringing into the best order he can all the countless decisions of occasions in the previous moment, and he tries to influence us behaviorly by bringing this order to bear upon us. This is the inherited environment in which we operate and it is very complex. Process people are very fuzzy about the extent of God's control here because there is a lot of evil and unpleasantness in the world that obviously cannot come from God, but not all the good and beautiful is from him either, at least not directly. But let us say that in the mind of the process believer God is doing absolutely, or relatively, or absolutely relatively everything he possibly can to make this a beautiful world and to give us satisfying and beautiful experiences until we perish (there is no future experience for us once we die, though God remembers all we've done forever). That is from the pole of the past.

From the pole of the future God can only work from possibilities that haven't yet come to be. He cannot know them as fact until you and I make them fact one way or another, but he can do his best to put ideas into our heads and hope we will come through for him. If we don't he is frustrated, but he constantly readjusts his frustrations with his victories and reorders the next set of lures in light of the new situation so that maximum beauty may be realized in a world that is imperfect and over which he does not have absolute control. This has been going on forever and will continue to go on forever (forget the "crack of doom" figure), so his lures to beauty will never be wholly successful. God always has had and always will have some universe or other, some better than others, but right now he's got this one and it is up to us to do our best to strive for the most beautiful things we can, not only to bring satisfaction and good feelings to ourselves personally, and to others, but to God himself, since he is dependent on us to give him the content of his own experience. (This raises another big problem we will take up later: Is God really a person, and if so can he be a person independent of us in any sense?)

Where does biblical prophecy fit into all this iffyness about the future? The price to be paid if we demand the right to put on the ring of invisibility in order to be free is that all the future God is not able to control behaviorly from his reorganization of data from the past must be left to sheer possibility. The future is open for him as for you and me. Of course, being God he knows all possibilities and we do not. Therefore he knows all the possible moves on the chessboard, though you make your moves with your ring on and he can't see you thinking and moving. But once you move he says, "Aha! I knew you would move this way or that and I've anticipated each possibility that would ensue. Now that I've readjusted according to plan B, make your next move, and try to listen to my lure next time. You'll be much happier if you do." (Note that not all process thinkers agree that God knows all possibilities about the future because this would seem to erase all genuine novelty. I would add that if he does know all possibilities, and if this is a finite universe, then in the infinity of time that God has experienced he would already have realized all possibilities as actual. This would pull the plug on the process system and cause it to crash.)

Something like that must go on in the mind of the process God. But observe that even if he knows a great deal more than you do about the future and its possibilities, right now he doesn't know which plan is going to go into operation because you and I and all the myriad emergent occasions of the universe haven't made our free decisions yet. (Another problem: we are not all of us in the same time zone, so some occasions will have made their decisions in the "present" while others have yet to make theirs in their present. Hence God would know some decisions in the present as already past before you got to the present that is yours—supposing of course that God is capable of being in all places of the universe at once and can participate in every relative kind of time you'll find distributed throughout the cosmos. Remember that in process thought God is limited to the speed of time, which makes it a tough assignment for him to be everywhere at once and get it all together. Confusing isn't it? But it is all part of the problem of the relativity of time and space. We will devote a section to this later on.)

What of biblical prophecy, then? It has to go. God can only know generally about the future, but since it is open because of our demand to be free there is no way God could give a certain picture of what lies ahead. Since the Scriptures give us certain prophecies of events to come, those that have already come to pass, like Christ's first coming, are considered by the process theologians to be prophecies after the fact, made up by eager followers to make it appear that such things happen. As for prophecies about the future yet to be, these are mythical and not to be taken for fact. One of the cardinal doctrines of process theology is that the only facts are past facts. There are only future possibilities. Nothing becomes factual until you and I make our invisible decisions. Then God and others can see them, but only as shells that are no longer living.

As a process friend of mine remarked, "The future cannot be known as fact, otherwise I would not be free because I could not do otherwise." As you can see, something has got to go; and since I insist on being free from an all-seeing and all-knowing and all-powerful God, it is that concept of God that God must be changed. Along with him goes the Bible as inspired and trustworthy, and prophecy as a part of the general discard. You may still want to say that God is all-powerful, but you must go on to say that God has all the power he could possibly have, given a universe in which the power is shared necessarily with other entities. But it amounts to the same thing in the end; a limited God who cannot make factual prophecies about the future.

In summary, process thought has presented us with a God who is unable to see a lot of things (all the present, as a matter of fact) because we are all invisible all of the time as we move along in our present immediacy. God can only know what we've left behind (the fossil minus the living creature within), and what may be true of us in the future. The best he can do is try to lure us with good and beautiful possibilities to wider social relationships. But don't be surprised if you overhear the process deity saying "Darn!" on occasion when you make a bad decision (he would never say damn because being a unitarian-universalist deity he would never damn anyone in the traditional sense). Of course you need to remember that if you happen to hear the process deity speaking it is not his immediate present you are hearing but his voice just past, for you cannot enter into his present any more than he can enter into your present. You might raise the question, "Does God then lose all his present immediacy as it now becomes past and as he moves on into the novelty of the future?" In order for God to have a genuine past, he must, because the past is what is no longer present. On the other hand, if God never loses any of his own immediate experience, then he has no past and simply gets bigger and bigger as he adds new presents for ever and ever. Of course in the process system he loses all the immediacy of our presents as they perish and become past, since it is impossible for him to enter into the invisible privacy of our immediate presents, as I've pointed out.

All these problems (which eventually forced me to doubt the truth of process theology) require a little more reflection. Let me suggest a new heading and continue our discussion there. The question will be whether God has to keep time with the rest of us. If he does he is in trouble.

If God Is In Time Can He Be Everywhere?

Charles Hartshorne has wanted to argue all along that God envelops absolutely everything in the universe in his own present experience, just as these occasions occur over vast stretches of time and space. But he also wants to say that God always has to move in time, because if he didn't our futures would be in his present and would be realized fact, and we would not be free. Now try to think for a moment what rate of speed God is limited to. Is it the speed of light ($C = 186,000$ miles per second)? Or some inconceivable faster velocity, like the super-speedy tachyons physicists are talking about? It really doesn't matter what speed we finally come up with, as long as it is at least as fast as the speed of light (God would not be God if he couldn't at least keep up with a beam of light). The point is that process theology stands or falls on its insistence that God is moving into a future that is in some sense unknown to him. He is processing at some temporal velocity because he has to. He can't get out of time because it is a necessary part of his nature. He's stuck in time with the rest of us because creativity says so, and creativity is Time with a capital T that determines the nature of everything. Process is an absolute, especially for God since he is affected most.

Do you see a problem here? Are you tempted to say, "You can't have your cake and eat it too?" I think you would be right if you did. I asked the question one day when I was thinking more clearly than I had for a long time, and I suddenly realized that if God is moving in time because he has to, he can't be everywhere at once. If God is everywhere at once he has everything in one simultaneous moment, and space and time do not limit him. It is interesting that classical Christian theologians have accepted God's claim in Scripture

348

that he is sovereign over all creation and perfectly knows past, present *where* and future, and therefore is everywhere at once. They have wrestled with the questions of the meaning of time and space and human freedom, but they have never given them pride of place, as process theology has done. They have traditionally begun with God and his rightful claim to sovereign power, not with the human demand to guarantee freedom and invisibility at God's expense.

The cost of putting on the ring is that you buy into an irrational system. Process thinkers are put out when I suggest this, because they think they are being logical and rational (far more than classical Christian thinkers) by making time absolute. The problem is that if time is absolute, not even God can claim to have a simultaneous experience of everything in the universe. Only if God is simultaneously everywhere can he comprehend everything, but in that case he transcends time. You cannot have it both ways. God reveals in Holy Scripture that he has created all things, sustains all things, and is able to participate in all things. Hence there is no question that time and space are meaningful to God. It is just that he is not subject to them (unless he chooses to be for a season, as in the incarnation of Christ). But as soon as you give pride of place to your own demands and require God to be in time because you want him out of your present and your future, don't expect that he will necessarily be around to remember your past. If he can get there, fine, but remember that he does have to travel great distances and may miss you on a distant planet. On the other hand, if you want him in every distant space as well as here on earth, you would do better to give up process theology and become a Christian.

There is one other little complication that should puzzle the process school, and that has to do with the idea of simultaneity. Because of relativity theory, modern physicists argue that there really isn't any perspective from which you could have a simultaneous bird's-eye view of the universe's present, because there is no such present, only relative time-zones that are impossible to synchronize in a moment of time. Time and space are always relative to an observer, and God could not observe the whole unless he were greater than the whole and had a privileged overview, in which case he would not be subject to time and space. But process thought wants to make God subject to time-space (creativity), and in so doing makes it

349

impossible for God to comprehend all of time and space. We have already asked what rate of speed the process system has in mind when it describes God processing. I would also like to ask (in view of what we have just said) what spatial perspective is God's preferred one as he looks out on as much of the world as he can see. Satisfying answers are not forthcoming to either of these questions because they cannot be. The process deity is a very limited, finite occasion (who happens also to be everlasting, if you can comprehend what that means).

We have discovered that putting on the ring of invisibility leads inevitably to one's enslavement to the tyranny of time and to the idolatry of mistaking the whole for the part. Whitehead himself warned of committing the "fallacy of misplaced concreteness," and it is a pity he did not take his own advice. By making creativity and atomicity absolute, that is, by conceiving of time-space and individual freedom as independent of God, process thought has contained the Creator and turned the biblical order upside down. But at tremendous cost. Now God is so limited and so impotent that he can't get there fast enough or get it all together. After all, if we will not allow God into our little private presents, we should hardly be surprised if all the time-space stuff of the universe is just too much for him to handle. The irony is that the process school promised us a God who cares and who is supposed to be tenderly with us, more than the old-tyrannical God of the Bible, but all it has delivered is a deity who can't run fast enough or squeeze into the right spaces to be of much help or to be worthy of our deepest worship.

Is The Process God Really God?

My last remark raises a truly disturbing question about the whole enterprise of process theology. It isn't just a matter of whether God can squeeze into all the spaces of the universe or travel fast enough to be of any help. It is more serious than that. It is a question of whether the process deity qualifies as God at all and whether in any real sense it is personal and a genuine acting agent. Here is the problem. We have already seen that process thought builds ordinary entities, occasions and persons from bottom up, that is, from the basic atomic units of "feeling" that are the building blocks of everything in the universe. A person like you or me, for instance,

Reflections on a Journey in Process

is not someone who begins as a person at conception, but who becomes a person as the result of a process of atomic building blocks or "feelings" that conglomerate together in increasing new units of complexity, creating the proper conditions for you or me to emerge as a person at the end of the process. We do not begin as persons, we end up as persons as we finally arise out of a complex field of atomic relationships. But when we do finally emerge as conscious persons we are a brand new cause on a higher level, not just the effect of prior causes. The reason for this, as you probably guessed, is to protect our right to be free; otherwise we would just be substituting one tyranny for another, the tyranny of behavioral conditioning for the tyranny of the biblical sovereign God. And process thought has as its number one priority the desire to be free from total causation so that we can put on the ring and make free choices.

In order to do this, process theology performs a little sleight of hand. It says that in the process of emerging as a person you are only partially conditioned by those atomic building blocks that provide your material, and when you appear as a conscious person you are a brand new causal agent in some very real sense. There is a mysterious leap (never explained) from the previous atomic occasions that contribute to you, to your emergence as a free person. (These leaps are called "epochs" and the theory the epochal theory of time.) This discontinuity or leap-frogging continues to go on many times every second (how many is debated by process people) even when you have become a conscious person, so that you are becoming a new free person many times over each second, as your old self peaks, perishes, and becomes grist for the new emerging self. We dealt with this problem earlier and observed that process thought simply is unable to account for any substantial continuity from self to self as "you" emerge (so as to be able to refer meaningfully to "you" as the same person over the long haul). Memory of the past and anticipation of the future are often employed as glue to hold the separate selves together. Presently we will see that process theology is really closer to Buddhism in this regard than to anything else and suffers from many of the same identity problems.

I have rehearsed the difficulty of identifying the self in process as a prelude to the problem of identifying God as substantial Self. The two prominent process thinkers, Whitehead and Hartshorne, handle the question of God's selfhood in slightly different ways but they amount to much the same thing in the end. Let's look at Whitehead's deity first. Remember that Whitehead begins with creativity as the largest container of all. In his most important work, *Process and Reality,* Whitehead speculates that after creativity comes a whole set of atomic possibilities (he calls them "sensa" though they are sheer possibilities and without any priority of order). Don't ask how they got there; just assume that Whitehead is cribbing from Plato, and Plato simply assumed that the world of ideas was there to begin with. At this point Whitehead introduces God. Remember that God has to work within time (creativity), and now sets to work on the unordered and unprioritized "sensa" or possibilities that will guide the actual world once it gets going.

But don't get the idea that God at this point is conscious or actual. Yes, you read me correctly. Whitehead speculates that at this logical stage of development God is only a "primordial" deity. The word has a ring of importance but must not be taken as anything substantial. It simply means that Whitehead is imagining God at this stage as pure possibility who is there to arrange the unordered sensa into a scale of preferences for the actual world to come. There is nothing at this point except a number of possible universes. The primordial God is imagining the best possible universe, and alternatives in case that one doesn't pan out. God is now without any actual universe, without substantial experience of anything, and is not even conscious.

Do you see any logical problems here? I'm sure you do. In looking at this with a sharper eye I began to see that Whitehead was using all sorts of ordinary concepts in an illegitimate way. For instance, he wanted to say that an unconscious deity of pure possibility arranges all possible universes on a scale of priorities. But some possible universes, like ours, which happens to have become actual, include conscious persons like you and me. Is it possible for an unconscious God to imagine a universe in which there are conscious persons? What would the mind of an unconscious God be like? Is it a legitimate use of language to take an operation that actual conscious persons perform, like ordering things in priorities, and apply that operation to a deity who cannot perform it? This seems very odd. Personally I think Whitehead was so intent on getting rid of the biblical God (he says some harsh things about this "despotic"

Deity in *Process and Reality*) that he kept the ring on too long and his mind grew fuzzy. It is clear to me that Whitehead's introduction of the primordial God, after he has given pride of place to creativity and the unordered possibilities (sensa), is a bold and desperate gambit to save the system from chaos. God is drawn in to give the process direction. But his primordial deity is no actual God and can do nothing personal because he is not a Person capable of ordering possibilities and planning luring programs for possible universes.

Some process folk have reacted in a rather feisty way when I pointed out this disturbing and illegitimate application of personal operations to an impersonal deity. They have responded by saying that in Whitehead's system the order of creativity⟶ sensa⟶ primordial God⟶ consequent God (I have yet to explain this term, which is Whitehead's actual God) is a purely logical relationship, not an actual temporal sequence. The actual (consequent) God and the primordial God must be seen as two sides to the same coin and as inseparable, they say. Well and good, I reply, but all the same Whitehead himself gives absolute priority to time (creativity), and once you do this all relationships have to be fitted into the temporal sequence or the whole system falls. The reason Whitehead placed creativity in the position the biblical God would rightly occupy is because he needed to buy an open future for the creature to be free. The primordial God poses no threat to human freedom. "He" (another illegitimate word) simply orders possibilities. He does not predestine actualities. In fact, the primordial God cannot know any actual world. He (it?) has to wait until we make our decisions and fill his balloon with actual gas.

Then and only then does God become actual. He needs us. He becomes an actual God as a consequence of our having chosen, acted and given him something to work on. Whitehead calls this the consequent God. He has actuality but is now limited by our freedom as to possible futures, whereas the primordial God is deficient in actuality and unlimited as to possibilities. There are serious problems with this notion of a consequent deity because he seems basically passive. We feed him data, but it is a question as to what he feeds us other than lures to possibility which we have the power to accept or reject. It is also a problem to figure out the exact relationship of the primordial God (who is supposed to be timeless) and the

353

consequent God who moves in time. It is all such a muddle that it hardly constitutes any competition for the biblical God, except for the agenda that process has set for itself, and that is the agenda of demanding the right to be free from God and to wear the ring of invisibility in the realms of the present and the future. As far as the nature of God is concerned, I fail to see how Whitehead's deity is personal or, for that matter, even possible. It suffers from a large identity problem as it moves from the primordial pole to the consequent pole and back again, without any substantial nature to guarantee its unity and integrity.

Hartshorne approaches the question a little differently but is in basic agreement with Whitehead about the priority of time in God's experience. If Whitehead was the Platonist, reflected in his primordial God of ideas, Hartshorne is the Aristotelian who emphasizes the consequent nature of God in the actual world. Hartshorne begins with God as Absolutely Related (AR) to everything that is. He is the God of Divine Relativity (the title of his most influential book). God's character, which guides the lures he holds out to the processing universe, is to be discerned in and abstracted from his actual relationships. Hartshorne does not begin with the primordial God of possibilities but with the actual God who is totally related to you and me and everything that is. Then he proceeds to abstract from the actual God those characteristics that define his style from moment to moment and everlastingly. On a big scale it is like taking you as you are in your present circumstances and noting what your lifestyle is from situation to situation, e.g., male or female, English-speaking, cheery, conscientious, morally upright, and the like. For Hartshorne these characteristics or attributes do not exist apart from a real embodied person, and likewise the attributes of holiness, beauty and everlastingness do not exist for God except as he is related to us in this necessary universe. We comprise God's body, his brain cells. as it were, and without us he would have no existence; that is, without some universe or other (he really doesn't need you and me personally) he would not be. Accordingly, for Hartshorne God has no independent status apart from the universe. He is not a substantial self who exists prior to the creation of the universe, and he experiences social relationships not as an inexhaustibly dynamic triune Family apart from creation but only in terms of the universe which is always a given for him.

You probably discern something here that bothered me increasingly until I finally left the process school. If you have no real substance as a person but are always defined in terms of some similar lifestyle in continually changing circumstances, then of course you have no soul and you perish as a living person when you die (God may remember what he can of you but you have no on-going thought or life). Not only does the process school fail to account for your lifestyle identity from moment to moment, but it really has a problem making sense of God and accounting for his eternal lifestyle. What happens when there are no conscious persons in the universe, for example? Does God have consciousness then? If he does, he must be the substantial and independent God the Bible speaks of; if he doesn't then he must fluctuate in the intensity of his experience, and in vast stretches of the evolutionary process where there are not conscious entities to provide him the raw material of his own consciousness he must be unconscious. But how can he then provide the necessary lures to higher evolution that lead to consciousness? Again, it's an awful muddle.

The Final Choice: Buddhism Or Christianity?

Honesty and good logic require that we do one of two things at this point. Either we return to biblical Christianity and the God of the Scriptures, or we move to an original form of Buddhism, called Theravada Buddhism, which dispenses with God altogether and tries to explain reality in terms of skeins of experience that come and go. In the latter school we arise by chance out of the momentary interweaving of these skeins, but of course they will come unwound again and then we will disappear because we have no substance as persons and no enduring souls. God doesn't exist either, so he cannot guarantee anything lasting. The sooner we realize that we are unsubstantial and have only a momentary appearance in the processing world, the more enlightened we will be. We will be fully enlightened when we realize that we are totally empty and that the empty is the ultimate. Then we will not hold on to anything but enjoy it for the moment and let it go, including ourselves, as we discipline our brief flame of life eventually to go out forever in the great void of Noflame (Nirvana).

This is the end result of putting on the ring of invisibility. I challenge you to accept it if you insist on wearing the ring of freedom and stand on your rights. Not only do you forfeit your substantial self and any hope of life after death, but you lose God in the process. He becomes invisible because there is no logical way he can be more than an abstraction in the weary procession of time, for he has no substance that endures. He fades out of the picture and becomes invisible. The final fade out comes when the rheostat of process is turned fully down in Nirvana.

Then everything is invisible. Everything is no thing, nothing. At last the ring of rebellion has exacted its price. There is nothing to be free or to be free from. It has all faded away, in invisible emptiness.

It was at this point that I realized the truth and decided like the prodigal son to come home. But first I had to repent and (like Frodo) throw the ring back into the fires of its original forging. Grace washed over me and I have never since doubted that God has his right to be sovereign. I will simply serve and let the freedom come by giving myself away. I will never chase it again.

I have been there and back again. It's good to be home.

The Stunted God
of Process Theology*

Carl F. H. Henry

Carl F. H. Henry

Carl F. H. Henry is a noted evangelical theologian, educator, lecturer, and author of more than twenty-five books. He holds two earned doctorates, a Ph.D. from Boston University and a Th.D. from Northern Baptist Seminary. His major six volume work on *God, Revelation and Authority* is available in Mandarin and Korean as well as in English. Dr. Henry was founding editor of *Christianity Today* from 1956-1968. He is currently lecturer-at-large for World Vision International.

Process theology is a significant alternative to the dialectical theology of Karl Barth and the existential theology of Rudolf Bultmann. Contrary to the neo-orthodox notion that the Christian faith is an internal commitment devoid of implications for external reality and history, process theology stresses anew the fact that religious truth is important for all of life and existence. Process theory links God to nature and history and appeals to objective reason. It is to be commended for its resistance both to the "God is dead" trend and to the neo-orthodox emphasis merely on a deity who is significant primarily for internal experience.

Unlike the contemporary disciples of Thomas Aquinas known as neo-Thomists, process theology rejects Aristotelian categories of substance and enthrones modern scientific categories of process and becoming. By correlating an evolutionary universe with a religious reality that guides the developmental process but yet is inseparable from it, process theology incorporates the creative process into the divine life and deprives deity of absolute transcendence.

While process theology avoids pantheism which directly identifies God with the universe, it nonetheless relates God more closely with nature, man and history than does biblical theism. It considers God an aspect of everything that is, yet in some respects also transcendent to everything. Charles Hartshorne calls this *pan-en-theism*, that is, all is in God, in contrast to pantheism which says all is God. For process theory, then, even though God is more than the universe, the universe is considered as necessary to God as God is to the universe.

Orthodox Christians, both Protestant and Catholic, deplore the way in which process thinkers reject the supernatural, spurn the objective reality of the Trinity, disavow the miraculous, and repudiate a Word of God mediated solely through Christ. They object to the elimination by most process theologians of Christ as the mediator through whom alone God speaks his word. Process theologians also assail the traditional insistence on divine decrees and election, on *creatio ex nihilo*, on miraculous redemption and on biblical eschatology. In place of divine decree and foreordination, process thinkers stress divine persuasion; they subordinate history and eschatological finalities broadly to the endless love of God. So great is the gulf between the two systems of theology that both can hardly lay claim to the title "Christian."

Other contributors to this volume have examined many of the more important departures from classical Christianity. A number have also focused on some of the significant philosophical and theological difficulties inherent in process thought. This chapter will develop some of my own concerns about the process concept of God and over how process thinkers believe they attain knowledge about God. I will then explore an aspect of biblical Christianity that many traditional Christian thinkers overlook. That is, the Bible does indeed affirm a "becoming" within the Godhead. But it does so on its own terms and in its own way: the eternal Logos becomes flesh (John 1:14), that is, becomes the God-man by assuming human nature in the Incarnation. And finally I will critique process theology's defective view of divine love along with its "solution" of the problem of evil.

The Concept of God

The process doctrine of God is heterodox in many ways. Process theologians deny the Christian doctrine of the Trinity according to which three persons—Father, Son, and Holy Spirit—exist eternally and coequally within the one divine essence. For process thinkers, Jesus Christ does not become the God-man; instead, God becomes ideal humanity.[1] Process theology blurs the distinction between divine and human activity. No specific actual event is understood by process thinkers as either wholly God's work or wholly man's work; every creaturely activity incarnates God's aims to a higher or lesser degree.

A defective and questionable view of divine perfection grounds many debatable process claims. Charles Hartshorne virtually slanders biblical truth when he asserts that by affirming God's complete perfection, revelational theism erases the value of man's achievements in God's sight. God's absolute perfection, Hartshorne declares, would require divine indifference to human life and work. Hartshorne sees in the process doctrine of God's growth and self-surpassibility a view in which "the world and our own efforts can contribute value to the divine life, and thus religion makes sense."[2] Hartshorne argues that no one can love a completely immutable, infinite or eternal deity.[3] We cannot in any event worship permanently what is but relative and changing; such entities in fact, are hardly worthy of even momentary worship. Moreover, if God created out of inner necessity as process theologians claim, why should we as creatures glorify and worship him? Would not God's creation of man and the world simply exemplify ontological determinism?

Schubert Ogden criticizes classical theism because its God "is lacking in all real internal relations to the contingent beings of which he is the ground," a criticism that stems, in part, from his insistence that God's being must be ontologically described in terms of changing divine relationships to man and the world.[4] Ogden's picture of evangelical theism is prejudiced and distorted and in some respects even a caricature. The fact is that neither metaphysical actuality nor logical consistency requires the verdict that a deity whose nature is defined by immutability, aseity and immateriality cannot as sovereign personal God voluntarily create and intimately relate himself to finite space-time realities. The absolute God of the Bible, who is unchanging, is not on that account aloof from his voluntary creation; he is no lofty Absolute disinterested in the affairs of his creatures.

Process theologians also err in their attempt to link evangelical theism with an immovable and uncompassionate Absolute. They seek to buttress their own alternative by claiming that the biblical writers believe in a changing God who in some respects depends upon the universe. But orthodoxy views the Bible as teaching rather that the living God is both eternally active in self-revelation and intimately involved in the plan of creation and redemption. By these activities God proposes to display his sovereign glory through the cosmos and human history and to lift a finite and fallen humanity to spiritual life.

Several considerations make it clear that process thinkers misidentify the God of biblical theism and of evangelical orthodoxy with the immovable divinity postulated by certain Greek philosophers and other more modern thinkers. (1) Unlike Greek views that forfeit the reality and importance of time and that consider space an undisputed eternal factor, biblical writers, on the other hand, affirm that the eternal God created the spatio-temporal universe and assign God an active role in nature and in human history. (2) Unlike ancient views that matter is intrinsically evil (Plato) and that deity is disinterested in the world (Aristotle), New Testament Christianity, by contrast, affirmed from its very beginnings a supernatural creator personally and universally active in nature and human affairs and specially manifested in his election-love of the Hebrews and in the incarnation, atonement and resurrection of Jesus Christ. (3) The Protestant Reformers rejected medieval scholastic attempts to expound the God of the Bible in speculative categories of abstract Being. (4) And today, like the biblical writers and the church fathers and the Reformers before them, modern evangelical theologians consider Scripture's insistence on God's active relation to the universe and his redemptive activity in history no less factual than they do Scripture's emphasis on God's absoluteness, nontemporal eternity, immutability and omniscience.

The Love of God

Process theology adds to its problems by diluting the love of God. On the one hand, it excludes miraculous divine redemption in deference to evolutionary continuity and scientific uniformity. On the other, it professes to universalize God's election love of the Hebrews. Yet in doing so process theology cannot avoid replacing *agape* with *eros* as the nature of divine love. It considers the universe in all its development as no less necessary to God than God is to the world. In the process view, God does not create or act in history out of self-giving love to confer blessing on the undeserving, but does so rather to expedite his own fulfillment.

For process theology, God is essentially and emphatically love. While this basic Christian affirmation is not to be denied, it is important to recognize that not all that passes for love is divine, that many expositions of God's love are not authentically biblical, and that love can be exaggerated at the expense of other divine perfections. Norman Pittenger considers God as love because he is infinitely related to his creation in necessary interdependence, and transmutes evil into good by absorbing it into his own nature.[5] From this it appears that Pittenger not only reduces the moral quality of love but also misunderstands the very nature of divine *agape*. If God "creates" out of inner necessity, and is motivated by *eros* rather than *agape*, his relationship to space-time realities is not that of the Judeo-Christian God. The New Testament nowhere portrays the climax of God's love as divine-human interdependence or as divine absorption of human wickedness. Scripture declares it, rather, to be God's costly redemption of sinners from the penalty and corruption of their evil ways, a redemption available only to those who turn to the Savior. The God of Judeo-Christian revelation is the God of loving kindness whose redemptive action in behalf of man, writes Gordon Kaufman, "is not called forth by the merit or value of man and the world, but simply because he loves. Far from deserving God's goodness, men are 'sinners' and his 'enemies' who trespass against his will and seek to thwart his purposes."[6]

Strangely enough, many aspects of process theology seem to revert to pre-Christian Greek thought, even if in the name of Christian metaphysics process theologians protest vociferously against that very philosophical perspective. Already in Hesiod's *Theogony*, for example, Eros appears as first among the gods. And in Empedocles Philia is the efficient cause of every union of cosmic forces, an idea that reappears in nineteenth-century theories of cosmic love. But what Christianity means by love is decisively and uniquely revealed in Jesus Christ. It is not uncharacteristic of secular religious philosophy to restate biblical *agape* in terms of a metaphysical *eros*.

Human Knowledge About God

While some process theologians occasionally profess concern for the authority of Scripture,[7] it is clear that they do not take such isolated claims seriously. They champion Scripture only when it supports particular features of their theological system. Process theologians invoke selected portions of Scripture, not to establish truth about God and his creation on the basis of an intelligible divine self-disclosure, but to lend a kind of sacred credence to conclusions based on pure conjecture. They appeal to Scripture only after rejecting what is incompatible with their own views. This arbitrary approach both forces on the Bible a view that Scripture opposes, and robs Scripture of cognitive revelational authority.

Since process theology rejects special or once-for-all divine self-revelation, it is faced with the task of offering an alternative account of how humans attain knowledge about God. Process thinkers appeal to experience and philosophical reasoning rather than to special revelation. An important plank in this experiential and speculative approach to God is their grounding of knowledge-claims about the deity in a postulated analogy between God and humankind. Process theology not only begins with the human self in its existential, psychological and epistemological situation, but it also considers the experimental basis of that self's fundamental concepts to be definitive for reality. Since the human self is both in a process of change involving distinct modes of past, present and future, and is related dependently to the world and to other selves, process thinkers advance a paradigm of reality in which God is a temporal and social being who stands in necessary as well as free relations to man and the universe. "Process" or "creative becoming" emerges as the basic category for interpreting all reality according to the analogy of finite selves.

But the process attempt to make God an analogue of humankind is replete with problems. Since man, for example, not only lives and suffers, but also comes into existence, why then should not God also? If we take seriously the fundamental concepts given in human experience should God not also be seen as subject to moral failure, and as vulnerable to affliction and death? If anything is fundamental to our temporal and social existence, surely it is the serious limitation of our creative becoming. The argument from analogy moreover can accomodate only novel origination, but not unique, miraculous creation.

Simply projecting our socio-temporal reality supremely upon God does not license us to pick-and-choose as process thinkers do. Even the suggestion that we find eminently in God the love that we find in the world ignores the fact the phenomenological analysis considers other forces more fundamental and persuasive for human decision and the social history of humanity. Christianity, moreover, finds *agape* uniquely mirrored only in the life of Jesus of Nazareth. The human race is not generally ruled by love but is expressly exhorted by the Great Commandment and its corollary to love God and neighbor. The light view of sin and the sentimental view of love imputed to deity by process thinkers carries highly subjective overtones. Modern thinking reflects diverse sociological premises, moreover, including the notion that mere incompatibility justifies divorce; the implications of this particular dimension for God's relationship to the world would surely lend a dramatically new dimension to process speculation.

Modern evolutionary thought considers man to be a self who has emerged from non-selfhood. If evolution is taken seriously, who knows whether man may not become dwarfed to insignificance? What presupposition confidently underwrites the speculative expectation that the presently existing human self analogically and permanently delineates the eminent image of the divine? If human nature is evolving and God's nature is projected as a generalization from human experience, may not divine reality embrace potentialities for change far beyond any we presently surmise? And in that event may not God become as subject to change as an airline schedule?

A major logical problem for process thinkers arises from their attempts to escalate quantitative differences between human selfhood and a Superself into qualitative differences. While they thus attempt to preserve literally such traditional metaphysical attributes of God as eternity, immutability, impassivity and immateriality, they actually redefine them within the requirements of process theory and preserve them only by linguistic obfuscation. Moreover, they substitute abstract philosophical projections for the concrete perfections of the self-revealed God and forfeit the Creator-creature relationship that biblical theism preserves.

The Being, Coming and Becoming of the Biblical God

Process theologians frequently refer to the classical Greek disjunction between being and becoming and then relegate classical Christian theism to the former category. One problem with this approach is its neglect of the fact that a doctrine of God grounded on Scripture will deal not simply with the *being* of God but also with the *coming* and *becoming* of God. To be soundly scriptural, any exposition of God must deal with all three: God's being, God's coming and God's becoming.

The Being of God

From the very first the Bible designates God as the transcendent ground of the universe. It depicts him as the eternal Sovereign who voluntarily comes to create the world and man, and comes also to redeem and to judge his creation. Yahweh not only announces a prospect of salvation but in dramatic fulfillment of his prophetic promise God also becomes what he was not, namely, the God-man of Nazareth.

When revealed religion speaks of the being of God, it differs profoundly from secular philosophical notions of being. What is theologically acceptable is not being-in-general, that is, being as an abstract philosophical construct, through which finite being is considered analogous to infinite being. What interests evangelical theism, rather, is the being of God as God has made himself known in his self-disclosure. The legitimacy of what we may say about God's being, essence, nature, substance, attributes, or whatever else, stems solely from the living God who makes himself known and from the divinely inspired Scriptures that characterize the finite universe as the creation of the self-manifesting supernatural God.

The Coming of God

Unless God in sovereign freedom comes in self-revelation, we have no definitive basis for speaking of God at all. The coming of God therefore speaks of his self-disclosure. In and through his revelation, God declares what we are authorized to say concerning the living God.

If we view God's being biblically, the coming of God can only indicate personal divine relationships to the created finite universe. God does not "come to himself"—far less "come to self-consciousness" through cosmic evolution—but relates himself condescendingly and contingently to man and the world as sovereign creator, preserver, redeemer and judge.

Ancient pagans presumed through cult rituals to summon their deities to appear in response to worshipers' desires. In the Bible, however, God as the sovereign creator and redeemer of man and the world appears on his own terms and in his own way. God who takes the initiative in self-revelation is not at the command of his creatures. The voluntary coming of God in sovereign determination, in personal presence and act, the coming of God in his Word, the coming of Messiah, the coming of God's Spirit, and the eschatological coming of God belong to the heart and substance of both Old and New Testaments.

Alongside his inner triune life of resplendent self-sufficiency, God's coming signals broadly his being-for-others that rises from his sovereign decree to create a universe with man in his image and to provide redemption for fallen sinners. Divine condescension characterizes his manifold relationships, a condescension evident in his creation of the universe out of nothing as a contingent reality that he ongoingly preserves alongside himself. It is seen in his self-revelation whereby he crosses the frontier between himself and the created world to make himself known to man. It is seen in the prophetic-apostolic Scriptures that articulate the divine claim and command in intelligible inspired words. Divine condescension is seen in God's mercifully promised redemption for rebellious mankind, in his incarnation in Jesus Christ and the mediator's death upon the cross, in his universal calling of sinners to repentance and the still open invitation to enter the kingdom of God. It is seen in his providential preservation of the faltering regenerate church in the midst of an ungodly world, in his hearing and answering the prayers of his people, in the 'season for repentance' built into God's historical judgments in anticipation of a final judgment of the nations. It will yet be seen in a crowning consummation of human destiny in the end-time reward of the righteous and of righteousness.

The Becoming of God

We have spoken of the being and of the coming of God as central Christian affirmation. Now we must emphasize the becoming of God as no less biblically central. In the Christian view divine becoming is a climactic reality that contrasts at once with ancient Greek notions of abstract being and becoming, and with modern process theology's misconceptions of divine becoming that postulate change in the very nature of God. The notion that God becomes the world, or that the cosmos should in whole or in part be considered divine, is from the biblical point of view unthinkable and profane.

The same erroneous views that identify God with the cosmos or with some aspect of the world also rule out in principle what is central to the New Testament revelation of God, namely, the doctrine of the divine becoming so forcibly stated in the prologue of John's Gospel: *The Word became flesh* (John 1:14). So centrally and strenuously does the New Testament insist on the exceptional and incomparable incarnation of God in Jesus Christ that it deplores as deceivers (2 John 7) and strangers to the living God (1 John 2:23) all who deny that God has come in the flesh. That *man* might be divinized was for disciplined Greek and Roman thought within the range of possibility; that God should assume human nature was out of question. In the Bible, God's coming—the divine movement toward the universe in creation, revelation and redemption—gains its climactic center in God's becoming, that is, in his extraordinary divine condescension and assumption of human nature. "In the beginning was the Word . . . the Word was made flesh" (John 1:1, 14)—this is the only doctrine of divine becoming authorized by Scripture and it ranges the Bible at once against both the whole realm of secular philosophy and the world of nonbiblical religions.

The biblical link between the being of God and God's coming and becoming is the promised and expected Messiah: "He that should come" (Matt. 11:3). The fundamental fact of the Gospels and the Epistles is not that multitudes came to Jesus or even that the disciples and early Christians did so, however requisite such human response is for personal salvation, but rather that God came in Christ (2 Cor. 5:18ff) and that history moves toward Christ's eschatological coming and the kingdom of Messiah.

The New Testament doctrine of divine becoming therefore differs in striking ways from that of contemporary process theology. The latter propounds a one layer view of reality more than a clear distinction between the supernatural and the natural, and it speaks of God's becoming in terms of an inner divine necessity of certain aspects of the divine nature rather than in terms of divine voluntarism; its formulation therefore centers elsewhere than in the once-for-all incarnation of God in Jesus Christ. Although process thought takes a variety of forms, it invariably rejects the orthodox thesis that the divine nature as such is immutable. It therefore sponsors an alteration of the very form of divinity, no less that of its content. This approach contrasts with the New Testament doctrine of divine becoming, in which Christ does not cling exclusively to the form of divinity, but voluntarily comes in the form of a man to unveil the inmost nature of the unchanging God. Process theology imports change and development into aspects of the very nature of God and consequently speaks of a growing God.

The Bible does indeed contain elements of process theology, or rather, of *procession* theology. But scriptural interest in divine procession has nothing whatever in common with philosophical theories that depict the universe as necessary to God. The Bible focuses instead on the interior life of the Godhead. When modern theology deals with God and process, it often expounds theories of how God intrinsically changes and develops, how aspects of the divine nature supposedly mesh into time-space realities and how the early church allegedly invented the doctrine of the Trinity. But the New Testament confines the terms ''begetting'' and ''procession'' to interrelationships between the persons of the Trinity, even as it speaks of divine ''becoming'' only in relation to the Incarnation. Discussion of divine procession is properly considered therefore under the theme of the Trinity rather than under that of creation and preservaton of the world. In the biblical view, moreover, the emphasis on the ''only begotten'' Son has to do with absolute uniqueness rather than with the notion of derivation. Likewise, when it emphasizes the procession of the Spirit from the Father and the Son, the Bible deals not with origination but with a subordination of office and work.

The biblical revelation of God's ''becoming'' therefore differs sharply from treatment of the phrase in recent process speculation. The fact of Jesus Christ as God come ''in the flesh'' to bring out who God permanently is, contrasts spectacularly with conjectural notions of change and growth in God that preclude our knowing and saying who and what in certain respects God permanently is. Any removal of the doctrine of God's once-for-all incarnation in Jesus Christ from centrality in discussing the being and becoming of God, any compromise of the doctrine that Jesus Christ alone is the embodied revelation of God, constitutes an assault on scriptural teaching. The reality of the incarnation of God in Christ is the linchpin of any authentically biblical discussion of divine becoming. Religious philosophers who profess to illumine the divine immutability, infinity and eternality of God in terms of speculative conceptions that mute this doctrine of incomparable incarnation can only distort the biblical view, however much they may deploy Scripture selectively to support partisan expositions. There is every reason to press those who occasionally stress the congruity of some of their conclusions with the Bible to indicate on just what basis of scriptural sensitivity they venture these traditional affirmations about God, and by what divine authority they reject other passages that contradict the perspective of process theology.

The Bible insistently reminds its readers that fallen man as God's enemy stands in dire need of a changed nature and of changed relationships; it uncompromisingly demands a change in man and in human society. The Bible therefore has a spirited interest in God and change. But the Bible cannot be detoured into conjectural theories of ontological change in God. It emphasizes instead that fallen man and the fallen universe will be changed (Heb. 1:12), that in the eschatological triumph of God "we shall all be changed" (1 Cor. 15:51f., 2 Cor. 3:18). The being and coming and becoming of God are the Bible's main motifs and its discussion of change illumines and brightens the plight of mortals precisely because the Sovereign of the universe does "not change" (Mal. 3:6, RSV).

Evil and the Process God

Process theologians consider their solution to the problem of evil better than that of traditional Christianity. While Whitehead and other process thinkers reject creation *ex nihilo*, they do insist, like Judeo-Christian thought (and in distinction from Plato), that matter is not intrinsically evil. They resist any suggestion of an ultimate dualism like Plato's demiurge who struggles to impose order on recalcitrant matter. But there is a sense in which Whitehead does ground evil in metaphysical necessity. He denies God's omnipotence because it would supposedly deprive temporal actual entities of their freedom. The autonomy and mutual obstruction of all entities together with the incompatibility of alternative potentialities is what becomes the source of evil; in short, evil is intrinsic to an evolutionary universe. Whitehead therefore merges the creation and the fall. In Judeo-Christian theology, on the other hand, God's omnipotence alone can guarantee freedom in the universe; any surrender of an absolute moral sovereign only confuses and masks the tragic dimension of moral evil.

What is the process alternative to an orthodox Christian view of evil? According to David Ray Griffin, God is doing his very best.[8] Moreover, Griffin suggests, God could not have created a universe in which there would be no evil.[9] What God is doing, according to Griffin, is transforming present evil into ideal aims in preparation for the next higher stage of the world.[10] But is this proposal a persuasive solution of the problem of evil? A nonomnipotent God could hardly be transforming a nonideal world into an ideal one, if a nonideal world is the best that he could create in the first place. Since Griffin's eschatology can assure no final outcomes he can only hope that the future will be better, not worse. He concedes, moreover, that for process theology belief in personal immortality is purely optional.[11] God's limited power would hold no promise of solving the problem of evil nor would God's limited knowledge on which Griffin insists. The fact is, Griffin's God himself becomes the problem.

If God is as intimately involved in nature and history as process thinkers contend, then their theory woefully obscures the gravity of evil. The more God is ontologically identified with man and history the more difficult it becomes to take the factor of tragedy in human experience seriously. If God is an aspect of all that happens, then no absolute distinction between good and evil is any longer possible. We must then find a divine ingredient not merely in Hitler but even in Satan. History's parade of tragedies, among them catastrophic wars, devastating famines and destructive natural evils, only abets skepticism over the god of process theology.

Process theology reduces sin to simply imperfection or maladjustment, and no longer views it as wicked and willful violation of God's will for man. The process view directly implicates divine agency in man's moral wrong, and thus removes sin from the searching condemnation of a righteous God. Norman Pittenger assures us that "God makes the best of everything, even of that which we can only describe as 'evil'."[12] The reader should not overlook the fact that Pittenger is repeatedly constrained to put the term "evil" in quotation marks. Pittenger's superficial, profoundly unbiblical devaluation of human sin and virtual elimination of divine indignation over human moral rebellion marks process theory as inauthentically Christian. It should give scant comfort to the victims of the Holocaust to say that God no less than man perpetrated their miseries, and this is God's way of achieving new divine possibilities. It seems evident that, at the very least, process theology views moral evil as potential good and as undeserving of divine judgment and death.

Daniel Day Williams contends that "God's capacity to involve himself in the suffering of his creatures and of his incarnate Son is the supreme manifestation of his divinity.[13] His suffering is the exhibition of his perfection which is love which cannot be impassible. Williams views the sufferings of Jesus as a "a disclosure of the suffering of God"[14] and as "the authentic expression and communication of love."[15] But in such a theory, Jesus's sufferings supremely exemplify suffering in general and lose their propitiatory-substitionary character.

However much process thinkers may relate all the evils in history to divine suffering love, these evils nonetheless become conditions that humans must bear because a self-satisfying deity could not avoid fashioning our universe. Humans, in other words, would have only instrumental and no intrinsic value; they would be creatures capable only of contributing to God's survival needs. While the omnipotently good God of the Bible does indeed create to reflect his own glory in and through the finite universe, he does so neither out of necessity nor for selfish ends, nor does he create a world and creatures whose moral rebellion is behaviorally determined.

Christian theism also stands in marked contrast to process theology's view that God suffers along with the world. Process theology can offer no final guarantee of victory; the ultimate outcome remains in doubt. The Bible affirms that God the Son suffers voluntarily and redemptively one-for-all for the sins of the world; his resurrection, moreover, anticipates a complete, final victory over all sin and oppression and Satan and unbelief. The future is not radically open, contingent on the world's self-determining freedom; rather, evil awaits its decisive conquest in the final victory of the good.

Conclusion

It becomes clear that process thinkers confuse the God of the Bible and of evangelical theism with the remote Absolute of past and present secular philosophy. On the basis of its own revelatory supports, Christianity can correlate a sovereign God whose eternal essence excludes further self-realization and whose essential glory is unaltered by the universe, with the fact that man is to glorify God through obedience to biblically revealed commands; it can correlate the absolute Creator whose relation to the world is transcendent, with the reality of the Father who in love revealed himself in Jesus Christ and who governs and guides the universe to its final goal. While it is true that some speculative medieval thinkers made concessions to secular philosophical notions of being, evangelical theists have consistently rejected any amalgam of the biblical view of God with conjectural pagan views. The contradictions that process theorists impute to evangelical theism rest on speculative imagination and not on factual information. The alternative offered by process theology to biblical theism and illicitly advanced as the definitive Christian view is conjectural; it is rooted not in theistic revelation but in philosophical postulation.

The God of the Bible is absolutely sovereign and omniscient. He at least has the advantage of knowing who he really is, since change and process do not apply to the Godhead. The living self-revealing God is eternally self-sufficient, the voluntary creator of the universe and sovereign monarch of all. He is the source of all the substance and structures of existence, the metaphysical ground of the true and the good, the God of election-love who enters into personal covenant with the ancient Hebrews and incarnates himself in Jesus Christ. He is the God who will one day consummate earthly judgment and redemption through the returning risen Redeemer. This emphasis on divine concern, and on God's relatedness to the world and man, could hardly come at a more propitious time than amid the overwhelming civilizational problems of the late twentieth century. Jesus of Nazareth left no doubt that human fortunes and misfortunes are of great concern to God and that our decisions and deeds make a difference not only in world affairs but also in God's attitude and actions toward us.

The biblical insistence that the true and living God still speaks in universal general revelation, and that the fall of humanity requires a special once-for-all revelation as well, illumines our world dilemmas, I believe, more consistently and coherently than any and all rival views. Only the self-revealing God can lead us even now toward a future that preserves truth and love and justice unsullied. All other gods including the God of process theology are either lame or walk backward.

NOTES

*Abridged from Carl F. Henry, *God, Revelation and Authority, Volume V and VI: God Who Stands and Stays, Parts One and Two* (Waco: Word Books, 1982 and 1983). Used by permission.

1. See Joe E. Barnhart, "Incarnation and Process Philosophizing," *Religious Studies* 3 (1967), pp. 225-232.

2. Charles Hartshorne, "What Did Anselm Discover?" in *The Many-Faced Argument*, ed. by John Hick and Arthur McGill (London: Macmillan, 1963), p. 332.

3. See Hartshorne's "Can There Be Proofs for the Existence of God?" in *Religious Language and Knowledge*, edited by Robert H. Ayers and William T. Blackstone (Athens: University of Georgia Press, 1972), p. 63.

4. Schubert Ogden, *The Reality of God and Other Essays* (New York: Harper and Row, 1966), p. 124.

5. See Pittenger's *Process Thought and Christian Faith* (New York: Macmillan, 1968), p. 33.

6. Gordon Kaufman, *Systematic Theology: A Historical Perspective* (New York: Charles Scribner's Sons, 1968), p. 88.

7. See Ogden, *The Reality of God* op. cit., p. 122.

8. David Ray Griffin, *God, Power, and Evil: A Process Theodicy* (Philadelphia: Westminster Press, 1976).

9. Ibid., p. 201f.

10. Ibid., p. 304f.

11. Ibid., p. 313.

12. Pittenger, op. cit., p. 32.

13. Daniel Day Williams, *The Spirit and the Forms of Love* (New York: Harper and Row, 1968), p. 160.

14. Ibid., p. 185.

15. Ibid., p. 167.

For Further Reading

Readers who desire to read further on the subject of process theology will find most of the important books and articles cited in the notes throughout this book. Readers who wish bibliographic help on more specialized topics would do well to begin by consulting the extensive bibliography at the end of *Process Philosophy and Christian Thought*, edited by Delwin Brown, Ralph E. James, Jr., and Gene Reeves (Indianapolis: Bobbs-Merrill, 1971). Since this work lists publications that appeared prior to 1970, information about the many books and articles published since then can be found by checking *The Philosopher's Index* and *Religion Index One: Periodicals* (formerly, *Index to Religious Periodical Literature*). Both are available in any good college library.

Royce Gruenler's views on process thought are expressed more fully in his technical study, *The Inexhaustible God: Biblical Faith and the Challenge of Process Theism* (Grand Rapids: Baker, 1983). More information about the views of Ronald Nash on the subject can be gleaned from his book, *The Concept of God* (Grand Rapids: Zondervan, 1983). There is obvious merit in allowing proponents of process thought to speak for themselves. Readers interested in getting right into the thick of things without first reading Whitehead and Hartshorne should study Lewis Ford's book, *The Lure of God: A Biblical Background for Process Theism* (Philadelphia: Fortress Press, 1978).

Many regard John B. Cobb, Jr. as one of the most influential process thinkers on the contemporary scene. He is a prolific writer and has persuaded many scholars, students, ministers and lay people to adopt the process point of view. One of his first important books, *A Christian Natural Theology Based on the Thought of Alfred North Whitehead* (Philadelphia: Westminster, 1965) is still challenging reading. A reading of Cobb's *Christian Natural Theology* followed by his later work, *Christ in a Pluralistic Age* (Philadelphia: Westminster, 1975) would help many readers to appreciate the wide-ranging implications of process thought for Christian theology and

377

missions. More recently, Cobb's attention has been directed toward political questions and liberation theology, a natural consequence of process theism.[1]

Schubert Ogden's *Christ Without Myth: A Study Based on the Theology of Rudolf Bultmann* (New York: Harper and Row, 1961) combines the radical New Testament thought of Bultmann with the radical process thought of Hartshorne. An easier introduction to Ogden's thought is his later book, *The Reality of God* (New York: Harper and Row, 1966).

Robert C. Neville's *Creativity and God: A Challenge to Process Theology* (New York: Seabury, 1980) is a fascinating study that criticizes Whitehead, Hartshorne, Ford, Cobb and Ogden. The author takes process thought beyond the men just named and suggests a new synthesis of religions, philosophies and cultures in the emerging world order, where the university and not the church is the center of creativity and mission. Gruenler discusses Neville extensively in his *The Inexhaustible God* (mentioned above).

One of the most widely read popularizers of process thought is Norman Pittenger. Whitehead's influence is apparent in Pittenger's *Christology Reconsidered* (London: SCM, 1970) and in his *The Divine Trinity* (Philadelphia: United Church Press, 1977). For the influence of process thought in modern liberal Roman Catholic circles, see David Tracy, *Blessed Rage for Order: The New Pluralism in Theology* (New York: Seabury, 1979).

The two men most responsible for the process movement in the twentieth century are, of course, Alfred North Whitehead and Charles Hartshorne. Perhaps the best introduction to Whitehead's concept of a social reality is his *Modes of Thought* (New York: Capricorn Books, 1958). Sooner or later, serious students of the subject must tackle Whitehead's *Process and Reality: An Essay in Cosmology* (New York: Harper and Row, 1957). Charles Hartshorne's most famous book is *The Divine Relativity: A Social Conception of God* (New Haven: Yale University Press, 1964). Some of the later chapters in his *The Logic of Perfection and Other Essays in Neoclassical Metaphysics* (La Salle, IL: Open Court, 1973) also provide provocative insights to his thought.

General introductions to the school are many. Two that are worth consulting are John B. Cobb, Jr., and David R. Griffin, *Process*

For Further Reading

Theology: An Introductory Exposition (Philadelphia: Westminster, 1976); and Paul Arthur Schilpp, ed., *The Philosophy of Alfred North Whitehead* (New York: Tudor, 1956).

NOTES

1. For an important critique of liberation theology, see Ronald H. Nash, editor, *Liberation Theology* (Milford, Michigan: Mott Media, 1984).

Index of Persons

On God's Knowledge. 243

Index of Subjects

Index of Subjects